Pantelis Golitsis
Damascius' Philosophy of Time

CHRONOI
Zeit, Zeitempfinden, Zeitordnungen
Time, Time Awareness, Time Management

—

Herausgegeben von

Eva Cancik-Kirschbaum, Christoph Markschies und Hermann Parzinger

im Auftrag des Einstein Center Chronoi

Band 7

Pantelis Golitsis

Damascius' Philosophy of Time

DE GRUYTER

ISBN 978-3-11-105318-9
e-ISBN (PDF) 978-3-11-105321-9
e-ISBN (EPUB) 978-3-11-105330-1
ISSN 2701-1453
DOI https://doi.org/10.1515/9783111053219

This work is licensed under the Creative Commons Attribution-NonCommercial-NoDerivatives 4.0 International License. For details go to https://creativecommons.org/licenses/by-nc-nd/4.0/. Creative Commons license terms for re-use do not apply to any content (such as graphs, figures, photos, excerpts, etc.) that is not part of the Open Access publication. These may require obtaining further permission from the rights holder. The obligation to research and clear permission lies solely with the party re-using the material.

Library of Congress Control Number: 2023933715

Bibliographic information published by the Deutsche Nationalbibliothek
The Deutsche Nationalbibliothek lists this publication in the Deutsche Nationalbibliografie; detailed bibliographic data are available on the Internet at http://dnb.dnb.de.

© 2023 the author(s), published by Walter de Gruyter GmbH, Berlin/Boston
The book is published open access at www.degruyter.com.

Printing and binding: CPI books GmbH, Leck

www.degruyter.com

Contents

Abbreviations — VII

Introduction — 1

1 Damascius as an exegete of Aristotle — 11
1.1 The philosophical vocation of Damascius — 11
1.2 The curriculum of Damascius — 13
1.3 Damascius' treatises *On Number, On Place,* and *On Time* — 16

2 Time as a uniting measure — 21
2.1 Being and activity of being: 2 + 1 measures — 23
2.2 Time as a measure of the duration of being: transforming the Aristotelian conception of time as a measure of the being of motion — 36
2.3 Time as a uniting measure from a contemporary point of view: McTaggart's B and C series and an ancient case for presentism — 42

3 Time all at once — 51
3.1 The indivisible 'now' and the present time — 53
3.2 The present time and the non-flowing 'now' — 61
3.3 The flowing time and the still essence of the higher times — 73
3.4 The whole of time in the heaven — 79

4 Epilogue: stillness and circularity as pertinent features of the Hellenic philosophy of time — 85

5 Appendix: Damascius, *On Time* — 91
    Δαμασκίου Περὶ χρόνου — 92
    Damascius, *On Time* — 93

Bibliography — 109
A Sources — 109
B Translations — 110
C Secondary Literature — 110

Index nominum — 114

Index locorum — 116

Abbreviations

Cat.	Aristotle, *Categories*
DK	H. Diels/W. Kranz (eds.), *Die Fragmente der Vorsokratiker.* Berlin: Weidmann, 1951⁶.
Parm.	Plato, *Parmenides*
Phys.	Aristotle, *Physics*
Plat. Theol.	Proclus, *Théologie platonicienne*
SVF	H. F. A. von Arnim (ed.), *Stoicorum veterum fragmenta*, 3 vols. Leipzig: Teubner, 1903–1905.

Introduction

The first person to think about time philosophically, i.e. in a more or less abstract way and searching to grasp the causality of time, was probably Anaximander. In positing 'the Unlimited' (together with its motion) as the only "ageless" element of the universe, this early Greek philosopher posited time (χρόνος), which, unlike the unlimited principle of all things, is generated, as that which determines the generation and corruption of beings.[1] Anaximander's notion of time was obviously linked to the common understanding of time as that in virtue of which living beings, once born, go through various stages of life, grow old, wither, and eventually pass away.[2] Every living being was thought to have its 'ages',[3] i.e. its life periods, the sum of which was coextensive with and, therefore, somehow regulative of the duration of its life. Such 'ages' were measured by 'time', for instance by the yearly cycle of the seasons or the year itself. The later philosophical concept of time as a 'number' (ἀριθμός) determinative of some thing's existence, a concept

---

1 Cf. Hippolytus, *Refutation of All Heresies*, I, 6.1–8 (= 12 A 11 DK): "[Anaximander] said that the principle of beings is some kind of existing unlimitedness, from which the heavens and the worlds that are within them are generated, while it itself is eternal and ageless, and that it contains all the worlds. He says that it contains also time, since both the generation and the corruption of beings is delimited. So, Anaximander says that the principle and the element of beings is the unlimited and was the first to use the name 'principle'. In addition to the unlimited, [he says that] motion is eternal, in which, he says, the heavens happen to be generated." (Οὗτος ἀρχὴν ἔφη τῶν ὄντων φύσιν τινὰ τοῦ ἀπείρου, ἐξ ἧς γίνεσθαι τοὺς οὐρανοὺς καὶ τοὺς ἐν αὐτοῖς κόσμους· ταύτην δὲ ἀίδιον εἶναι καὶ ἀγήρω, ἣν καὶ πάντας περιέχειν τοὺς κόσμους. λέγει δὲ ⟨καὶ⟩ χρόνον [sc. περιέχειν], ὡς ὡρισμένης καὶ τῆς γενέσεως τοῖς οὖσι καὶ τῆς φθορᾶς. οὗτος μὲν οὖν ἀρχὴν καὶ στοιχεῖον εἴρηκεν τῶν ὄντων τὸ ἄπειρον, πρῶτος τοὔνομα καλέσας τῆς ἀρχῆς· πρὸς δὲ τούτῳ κίνησιν ἀίδιον εἶναι, ἐν ᾗ συμβαίνει(ν) γίνεσθαι τοὺς οὐρανούς.) It is interesting to notice that, according to the Orphic theogony of Hieronymus and/or Hellanicus, it is Time itself, i.e. the third principle born from Water and Earth, which is qualified as "ageless" (Χρόνος ἀγήραος); cf. Damascius, *On the First Principles*, III, 160.17–161.8.
2 Cf. Aristotle, *Phys.*, IV 13, 222b 16–25: "All things come into being and pass away in time [...]. It is clear then that time will be in itself cause of destruction rather than of coming into being [...]. A sufficient evidence of this is that nothing comes into being without itself moving somehow and acting, but a thing can be destroyed even if it does not move at all. And this is what we are accustomed to mean by a thing's being destroyed by time." (Ἐν δὲ τῷ χρόνῳ πάντα γίγνεται καὶ φθείρεται [...]. δῆλον οὖν ὅτι φθορᾶς μᾶλλον ἔσται καθ' αὑτὸν αἴτιος ἢ γενέσεως [...]. σημεῖον δὲ ἱκανὸν ὅτι γίγνεται μὲν οὐδὲν ἄνευ τοῦ κινεῖσθαί πως αὐτὸ καὶ πράττειν, φθείρεται δὲ καὶ μηδὲν κινούμενον. καὶ ταύτην μάλιστα λέγειν εἰώθαμεν ὑπὸ τοῦ χρόνου φθοράν. Translation by Hardie, slightly modified.) In chapter 13 of book IV of the *Physics*, Aristotle reviews common notions about time.
3 See, for instance, the Hippocratic medical text *Hebdomads*, in which the human lifespan is divided into seven seven-year periods. See further Singer (2022: 35–66).

Open Access. © 2023 the author, published by De Gruyter. This work is licensed under the Creative Commons Attribution-NonCommercial-NoDerivatives 4.0 International License.
https://doi.org/10.1515/9783111053219-002

conspicuous in Greek philosophy since Plato,[4] originates from this archaic intuition about time.

Philosophers subsequent to Anaximander related time to heaven, which provided the most stable and most easily cognizable temporal unit: the day and night (or sidereal time). Aristotle reports that some earlier philosophers, possibly the Pythagoreans,[5] thought that time *is* the rotation of the heaven.[6] Plato says in the *Timaeus* that "time came into existence along with the heaven",[7] presumably thinking of the time period determined by a complete revolution of the outermost heavenly sphere,[8] and also that the Sun and the Moon and the other five planets

---

[4] Plato says in the *Timaeus* that "god", i.e. the Demiurge who contemplates the intelligible Living Being, "kindled a light which now we call the Sun, to the end that it might shine, so far as possible, throughout the whole Heaven, and that all the living creatures entitled thereto might participate in number." (*Timaeus*, 39b 4–7: [...] | φῶς ὁ θεὸς ἀνῆψεν ἐν τῇ πρὸς γῆν δευτέρᾳ τῶν περιόδων, ὃ δὴ νῦν κεκλήκαμεν ἥλιον, ἵνα ὅτι μάλιστα εἰς ἅπαντα φαίνοι τὸν οὐρανὸν μετάσχοι τε ἀριθμοῦ τὰ ζῷα ὅσοις ἦν προσῆκον. Translation by Lamb.) In his commentary on Plato's *Timaeus*, the late Platonist Proclus speaks of "the essential time (οὐσιώδης χρόνος, i.e. time not as pertaining to something else but as an essence or substance) in virtue of which all things are numbered by the greater or smaller numbers that determine their lifespan; so, for instance, an ox lives this long but a man that long, while the Sun or the Moon return to the start of the cycles in such and such a time, and Saturn and the other planets complete their own cycles in accordance with other measures." (*In Timaeum*, III, 19.28–32: [...] τοῦ οὐσιώδους χρόνου, δι' ὃν πάντα ἀριθμεῖται μείζοσι καὶ ἐλάσσοσι τῆς ἑαυτῶν ζωῆς ἀριθμοῖς, ὡς βοῦν μὲν τοσόνδε ζῆν χρόνον, ἄνθρωπον δὲ τοσόνδε, ἥλιον δὲ ἐν τοσῷδε ἀποκαθίστασθαι καὶ σελήνην καὶ Φαίνοντα καὶ ἄλλους κατ' ἄλλα μέτρα ποιεῖσθαι τὰς ἑαυτῶν περιόδους. Translation by Baltzly, slightly modified.) Thus, 'number' is formative. It is not an abstract entity or a predicate of plurality, as in modern thought, but has an "active power" (δύναμις δραστήριος), as the late Platonist Iamblichus said before Proclus (see Chapter 1, n. 36). On the essential time and its causal power in Proclus see Vargas (2021). On Iamblichus see Hoffmann (1980).

[5] Simplicius reports that some interpreters associated the Pythagoreans with the most naïve of the ancient doctrines on time discussed by Aristotle, namely the doctrine that time is the heavenly sphere itself. But Simplicius discards this interpretation as originating from a misunderstanding of time defined by the Pythagorean Archytas as "τὸ διάστημα of the nature of the universe", διάστημα being misinterpreted as *spatial* extension; cf. Simplicius, *In Phys.*, 700.19–21. ('Archytas' was, in fact, an allonymous Neopythagorean philosopher.)

[6] Cf. Aristotle, *Phys.*, IV 10, 218a 33-b 1: "Some say that [time] is the motion of the universe" (Οἱ μὲν γὰρ τὴν τοῦ ὅλου κίνησιν εἶναί φασιν.) This doctrine is sometimes wrongly associated with Plato.

[7] Plato, *Timaeus*, 38b 6: Χρόνος δ' οὖν μετ' οὐρανοῦ γέγονεν.

[8] Cf. Plato, *Timaeus*, 39c 1–2: "In this wise and for these reasons were generated Night and Day, which are the [time] period of the single and most intelligent circuit." (Νὺξ μὲν οὖν ἡμέρα τε γέγονεν οὕτως καὶ διὰ ταῦτα, ἡ τῆς μιᾶς καὶ φρονιμωτάτης κυκλήσεως περίοδος. Translation by Lamb, modified.) In accordance with Eudoxus' theory of the concentric spheres, Plato believed that, unlike the outermost celestial sphere which moves with a single motion, the seven planets (Saturn,

came into existence "for determining and preserving the numbers of time",⁹ i.e. the year, the month and other temporal units, which, "save for a few", nobody has understood.¹⁰ Aristotle provided in his *Physics* a more sophisticated account, which resulted in the conviction that time is a number only extrinsically related, as a concomitant of the human soul, to things in motion.¹¹ It is our mind, he argues,¹² which actually cognizes time by individuating limits of time (later called 'indivisible nows') as anterior and posterior cuts in some thing's motion. Still, Aristotle, too, recognized that human souls cognize one rotation of the outermost celestial sphere as the fundamental temporal unit.¹³ The Stoic philosopher Chrysippus subsequently defined time as "the interval that is concomitant to the motion of the cosmos",¹⁴ the 'pace', we may say, with which the outermost heavenly sphere is moving. The understanding of time as a recurring 'interval' (διάστημα) of tiniest

---

Jupiter, Mars, Venus, Mercury, Sun, Moon) were carried by more than one spheres and were therefore moving in more than one circuits.

9 Plato, *Timaeus*, 38c 6: [...] εἰς διορισμὸν καὶ φυλακὴν ἀριθμῶν χρόνου.

10 Cf. Plato, *Timaeus*, 39c 3-d 2: "Month [was generated], every time that the Moon having completed her own orbit overtakes the Sun; and Year, as often as the Sun has completed his own orbit. Of the other stars the revolutions have not been understood by men (save for a few out of the many); wherefore they have no names for them, nor do they compute and compare their relative measurements, so that they are not aware, as a rule, that the 'wanderings' of these bodies, which are hard to calculate and of wondrous complexity, constitute [a] time." (Μεὶς δὲ ἐπειδὰν σελήνη περιελθοῦσα τὸν ἑαυτῆς κύκλον ἥλιον ἐπικαταλάβῃ, ἐνιαυτὸς δὲ ὁπόταν ἥλιος τὸν ἑαυτοῦ περιέλθῃ κύκλον. τῶν δ' ἄλλων τὰς περιόδους οὐκ ἐννενοηκότες ἄνθρωποι, πλὴν ὀλίγοι τῶν πολλῶν, οὔτε ὀνομάζουσιν οὔτε πρὸς ἄλληλα συμμετροῦνται σκοποῦντες ἀριθμοῖς, ὥστε ὡς ἔπος εἰπεῖν οὐκ ἴσασιν χρόνον ὄντα τὰς τούτων πλάνας, πλήθει μὲν ἀμηχάνῳ χρωμένας, πεποικιλμένας δὲ θαυμαστῶς. Translation by Lamb, slightly modified.) In virtue of its admitting a 'number', in other words, of its being a temporal unit, a 'time', cannot be but regular and calculable.

11 Cf. Aristotle, *Phys.*, IV 14, 223a 25–26: "If nothing but soul, or in soul intelligence, is by nature qualified to count, there would not be time unless there were soul." (Εἰ δὲ μηδὲν ἄλλο πέφυκεν ἀριθμεῖν ἢ ψυχὴ καὶ ψυχῆς νοῦς, ἀδύνατον εἶναι χρόνον ψυχῆς μὴ οὔσης.)

12 Note that, in his commentary on Plato's *Timaeus*, Proclus dismisses all those, i.e. Aristotle and the Peripatetic philosophers, "who posit time as a bare conception or make of it an incidental property." (Proclus, *In Timaeum*, III, 21.5–6: Οὐκ ἄρα ἀκολουθητέον τοῖς ἐν ψιλαῖς ἐπινοίαις αὐτὸν ἱστᾶσιν ἢ συμβεβηκός τι ποιοῦσιν.) In the vein of the Peripatetics, Porphyry had earlier considered that the existence of time is dependent on the motion of the universal soul; cf. Porphyry, *Launching Points towards the Intelligibles*, §44, lin. 45–46: "Time subsists as subordinate to the motion of the Soul, whereas eternity subsists as subordinate to the abiding of Intelligence in itself." (Τῇ μὲν οὖν ταύτης κινήσει παρυφίσταται χρόνος, τῇ δὲ τοῦ νοῦ μονῇ τῇ ἐν ἑαυτῷ ὁ αἰών.)

13 Cf. Aristotle, *Phys.*, IV 14, 223b 18–20 (quoted in Ch. 2, n. 2).

14 *SVF* II, 509 (p. 164.15–17): Ὁ δὲ Χρύσιππος χρόνον εἶναι [...] τὸ παρακολουθοῦν διάστημα τῇ τοῦ κόσμου κινήσει.

extension, undivided but divisible in thought, which is traceable back to Plato's *Parmenides*, was of great significance for all post-Aristotelian theories of time.

We will review various details of these doctrines later. In these introductory pages we should notice that the philosophy of time on which this book focuses, namely the philosophy of time of the late ancient philosopher Damascius, the last 'Platonic successor', both reassumed and rejuvenated the rich and long-established Greek thinking about time.[15] That time orders the duration of life—the sum of the "leaps of generation", as he says—of a sublunary substance is a basic component of Damascius' thought. That the sublunary time is shaped by a recurring extended but undivided 'now', which leaps along with the 'leaps' that make up the rotation of the heaven, is at the core of his notion of flowing time. Damascius distinguished, however, between different perceptions of time and offered novel perspectives, which can even be interpreted as anticipating modern and contemporary theories. The A series (the placement of a single event in time as variously future, present and past), the C series (the permanent relations to one another of those realities which in time are events) and the B series (the tenseless earlier and later which is generated through the combination of the C series with the A series) of McTaggart's analysis are distinguished for the first time explicitly in Damascius' philosophy of time.[16] This late Platonist was also the first to make a case for presentism, i.e. the view that there are no past or future entities, but this only with regard to the activity and the essence of the heavens. Damascius was an innovative philosopher. The greatest merit of his philosophy of time, however, is his deep reflection on what it is for a living being to have its being in becoming—as it happens with us human beings—and how this relates to temporality, temporalization, perpetuity and, finally, stillness.

Damascius was a Platonist and, what is more, a concordist Platonist: he thought that Aristotle's philosophy does not contradict the philosophy of Plato.[17] Still, he was a committed Platonist. He therefore philosophized about the sensible realm of human experience on the assumption that it is the faithful image of an extremely complex intelligible model, which only the pure human intellect could access, albeit with labour. Inspired by Iamblichus, Damascius thought that time has an ordering power, which enables a generated living creature to have its being in becoming. In doing so, time indeed emerges as an image of eternity. It

---

15 Nonetheless, Damascius' philosophy of time was left without posterity.
16 Sambursky (1968: 167) identifies McTaggart's C series with "the time of the intelligible world in the doctrine of Iamblichus and his School". This interpretation is far-fetched and does not do justice either to McTaggart's analysis or to the theory of the Late Platonists; see Sorabji (1983: 37–39).
17 I argue for this in my "From Athens to Alexandria: What Damascius Learned from Ammonius" (to be published in *The International Journal of the Platonic Tradition* [2024]).

is in virtue of time that a generated living being, like each one of us, *comes to be* until it perishes. It is in virtue of eternity that a non-generated living being, like any intelligible form, *is*. As he also did with place,[18] Damascius undertook to discover the essence of time by considering its utility. In doing so, he reversed the methodological primacy of essence, established by Aristotle. Damascius contended that, just as the model of time, i.e. eternity, is necessary for the well-being of the intelligible forms, so time is necessary for the well-being of the common form that inheres in all generated and perishable substances. Duration, spatiality and plurality are types of disintegration that pertain to whatever departs from the intelligible existence. Number, place and time are thought by Damascius to intervene as measures in order to bring about unity and order in the bodily world.

Nevertheless, as in other domains of his philosophy, Damascius went with his theory of time well beyond this kind of Platonic dualism. He thought that midway between time as a uniting power of the durative existence of the generated substances and eternity as the timeless existence of intelligible forms, stands not only the flowing time that runs along with the rotation of the heaven, but also a time that is "everlastingly totally present",[19] a claim to which even his pupil Simplicius did not consent.

The following chapters will endeavour to show the richness and deepness of Damascius' philosophy of time by going back to his sources and into the fundamental concepts that shaped his thought: 'the indivisible now' of Aristotle's *Physics* versus 'the present time' of Plato's *Parmenides*, 'the flowing now' versus 'the non-flowing now' and 'the flowing time' versus 'the whole of time'. Damascius fully developed his thoughts about time in his treatise *On Time*, which is unfortunately lost. I edit, translate and annotate the preserved fragments of this treatise, as well as the testimonies, which are due to Simplicius,[20] in the Appendix.

It will be helpful to the reader to know from the beginning that, in contrast with the modern straightforward distinction between absolute and relative time,

---

18 See Hoffmann/Golitsis (2016: 539). Cf. Simplicius, *In Phys.*, 624.18–20: "If the utility of place be not well defined, we cannot know whether place is a body or incorporeal, nor whether it is divisible or indivisible in its nature." ([…] τῆς τοῦ τόπου χρείας μὴ διορισθείσης καλῶς, οὔτε ἢ σῶμα ὁ τόπος οὔτε εἰ ἀσώματον, οὔτε εἰ διαστατὴν ἔχει φύσιν οὔτε εἰ ἀδιάστατον, καταμαθεῖν ἔστι. Translation by Urmson, modified.) *In Phys.*, 625.1–3: "Let us expound that [doctrine, i.e. Damascius'] too. We shall of necessity need a longer discussion on account of the novelty of his theory, which seeks to discover the essence of place from its utility." (Φέρε καὶ ἐκείνην ἐκθώμεθα μακροτέρων ἐξ ἀνάγκης δεόμενοι λόγων διὰ τὸ καινοπρεπὲς τῆς ὑποθέσεως ἐκ τῆς χρείας τοῦ τόπου βουλομένης αὐτοῦ τὴν οὐσίαν εὑρεῖν. Translation by Urmson, modified.)
19 Damascius, *apud Simplicium, In Phys.*, 780.5.
20 On Simplicius' digressions on place and on time, which include fragments of Damascius' *On Place* and *On Time*, see Golitsis/Hoffmann (2023).

or objective and subjective time,[21] the late ancient Platonists accepted a plurality of times. They quickly overruled Aristotle's subjective time[22] and thought that time exists objectively but at many levels. The most characteristic account in this respect is perhaps to be found in a passage of Proclus' commentary on the *Timaeus*. Reflecting upon Plato's dismissal of the use of tensed words when it comes to the divine intelligible Forms, Proclus gives a panorama of the existing times, which culminates in Time as god (or "fontal" time). This god, he explains, comes from Hecate, the great Goddess who presides over all life and motion, and is itself the monad that presides over all times, even over the time that measures the existence of completely perishable things (such as hair and nails):

> For what reason, therefore, do [the words] 'was' and 'will be' not apply to the intelligibles? It is because the very measure of the intelligibles [i.e. eternity] is both unshaken and unmoved and this measure makes what is measured by it wholly transcend change. For what reason, then, does *"solely [the word] 'is' apply"* to the intelligibles *"according to true speech"*?[23] Because what the intelligibles *are*, they always *are*. They neither lose anything nor do they gain: not with respect to essence or life or cognition—much less with respect to their very unification. Is it therefore the case that of these three—'was', 'is', and 'will be'—it is not fitting to apply the extreme in the case of the intelligibles but only the middle? Or is it the case that none [of these words may be used]? The reason for the latter is that the sense of 'is' that is coordinate with 'was' and 'will be' is not fitting for the intelligibles, but only [the sense of 'is'] that transcends all of these. Only the sense of 'is' that has no trace whatsoever of time and is determined in accordance with the eternal measure itself ought to be assigned to the gods and the intelligibles. The case is parallel to that of [the meaning of the word] 'always' where there was one sense that was eternal and another that was temporal. So, too, there is a dual sense of 'is' where one sense applies to genuine beings [i.e. the intelligibles], while the other applies

---

21 See Detel (2021).
22 Most characteristically expressed through the incubation of the people sleeping in the vicinity of the buried children of Hercules in Sardinia, to which Aristotle refers in *Phys.*, IV 11, 218b 21–27: "But neither does time exist without change; for when the state of our own minds does not change at all, or we have not noticed its changing, we do not realize that time has elapsed, any more than those who are fabled to sleep among the heroes in Sardinia do when they are awakened; for they connect the earlier 'now' with the later and make them one, cutting out the interval because of their failure to notice it." (Ἀλλὰ μὴν οὐδ' ἄνευ γε μεταβολῆς· ὅταν γὰρ μηδὲν αὐτοὶ μεταβάλλωμεν τὴν διάνοιαν ἢ λάθωμεν μεταβάλλοντες, οὐ δοκεῖ ἡμῖν γεγονέναι χρόνος, καθάπερ οὐδὲ τοῖς ἐν Σαρδοῖ μυθολογουμένοις καθεύδειν παρὰ τοῖς ἥρωσιν, ὅταν ἐγερθῶσι· συνάπτουσι γὰρ τῷ πρότερον νῦν τὸ ὕστερον νῦν καὶ ἓν ποιοῦσιν, ἐξαιροῦντες διὰ τὴν ἀναισθησίαν τὸ μεταξύ. Translation by Hardie.)
23 Cf. Plato, *Timaeus*, 37e 5–38a 2: "For we say that it 'is' or 'was' or 'will be', whereas, according to true speech, solely [the term] 'is' applies to the eternal essence; 'was' and 'will be', on the other hand, are [terms] properly applicable to the generation that proceeds in time." (Λέγομεν γὰρ δὴ ὡς ἦν ἔστιν τε καὶ ἔσται, τῇ δὲ [sc. τῇ ἀιδίῳ οὐσίᾳ] τὸ ἔστιν μόνον κατὰ τὸν ἀληθῆ λόγον προσήκει, τὸ δὲ ἦν τό τ' ἔσται περὶ τὴν ἐν χρόνῳ γένεσιν ἰοῦσαν πρέπει λέγεσθαι.)

to things within the cosmos. Therefore, when Plato says that *"solely [the term] 'is' applies to the eternal essence according to true speech"*, by changing the position of 'solely' we may discover a more scientific statement: 'that which solely is applies to the eternal essence'—that is, the sense of 'is' that is in itself and transcends any relation to the forms of time [i.e. the past, the present, and the future]. How then did it turn out that human beings came to be so mistaken as to project back up toward the intelligible gods [words] that are not at all fitting for them? The general cause is the forgetting about divinity that in our case supervenes upon the shedding of [the soul's] wings, falling down, and associating with mortal bodies. It was for this reason that Plato said: *"We apply them* [sc. the tensed words] *wrongly, without noticing, to eternal essence"*.[24] But the Theurgists are surely not affected in this way: it is not licit for them. Rather, they celebrate Time himself as a god, and they regard (v) one time as 'connected with the zones', as we said, and (iv) another as 'independent of the zones', [i.e. the time] which measures the period of the third of the aetherial worlds. Yet (iii) another [time] is set over the intermediate one among these worlds, a certain archangelic time. (ii) Another [time that is called] archic rules over the very first of the aetherial worlds, while above all these [times] is (i) another [time], the fontal [time], which directs and rotates the empyrean world and also determines its period. This [fontal time] proceeds from the fontal goddess [i.e. Hecate] who gives birth to all life, as well as to all motion. This goddess brought forth also the fontal time and set it over all things in motion as a measure of the periods of every one of them right down to the ultimate [generated things]. After all, these too are measured by periods, even if they are entirely destroyed.[25]

---

24 Plato, *Timaeus*, 37e 4–5. Note that eternity is not the same as perpetuity.
25 Proclus, *In Timaeum*, III, 42.16–43.24: Διὰ τί οὖν τὸ ἦν καὶ τὸ ἔσται οὐχ ἁρμόζει τοῖς νοητοῖς; ὅτι τὸ μέτρον αὐτῶν αὐτό τέ ἐστιν ἀστεμφὲς καὶ ἀκίνητον καὶ τὰ μετρούμενα ὑφ' ἑαυτοῦ πάσης ἐξῃρῆσθαι ποιεῖ μεταβολῆς. διὰ τί δὲ τὸ ἔστι κατὰ τὸν ἀληθῆ λόγον αὐτοῖς προσήκει μόνον; ὅτι ἄ ἐστιν ἔστιν ἀεί, οὐδὲν οὔτε ἀφιέντα οὔτε προσλαμβάνοντα οὔτε κατ' οὐσίαν οὔτε κατὰ ζωὴν οὔτε κατὰ τὴν νόησιν οὔτε πολλῷ πλέον κατ' αὐτὴν τὴν ἕνωσιν. ἆρ' οὖν τῶν τριῶν τούτων, τοῦ ἦν ἔστι τε καὶ ἔσται, τὰ μὲν ἄκρα οὐ προσήκει λέγειν ἐπὶ τῶν νοητῶν, μόνον δὲ τὸ μέσον, ἢ οὐδαμῶς; οὐδὲ γὰρ τὸ ἔστι τὸ συνταττόμενον τῷ τε ἦν καὶ τῷ ἔσται προσήκει τι τοῖς νοητοῖς, ἀλλ' ὃ πάντων μὲν τούτων ἐξῄρηται, χρόνου δὲ οὐδεμίαν ἔμφασιν ἔχει, κατ' αὐτὸ δὲ τὸ αἰώνιον ὥρισται μέτρον, ἀπονεμητέον ἐστὶ τοῖς θεοῖς καὶ τοῖς νοητοῖς· ὥσπερ γὰρ τὸ ἀεὶ τὸ μὲν ἦν αἰώνιον, τὸ δὲ χρονικόν, οὕτω καὶ τὸ ἔστι διττόν ἐστι καὶ τὸ μὲν τοῖς ὄντως οὖσιν ἁρμόζει, τὸ δὲ τοῖς ἐγκοσμίοις πράγμασιν. ὅταν οὖν λέγῃ "τῇ δὲ τὸ ἔστι μόνον κατὰ τὸν ἀληθῆ λόγον προσήκει", τὸ μόνον μεταθέντες ἐπιστημονικώτερον εὑρήσομεν τὸν λόγον· 'τῇ δὲ τὸ μόνον ἔστι προσήκει', τουτέστι τὸ καθ' ἑαυτὸ καὶ ἐξῃρημένον τῆς πρὸς τὰ εἴδη τοῦ χρόνου συντάξεως. πόθεν οὖν ἐπῆλθε τοῖς ἀνθρώποις τηλικαῦτα πλημμελεῖν καὶ τὰ μηδὲν προσήκοντα τοῖς νοητοῖς θεοῖς ἐπ' αὐτοὺς ἀναπέμπειν; τὸ μὲν ὅλον αἴτιον ἡ λήθη τῶν θείων ἡ διὰ τὴν πτερορρύησιν καὶ τὴν πτῶσιν καὶ τὴν τῶν ἐπικήρων σωμάτων κοινωνίαν ἡμῖν ἐπιγεγενημένη· διὸ καὶ αὐτὸς οὗτος ἔφη "λανθάνομεν φέροντες ἐπὶ τὴν ἀίδιον οὐσίαν οὐκ ὀρθῶς". ἀλλ' οὐχ οἵ γε θεουργοὶ ταῦτα πεπόνθασιν· οὐ γὰρ θέμις αὐτοῖς· ἀλλὰ τὸν χρόνον αὐτὸν ὑμνήκασιν ὡς θεόν, καὶ ἄλλον μὲν τὸν ζωναῖον, ὡς εἴπομεν, ἄλλον δὲ ἄζωνον, μετροῦντα τὴν περίοδον τοῦ τρίτου τῶν αἰθερίων, ἄλλον δὲ τὸν ἐπὶ τοῦ μέσου τῶν κόσμων ἐκείνων, ἀρχαγγελικόν τινα χρόνον, ἄλλον δὲ ἀρχικὸν αὐτῷ ἐφεστῶτα τῷ πρωτίστῳ τῶν αἰθερίων, ἐφ' ἅπασι δὲ τούτοις πηγαῖον ἄλλον, ὃς τὸν ἐμπύριον κόσμον ἄγει καὶ περιάγει καὶ ἀφορίζει τὴν ἐκείνου περίοδον, ἀπ' αὐτῆς προελθὼν τῆς πηγαίας θεοῦ τῆς πᾶσαν μὲν ζωήν, πᾶσαν δὲ κίνησιν τεκούσης· αὕτη γὰρ παρήγαγε καὶ τὸν πηγαῖον χρόνον καὶ πᾶσι τοῖς κινουμένοις ἐπέστησε μετροῦντα τὰς πάντων περιόδους μέχρι

Proclus distinguishes here between five different times—(i) the fontal time, (ii) the archic time, (iii) the archangelic time, (iv) the azonic time, and (v) the zonic time—in accordance with the sacred theology revealed by the Chaldean theurgists,[26] a theology that was fully espoused by the last Hellenes (such as Proclus and Damascius). In fact, the Chaldeans distinguished between seven 'worlds'—one empyrean, three aetherial, and three hylic (according to the Neoplatonist interpretation)[27]—to which seven different times should correspond. The time firstly mentioned by Proclus, i.e. the time "connected with the zones", probably corresponds to the times of the first two hylic worlds, i.e. the time that measures the motion of the outermost sphere of the fixed stars (i.e. the sidereal time) and the time of the (supralunary) planetary motions (the year, the month, and other 'unknown' temporal units). Further down is the time of the third hylic world, i.e. the sublunary time. Although Damascius believed that the source of all time(s), i.e. Time as god, is to be found not in the great Hecate but in the Demiurge,[28] there can be no doubt that he accepted this plurality of times. But he seems to have been mostly concerned with the times of the 'hylic' worlds, as well as with a further time which he himself grasped, a time that should perhaps be situated between what Proclus calls the 'azonic time' and the 'zonic time'. This integral time, which pertains to the activity of being of the heaven, as well as the supralunary and the sublunary times, constitute the object of the present book.

**

The research that led to the publication of the present book and the publication itself were made possible thanks to a twelve months fellowship granted by the Einstein Center Chronoi in Berlin. Although a major part of my fellowship took place

---

τῶν ἐσχάτων, ἃ δὴ καὶ αὐτὰ κατὰ περιόδους μετρεῖται, κἂν ᾖ τῶν παμφθόρων πραγμάτων. Translation by Baltzly, modified.

[26] This theology was delivered through the *Chaldean Oracles*, an apocryphal text of the second century AD, which we know fragmentarily mainly through quotations by the Late Platonists. See, in general, Seng (2016). On Proclus' interpretation of the *Chaldean Oracles* see lately Spanu (2021).

[27] Cf. *Chaldean Oracles*, fr. 57, with Michael Psellos, *General and concise exposition of the doctrines of the Chaldeans*, p. 146.9–12.

[28] Cf. Damascius, *In Parm.*, III, 181.7–182.9. Damascius thought that, since time is not properly a life-giver but rather "measures" (the life of) the enmattered forms, is organically related to the Demiurge, who contemplates the intelligible forms in the "complete Living Being" (Plato, *Timaeus*, 31b 1: τὸ παντελὲς ζῷον). Cf. Damascius, *In Parm.*, III, 181.11–13: "I do not think that the fontal time is in the great Goddess [i.e. Hecate] but rather in the Demiurge." (Οὐκ οἶμαι τὸν πηγαῖον χρόνον ἐν τῇ μεγάλῃ εἶναι θεῷ, ἀλλὰ μᾶλλον ἐν τῷ δημιουργῷ.) See further Chapter 3, n. 85.

during the restrictive conditions imposed by the pandemic, the EC Chronoi has been a stimulating place, both virtually and physically, for doing research, giving talks, discussing and learning from scholars who approach time and time-awareness from different perspectives. I wish to thank all the Chronoi fellows for their interest in my work and, especially, Eva Cancik-Kirschbaum, Christoph Markschies and Hermann Parzinger for welcoming this little philosophical book in the Chronoi series. I also thank for their queries and comments the participants in Stephen Menn's colloquium at the Humboldt Universität, where I was invited to present some parts of my research on Damascius' philosophy of time. My warmest thanks are also extended to Irene Sibbing-Plantholt, Stefanie Rabe and Yosef Elharar for their assistance and their kindness, as well as to Gene Trabich for scrutinizing my text and to Paraskevi Naka for her help with the indices. Any shortcomings are, of course, my own responsibility.

1 Damascius as an exegete of Aristotle

1.1 The philosophical vocation of Damascius

Damascius of Damascus, the last Head of the Platonic School in Athens (πλατωνικὸς διάδοχος),[1] is known among contemporary Hellenists and historians of philosophy for his philosophical and scholarly commitment to Plato. He himself qualifies himself as a Platonist, using a distinct philosophical vocabulary, in the following passage of his lost treatise *On Time*:

> But we [i.e. Platonists] who agree that whatever receives its existence from something else is generated and becoming would reasonably not call this eternity, but time, positing this as the first image of eternity.[2]

It is Plato who calls time "an image of eternity",[3] and we will see in the following chapters why Damascius thinks that there is a first and, therefore, also a second image of eternity. For the time being, what needs to retain our attention is that Damascius understood generation and becoming not in the manner of Peripatetic philosophers, such as Alexander of Aphrodisias, who thought that generation occurs in time and therefore cannot be predicated to time, given that time is eternal, but in accordance with the *Timaeus*, where Plato has the Pythagorean Timaeus say that "everything which becomes must of necessity become in virtue of *some cause*; for without a cause it is impossible for everything to attain generation".[4] Time has a cause and is therefore generated but certainly not in time.

Damascius' pupil Simplicius of Cilicia—and presumably the next 'Platonic successor', had the Athenian School not been closed in 529—says of his master that

---

[1] That is, 'Platonic successor'. There was neither institutional nor geographical continuation between Plato's (Ancient) Academy and the (Late antique) Platonic School of Athens; see Glucker (1978). The πλατωνικὸς διάδοχος was the intellectual heir of Plato and the genuine expounder of his doctrines. When the emperor Justinian banned the teaching activities of the School in 529, the 'successor' of Plato was Damascius. Because of this banning and other persecutions against Hellenes in Athens, Damascius and his fellow philosophers fled to the court of Chosroes in Ctesiphon in 531/532. There is some controversy as to the place in which they settled later. Damascius, at any rate, returned to his native Syria. See lately Golitsis (2015) for discussion of these matters.
[2] Damascius *apud Simplicium, In Phys.*, 781.11–13: Ἡμεῖς δὲ οἱ τὸ ὑπὸ ἑτέρου ὑφιστάμενον γενητὸν εἶναι καὶ γινόμενον ὁμολογοῦντες εἰκότως ἂν οὐκ αἰῶνα καλοῖμεν αὐτὸν ἀλλὰ χρόνον, αἰῶνος εἰκόνα πρώτην τιθέμενοι ταύτην.
[3] Cf. Plato, *Timaeus*, 37d 5.
[4] Plato, *Timaeus*, 28a 4–6: Πᾶν δὲ αὖ τὸ γιγνόμενον ὑπ' αἰτίου τινὸς ἐξ ἀνάγκης γίγνεσθαι· παντὶ γὰρ ἀδύνατον χωρὶς αἰτίου γένεσιν σχεῖν.

"he put many labours in philosophy".[5] By this, Simplicius probably meant Damascius' wide lecturing and writing on philosophy, as compared to the exegetical endeavours of previous 'Platonic successors', that is, Isidore of Alexandria, who had succeeded Marinus of Neapolis, who in turn had succeeded the great Proclus of Lycia.[6] Damascius' lectures on Plato's *Phaedo* and Plato's *Philebus* recorded by his pupils, as well as a major part of his commentary on Plato's *Parmenides* and a related autonomous treatise *On the First Principles*, survive today.[7] Several references in these works reveal that Damascius had also lectured on the *Republic*, the *Phaedrus*, the *Sophist*, the *Timaeus*, and possibly the *Laws*,[8] whereas the Alexandrian philosopher Olympiodorus made extensive use of Damascius' (lost) commentary on the *First Alcibiades* in his own commentary on this Platonic dialogue, mostly reporting Damascius' criticisms of Proclus' explanations.[9] Damascius' surviving works were transliterated in the ninth/tenth century in the Constantinopolitan *scriptoria* and were handed down to the Renaissance Platonists, as well as to their modern and contemporary peers, thanks to Cardinal Bessarion's legacy to the Republic of Venice.[10] Still, as an intellectual living in the Eastern part of the Mediterranean in the end of Antiquity, Damascius could not possibly bypass Aristotle, not only exegetically but also philosophically. As we shall see in the next chapter, one of the basic elements of his (Platonic) system, namely the three modes of distension, i.e. plurality, extension, and duration, according to which the perceptible world in its fundamental structure is an image of the intelligible world, is built upon the Aristotelian distinctions between number and measure, position and order, and essence and activity.

---

[5] Simplicius, *In Phys.*, 625.1: πολλοὺς πόνους εἰσαγαγὼν φιλοσοφίᾳ.

[6] One may also think that Simplicius contrasted Damascius' deep interest in philosophy with the preference for theurgy over philosophical activity of some members of the Athenian School, such as the notorious Hegias (see n. 16). This does not imply, of course, that Damascius was hostile to theurgic practice, as Porphyry, the pupil and biographer of Plotinus, was. Damascius was seriously interested in the *Chaldean Oracles* and at least planned to write a commentary on them, as Proclus and Syrianus had done before him; see Westerink/Combès (1991: p. 227, n. 3).

[7] Respectively edited by Westerink (1977); Westerink (1959); Westerink/Combès (1997–2003); Westerink/Combès (1986–1991).

[8] See the auto-references assembled in Westerink-Combès (1986: xxxiv, n. 1–5).

[9] See Westerink-Combès (1986: xlvi).

[10] All Renaissance copies of Damascius' works go back to two exemplars of the so-called 'philosophical collection' of the ninth/tenth century, namely *Marcianus gr.* 196 and *Marcianus gr.* 246, which in the fifteenth century belonged to Bessarion. On the 'philosophical collection' see now Bianconi/Ronconi (2020). There are no further properly Byzantine copies of these manuscript. This testifies of the poor reception of Damascius in Byzantium. Michael Psellos in the eleventh century, however, did have some knowledge of Damascius' works.

Simplicius qualifies his master Damascius not only as φιλόπονος, i.e. 'lover of (philosophical) toil', but also as ἀνὴρ ζητητικώτατος,[11] i.e. 'most disposed to inquiring'. This inquiring, which is related to the dialectical skills that Damascius acquired thanks to his master Isidore of Alexandria,[12] is mostly evident in Damascius' commentary on Plato's *Parmenides* and his treatise *On the First Principles*. But it is also at work, as we will see in the following chapters, in his treatise *On Time*. This kind of extreme inquiry (ζήτησις) involved questioning received doctrines and interpretations of doctrines not in a sterile aporetic manner, that is, for the sake of questioning, but for the sake of intellectually perceiving entities that were previously not perceived.[13] As we shall see, in the core of his philosophy of time, namely the doctrine of 'the whole of time', where no difference between past, present and future occurs, Damascius endeavoured to grasp such an entity: no one had perceived this entity before.

1.2 The curriculum of Damascius

Born in Damascus around 460 A.D.,[14] apparently to a wealthy family, Damascius and his brother Julian studied rhetoric in Alexandria. Damascius subsequently taught this discipline for nine years in Alexandria and Athens, as Photius reports in his *Bibliotheca*.[15] It was probably in Athens that he became a close friend of Isi-

---

11 Simplicius, *In Phys.*, 624.38.
12 Cf. Photius, *Bibliotheca*, codex 181 ("On the life of the philosopher Isidore"), 127a 10 – 14 (= Damascius, *The Philosophical History*, Test. III Athanassiadi, lin. 91 – 95): "[Damascius] claims that he acquired his strength in the practice of dialectic from his conservations with Isidore, whom he declares to have eclipsed in the power of his discourse all men born in that generation." (Τῆς μέντοι διαλεκτικῆς τριβῆς τὰς Ἰσιδώρου συνουσίας τὴν ἰσχὺν αὐτῷ διατείνεται παρασχεῖν, ὃν καὶ ἐπὶ τῇ τοιαύτῃ τῶν λόγων δυνάμει πάντας ἀνθρώπους, ὅσους ὁ κατ' ἐκείνην τὴν γενεὰν ἤνεγκε χρόνος, ἀποκρύψασθαί φησιν. Translation by Athanassiadi.)
13 See further Tresson-Metry (2012); Ahbel-Rappe (2018).
14 See Hoffmann (1994) for a detailed biobibliography of Damascius. See also Trabattoni (1985).
15 Cf. Photius, *Bibliotheca*, codex 181, 126b 40 – 127a 10 (= Damascius, *The Philosophical History*, Test. III Athanassiadi, lin. 81 – 91): "Damascius studied the art of rhetoric under Theo for three whole years, and taught rhetoric for nine years. In geometry, arithmetic and the other sciences he was taught in Athens by Marinus, the successor of Proclus; in philosophy Zenodotus (also a successor of Proclus, second to Marinus) was his master in Athens, and Ammonius, son of Hermeias, in Alexandria, who, he says, greatly surpassed all his contemporaries in philosophy and especially in the sciences. Damascius mentions him as the man who taught him the Platonic writings and Ptolemy's astronomical syntaxis." (Ὁ δὲ Δαμάσκιος τήν τε ῥητορεύουσαν τέχνην ὑπὸ Θέωνι τρία ἔτη ὅλα διεπόνησε καὶ προὔστη διατριβῶν ῥητορικῶν ἐπὶ ἔτη θ'. Γεωμετρίας δὲ καὶ ἀριθμητικῆς καὶ τῶν ἄλλων μαθημάτων Μαρῖνον τὸν διάδοχον Πρόκλου ἐν Ἀθήναις ἔσχε διδάσκαλον. Τῆς τε

dore of Alexandria, who was studying there with Proclus. Isidore seems to have been to Damascius what Socrates has been to Plato: he converted him to philosophy.[16] As a Hellene and an acquaintance of Isidore, Damascius became familiar with the members of the Athenian Platonic School: the aged Proclus, who was 'Platonic successor' by the time of Damascius' arrival in Athens, Marinus, who taught to Damascius the mathematical sciences and eventually became Proclus' successor, and Zenodotus,[17] who taught philosophy to Damascius.[18] When Marinus was about

---

φιλοσόφου θεωρίας ὅ τε Ζηνόδοτος αὐτῷ καθηγεμὼν Ἀθήνησι καὶ αὐτὸς ἐγεγόνει (διάδοχος δὲ καὶ οὗτος Πρόκλου, τὰ δεύτερα Μαρίνου φέρων) καὶ Ἀμμώνιος ἐν Ἀλεξανδρείᾳ ὁ Ἑρμείου, ὃν οὐ μικρῷ μέτρῳ τῶν καθ' ἑαυτὸν ἐπὶ φιλοσοφίᾳ φησὶ διαφέρειν, καὶ μάλιστα τοῖς μαθήμασι. Τοῦτον καὶ τῶν Πλατωνικῶν ἐξηγητὴν αὐτῷ γεγενῆσθαι Δαμάσκιος ἀναγράφει, καὶ τῆς συντάξεως τῶν ἀστρονομικῶν Πτολεμαίου βιβλίων. Translation by Athanassiadi, slightly modified.)

16 In his *Philosophical History* (quoted as *On the life of the philosopher Isidore* by Photius), which we know fragmentarily through the *Suidae Lexicon* and Photius' *Bibliotheca*, Damascius praises Isidore's disinterest in rhetoric ("he left to others the graceful display of words") and his ability "to pronounce concepts rather than words and, indeed, to bring to light [i.e. via their knowingness] the very essences of the things themselves"; cf. Damascius, *The Philosophical History*, fr. 37 D Athanassiadi, lin. 4–7 (=*Life of Isidore*, fr. 85 Zintzen, lin. 5–10): τὴν δὲ τῶν ὀνομάτων εὐρυθμίαν ἀφιεὶς [sc. ὁ Ἰσίδωρος] ἑτέροις πρὸς ἐπίδειξιν εἴχετο τῶν πραγμάτων, οὐ λόγους τὸ πλέον ἢ νοήσεις φθεγγόμενος, οὐδὲ νοήσεις μᾶλλον ἢ τὰς οὐσίας αὐτῶν τῶν πραγμάτων ἄγων εἰς φῶς. Translation by Athanassiadi. Cf. also Damascius, *The Philosophical History*, fr. 59 A Athanassiadi (=*Life of Isidore*, fr. 131–133 Zintzen): "A feeling of great joy came upon Isidore as he caught sight of Proclus, whose appearance was both grave and formidable, so that he seemed to be gazing on the very face of philosophy itself. Proclus too marvelled at Isidore's face as being divine and full of the philosophical life within. His eyes betrayed the mobility of his mind and at the same time there ran through them a charming gravity and an unaffected modesty which made the philosopher turn to himself and immediately made the young man an old friend of Proclus." (Ὁ δὲ Ἰσίδωρος εὐφραίνετο ὁρῶν τὸν Πρόκλον, αἰδοῖόν τε ἅμα καὶ δεινὸν ἰδεῖν, αὐτὸ δοκῶν ἐκεῖνο ὁρᾶν τὸ φιλοσοφίας τῷ ὄντι πρόσωπον. καὶ ὁ Πρόκλος ἐθαύμαζε τὸ Ἰσιδώρου πρόσωπον, ὡς ἔνθεον ἦν καὶ πλῆρες εἴσω φιλοσόφου ζωῆς. οἵ τε ὀφθαλμοὶ τὸ τῆς διανοίας εὔτροχον ἀποσαφοῦντες καὶ ἅμα αὐτοῖς ἐπιθέουσα σεμνότης ἡδεῖα καὶ ἄπλαστος αἰδὼς ἐπέστρεφε πρὸς αὐτὸν [scripsi : αὐτὸν Photius : ἱκανῶς Athanassiadi] τὸν φιλόσοφον καὶ ἤδη γνώριμον ἐποίει αὐτῷ τὸν νεανίσκον. Translation by Athanassiadi, modified.) The last phrase points to Proclus' recognition of a soulmate and a true philosopher, as he himself was, in the face of Isidore.

17 Zenodotus was the "beloved pupil" (παιδικά) of Proclus, as Zeno was of Parmenides; cf. Plato, *Parm.*, 127b 6. It seems that Zenodotus would have succeeded Marinus but must have died unexpectedly before Marinus, probably leaving the office of the "sub-head" of the School (ὁ τὰ δεύτερα φέρων; see below, n. 24) to Hegias. As Hegias aspired to be a theurgist disinterested in philosophy (cf. Damascius, *The Philosophical History*, fr. 145 A Athanassiadi: "We had never heard of philosophy being so despised in Athens as we saw it dishonoured in the time of Hegias" [εἰς τοσοῦτον γὰρ ἀκηκόαμεν φιλοσοφίαν καταφρονηθεῖσαν οὐδὲ πώποτε Ἀθήνησιν, ὅσον ἑωράκαμεν ἀτιμαζομένην ἐπὶ Ἡγίου]; cf. also fr. 150 Athanassiadi), Marinus summoned Isidore to be his successor. Isidore had once denied his succeeding Proclus in favour of Marinus.

18 See n. 14.

to die, Damascius was sent to Alexandria with the mission to convince his old friend and tutor Isidore to assume the direction of the Athenian Platonic School.[19] Damascius settled anew in Alexandria, where he continued his philosophical studies with Ammonius, who also taught him astronomy.[20] Damascius says that Ammonius taught him Plato,[21] which means that he had completed by then the Aristotelian curriculum.[22] This implies that he had studied Aristotle in Athens with Zenodotus, as Isidore had done before him with Marinus.[23] Ammonius was a committed concordist, i.e. he firmly believed that Aristotle did not contradict Plato but expressed the same philosophical ideas differently and from a different perspective.[24] This concordist spirit is evident also in Damascius.

Thus, Damascius was thoroughly acquainted with Aristotle, first of all, thanks to his philosophical studies. Later, he himself must have taught Aristotle, while Isidore as the 'Platonic successor' was lecturing on Plato.[25] But it is only with some exaggeration that it can be asserted that Damascius composed or published full-fledged commentaries on Aristotle's treatises. The most conspicuous case is an alleged commentary on the (first book of) *Meteorology*,[26] which John Philoponus dis-

---

19 According to the reconstruction first proposed by Asmus (1911: 118). Cf. Damascius, *The Philosophical History*, fr. 148 C Athanassiadi (= Damascius, *Life of Isidore [ap. Photium, Bibl. codd. 181, 242]*, fr. 226 Zintzen).
20 See n. 14.
21 See n. 14.
22 At least since Porphyry the study of (select) Aristotelian treatises was seen as preparatory for the study of Plato and was integrated in the philosophical curriculum. See Goulet-Cazé (1982) and Hadot (1992).
23 Cf. *Suidae Lexicon*, III 324, 16, s. v. Μαρῖνος (= Damascius, *The Philosophical History*, fr. 38 A Athanassiadi): "This man [i.e. Marinus] took over Proclus' school and taught Isidore the philosopher the writings of Aristotle; when Isidore came to Athens for the second time, after the death of their common master [i.e. Proclus] [...]." (Οὗτος Πρόκλου διατριβὴν παραδεξάμενος καὶ Ἰσιδώρου τοῦ φιλοσόφου τῶν Ἀριστοτέλους λόγων καθηγησάμενος, ἐλθόντι τὸ δεύτερον Ἀθήναζε, τοῦ κοινοῦ διδασκάλου τετελευτηκότος [...].)
24 On Ammonius' concordism see Golitsis (2017a) and Golitsis (2019).
25 There is no direct testimony that Damascius actually succeeded Isidore. But it is hard to imagine that some other (unknown) philosopher was nominated 'successor' by Isidore. At any rate, there seems to have been a scholarly tradition according to which the Head of the School lectured on Plato, whereas the "sub-head" (ὁ τὰ δεύτερα φέρων) lectured on Aristotle: (a) when Proclus was still living, Marinus taught Aristotle to Isidore (see n. 22); (b) when Damascius left from Athens, having studied philosophy with Zenodotus, who was ὁ τὰ δεύτερα φέρων with regard to the διάδοχος Marinus, he had not yet entered the Platonic part of the curriculum (see n. 14). If this is right, Damascius' numerous commentaries on Plato should be related to his teaching activity as 'Platonic successor'. Damascius' pupil Simplicius, as a sub-head, would then lecture on Aristotle.
26 See Westerink/Combès (1986: xxxix–xli). There is no real evidence that Damascius wrote commentaries (or lectured) on Aristotle's *Categories*, as (prudently) surmised by Westerink/Combès

cusses in his own commentary on the same treatise.²⁷ Philoponus, however, does not use Damascius' text as an exegetical instrument but focuses critically on Damascius' theological and symbolic interpretations, namely of the causal power of the planets,²⁸ the supernatural motion of the comets, and the Milky Way as a path of purified souls. All this suggests that Damascius did not write a commentary on the *Meteorology* but rather composed separate 'theological' treatises on certain meteorological phenomena, which were of particular interest to him. As Aristotle famously dealt with these phenomena in his *Meteorology*, Damascius would naturally begin his treatises by discussing Aristotle's relevant accounts. At least, this procedure is more or less verified by his treatises *On Number, On Place*, and *On Time* (Περὶ ἀριθμοῦ, Περὶ τόπου, Περὶ χρόνου), the last two of which are fragmentarily preserved through quotations by Simplicius in his commentary on Aristotle's *Physics*. Number, place and time are, of course, conspicuous concepts in the Greek philosophical tradition; Damascius' reflections on them, however, take, as we shall see in the following chapter, Aristotle's *Categories* and *Physics* as their basis.

1.3 Damascius' treatises *On Number, On Place*, and *On Time*

The scholars who are familiar with Damascius' "Περὶ ἀριθμοῦ, τόπου καὶ χρόνου", as quoted by Simplicius, usually believe that this text formed a single treatise (μονόβιβλον). This, however, is contradicted by Simplicius' own testimony:

> At this point I ask to be excused by my master Damascius who, in the treatises (συγγράμμασιν) that he has written about number, place and time, wants that the measures be not four but three: number, place, and time.²⁹

The plural (συγγράμματα) leaves no doubt that Damascius wrote three different treatises. Simplicius uses the singular (βιβλίον, σύγγραμμα) when he wants to

---

(1986: xxxvi–xxxvii). The attribution of the first book of the commentary on Aristotle's *On the Heavens*, actually written by Simplicius, to Damascius is clearly an accident in the manuscript tradition of the text; see Hoffmann (1994: 577–578) and Golitsis (2008: 21–22).

27 Cf. Philoponus, *In Meteora*, 44.21–36; 97.20–21; 116.36–117.39.
28 As we will see in the next chapter, number, place and time have also causal powers for Damascius (who takes this doctrine from Iamblichus).
29 Simplicius, *In Phys.*, 774.30–31: Παραιτοῦμαι δὲ ἐνταῦθα τὸν ἐμαυτοῦ καθηγεμόνα Δαμάσκιον οὐ τέτταρα βουλόμενον εἶναι τὰ μέτρα ἀλλὰ τρία ἀριθμὸν καὶ τόπον καὶ χρόνον ἐν τοῖς περὶ ἀριθμοῦ καὶ τόπου καὶ χρόνου γεγραμμένοις αὐτῷ συγγράμμασιν.

refer separately to Damascius' treatise *On Place* and to Damascius' treatise *On Time*.[30]

Nonetheless, the treatises *On Number, On Place*, and *On Time* were conceptually related through the concept of 'measure' (μέτρον) as an ontological principle of equality and unity—a concept that Damascius drew from Iamblichus of Chalcis, who was for him a constant source of inspiration.[31] Here are Iamblichus' own words about time as measure:

> And we may posit that time is a measure, of course not by [merely] measuring locomotion, or by being [itself] measured by motion,[32] or by [merely] manifesting or being manifested by the [celestial] rotation,[33] but by being *the cause and unifier* of all these things together.[34]

Iamblichus goes beyond the Aristotelian and the Platonic conception of time as a measure of locomotion and rotation in order to conceive an instance of time at a higher level as a "cause and unifier" of all celestial and sublunary activities, that is, as a transcendent principle of unity.[35] Simplicius calls this imparticipable principle

---

30 Cf. Simplicius, *In Phys.*, 644.25–26: "It would probably not be a bad thing to listen also to Damascius' words in his book *On Place*, where he writes [...]." (Οὐδὲν δὲ ἴσως χεῖρον καὶ τῶν αὐτοῦ λόγων ἀκούειν ἐν τῷ περὶ τόπου βιβλίῳ γράφοντος ὧδε.) *In Phys.*, 800.20–21: "But let him who is not satisfied with the above as solutions of the aporiae read the treatise *On Time* by the philosopher Damascius." ('Ἀλλ' ὅτῳ ταῦτα πρὸς διάλυσιν μὴ ἀρκεῖ τῶν εἰρημένων, ἐντυγχανέτω τῷ τοῦ φιλοσόφου Δαμασκίου Περὶ χρόνου συγγράμματι.) Note that Proclus had also written a treatise *On Place*.

31 Much of Damascius' commentaries reintroduce Iamblichean ideas in order to rectify or improve Proclus' explanations. Cf. Simplicius, *In Phys.*, 795.15–17: "Damascius, because of his love of [philosophical] toil and his [intellectual] sympathy with Iamblichus, did not hesitate to criticize many of Proclus' doctrines." ('Ο δὲ Δαμάσκιος διὰ φιλοπονίαν καὶ τὴν πρὸς τὰ Ἰαμβλίχου συμπάθειαν πολλοῖς οὐκ ὤκνει τῶν Πρόκλου δογμάτων ἐφιστάνειν.) An intellectual sympathy with Iamblichus was previously distinctive of Damascius' beloved master, namely Isidore; cf. Damascius, *The Philosophical History*, fr. 34 A and 34 D Athanassiadi (cf. Damascius, *Life of Isidore*, fr. 77 Zintzen and Damascius, *Life of Isidore [ap. Photium, Bibl. codd. 181, 242]*, fr. 33 Zintzen).

32 As Aristotle thought; cf. Aristotle, *Phys.*, IV 12, 220b 14–16: "Not only do we measure the motion by the time, but also the time by the motion, because they bound each other." (Οὐ μόνον δὲ τὴν κίνησιν τῷ χρόνῳ μετροῦμεν, ἀλλὰ καὶ τῇ κινήσει τὸν χρόνον διὰ τὸ ὁρίζεσθαι ὑπ' ἀλλήλων.)

33 As Plato thought; cf. Plato, *Timaeus*, 38a 7–8: "[...] time [...] imitates eternity and circles round according to number." ([...] χρόνου [...] αἰῶνα μιμουμένου καὶ κατ' ἀριθμὸν κυκλουμένου.)

34 Iamblichus *apud Simplicium, In Phys.*, 794.18–20 (quoting from Iamblichus' commentary on the *Timaeus*): Καὶ θείη ἄν τις αὐτὸν [sc. τὸν χρόνον] εἶναι μέτρον οὔ τοι κατὰ τὸ μετροῦν τὴν φορὰν ἢ τῇ κινήσει μετρούμενον ἢ δηλοῦν τὴν περιφορὰν ἢ δηλούμενον, ἀλλὰ κατὰ τὸ αἴτιον καὶ ἓν ὁμοῦ δὴ πάντων τούτων.

35 This is the time which the Theurgists (i.e. the *Chaldean Oracles*) celebrate as a god, as Proclus explains; cf. *In Timaeum*, III, 20.22–30: "But the Theurgists would not say such things [i.e., as Aristotle and the Peripatetics claim, that time is the cause of corruption rather than generation, of

"the primary time" (ὁ πρῶτος χρόνος), which, by being participated, orders the duration of all generated things.³⁶ Moreover, in his commentary on Aristotle's *Categories*, Iamblichus defined place as an "incorporeal essence" with an "active power", which delimits and perfects the bodies by preventing them from draining away towards the unlimited.³⁷

Damascius was undoubtedly inspired by those Iamblichean concepts. He wrote the treatises *On Number*, *On Place*, and *On Time*, in order to show that number, place and time are not ontologically dependent on a body, as they are (or, in a concordist Neoplatonic perspective, seem to be) in Aristotle. For the Stagirite, a number counts entities that are either bodies or somehow related to bodies, place is the first boundary of the surrounding body, and time is the measure of a body's motion. For Damascius, however, number, place and time are superior to bodies, as they were for Iamblichus too. Number, place and time are self-stand-

---

oblivion rather than preservation, and that it is a cause incidentally and not *per se*], since they doubtless say that [time] is a god and have given us the invocation whereby it is possible to move this god to appear to us in person, and they celebrate this god as [...] 'eternal'. He is eternal not merely as an image of Eternity, but as antecedently comprehending and cognizing in an eternal manner the sum total number for all the things in the cosmos that undergo motion, thanks to which he draws round all the things that are moved and brings them back to the beginning of their regular cycles, whether they be swift or slow." (Ἀλλ' οὐχ οἱ θεουργοὶ ταῦτα φαῖεν ἄν, οἵ γε καὶ θεὸν αὐτὸν εἶναί φασι καὶ ἀγωγὴν αὐτοῦ παρέδοσαν ἡμῖν, δι' ἧς εἰς αὐτοφάνειαν κινεῖν αὐτὸν δυνατόν, καὶ ὑμνοῦσι [...] ⟨τοῦτον⟩ τὸν θεὸν καὶ αἰώνιον, οὐ μόνον ὡς αἰῶνος εἰκόνα, ἀλλὰ καὶ ὡς αὐτὸν αἰωνίως προειληφότα καὶ νοοῦντα τὸν σύμπαντα τῶν ἐν τῷ κόσμῳ κινουμένων ἁπάντων ἀριθμόν, καθ' ὃν πάντα τὰ κινούμενα περιάγει καὶ ἀποκαθίστησι περιόδοις θάττοσιν ἢ βραδυτέραις. Translation by Baltzly.)

36 Cf. Simplicius, *In Phys.*, 784.18–22: "From the analogy with eternity I myself have also come to conceive of the primary time which transcends all things that are in time and which temporalizes them by their participation in itself, that is, which arranges and measures the duration of their being and which makes the parts of that duration have an order." (Ἀπὸ δὲ τῆς τοῦ αἰῶνος ἀναλογίας εἰς ἔννοιαν ἦλθον καὶ ἐγὼ τοῦ πρώτου χρόνου τοῦ ὑπὲρ πάντα τὰ ἔγχρονα ὄντος καὶ ταῖς ἑαυτοῦ μεθέξεσιν ἐκεῖνα χρονίζοντος, τουτέστι τὴν τοῦ εἶναι παράτασιν αὐτῶν εὐθετίζοντος καὶ μετροῦντος καὶ τάξιν ἔχειν ποιοῦντος τὰ τῆς τοιαύτης παρατάσεως μόρια.)

37 Cf. Iamblichus *apud* Simplicium, *In Cat.*, 361.15–20: "For if place were inert, having its being in infinite void and extension, without having [itself] any subsistent reality, then it would also receive its delimitation from without. But if it has an active power and a determinate incorporeal essence, and if it does not permit the distension of bodies to proceed more or less unlimitedly, but rather delimits them within itself, then plausibly it will also furnish bodies with their limit from itself." (Εἰ μὲν γὰρ ἦν ἀδρανὴς ὁ τόπος ἐν ἀπείρῳ κενῷ καὶ διαστήματι ἄνευ τινὸς ὑποστάσεως ἔχων τὸ εἶναι, καὶ τὸν ὅρον ἂν ἔξωθεν παρεδέχετο·εἰ δὲ καὶ δραστήριον ἔχει δύναμιν καὶ οὐσίαν ἀσώματον ὡρισμένην καὶ τὴν τῶν σωμάτων διάστασιν οὐκ ἐᾷ μᾶλλον καὶ ἧττον εἰς ἄπειρον προχωρεῖν, ἀλλ' ἐν ἑαυτῷ ὁρίζει, εἰκότως ἂν καὶ τὸ πέρας ἀφ' ἑαυτοῦ τοῖς σώμασιν ἐπάγοι. Translation by Gaskin, modified.)

ing incorporeal uniting measures that coexist with bodies—hence, they are also called 'corporiform' (σωματοειδῆ)—and thus prevent them from sinking into complete indeterminacy.[38] Damascius also espoused Iamblichus' conception of an intellectual time (Simplicius' "first time", which we mentioned earlier). But he was no sterile reader of Iamblichus. In-between this transcendent time and time as a measure immanent in the rotation of the heaven, Damascius posited a further time, namely the time that exists all at once in the essence of the heaven.

I will discuss the preserved fragments of Damascius' *On Time* in the next two chapters and will try to put them in a sequence in the Appendix. As Damascius' doctrine of time as an (immanent) measure is closely related to his doctrine of place as an (immanent) measure, his *On Place* will be also discussed in the following chapter. Unfortunately, Simplicius has not preserved for us any fragment from Damascius' *On Number*. But we may reasonably guess that it, too, was inspired by Iamblichus. In his commentary on the *Categories*, while commenting on Aristotle's concept of discrete quantity, i.e. the number,[39] Iamblichus speaks of a number that coexists with the things that are numbered but has a "proper essence",[40] as place and time have. In general, we may surmise that, in all three treatises, Damascius' strategy would be, first, to determine the 'measures', against (a superficial reading of) Aristotle, as distinct ontological items with the help of Iamblichean concepts, and then to distinguish these immanent measures from their causes, which may

---

[38] For a succinct presentation of the doctrine of the uniting measures see Hoffmann/Golitsis (2016).

[39] Cf. Aristotle, *Cat.*, 6, 4b 20–25: "Quantity is either discrete or continuous. Moreover, some quantities are such that each part of the whole has a relative position to the other parts; others have within them no such relation of part to part. Instances of discrete quantities are number and speech; of continuous, lines, surfaces, solids, and, besides these, time and place." (Τοῦ δὲ ποσοῦ τὸ μέν ἐστι διωρισμένον, τὸ δὲ συνεχές· καὶ τὸ μὲν ἐκ θέσιν ἐχόντων πρὸς ἄλληλα τῶν ἐν αὐτοῖς μορίων συνέστηκε, τὸ δὲ οὐκ ἐξ ἐχόντων θέσιν. ἔστι δὲ διωρισμένον μὲν οἷον ἀριθμὸς καὶ λόγος, συνεχὲς δὲ γραμμή, ἐπιφάνεια, σῶμα, ἔτι δὲ παρὰ ταῦτα χρόνος καὶ τόπος. Translation by Edghill.)

[40] Cf. Iamblichus *apud Simplicium, In Cat.*, 130.14–19: "Iamblichus says: 'Like the other enmattered forms, number too is present in, and co-exists with, the things that are enumerated; but it does not have a mere existence in them, nor is its existence supervenient on them as a consequence, nor does it arrive with the status of an accident, but it has *some essence of its own* along with the things [enumerated], according to which it determines the things that participate [in it] and arranges them according to the measure that is appropriate [to them]'." (Ὁ δὲ Ἰάμβλιχός φησιν ὅτι "ὥσπερ τὰ ἄλλα ἔνυλα εἴδη, οὕτως καὶ ὁ ἀριθμὸς πάρεστι μὲν καὶ συνυπάρχει τοῖς διαριθμουμένοις πράγμασιν, οὐ μέντοι ἐν αὐτοῖς ἁπλῶς ἔχει τὴν ὑπόστασιν, οὐδὲ ἐπιγινομένην αὐτοῖς κατ' ἐπακολούθησιν οὐδὲ ἐν συμβεβηκότος τάξει παραγινομένην, ἔχουσαν δέ τινα ἰδίαν μετὰ τῶν πραγμάτων οὐσίαν, καθ' ἣν ἀφορίζει καὶ πρὸς τὸ οἰκεῖον μέτρον συντάττει τὰ μετέχοντα". Translation by Fleet, modified.)

exist at multiple levels of the (Platonically described) non-perceptible reality; finally, to identify the highest of these causes as gods within the Hellenic and the Barbaric (Chaldean, Egyptian and Phoenician) theology.

We cannot know when Damascius wrote his treatises *On Number*, *On Place*, and *On Time*. A first reasonable guess would be that they were written in Athens early in his career, when Damascius was focusing his philosophical activity on Aristotle, and, at any rate, before 531/532, when Damascius, together with Simplicius and five other fellow Platonists, left Athens for the Sassanid Empire. An early dating, however, seems less convincing than a late one. As Simplicius reports, he was objecting to the idea of "time existing all at once" to Damascius himself, when the latter "was still alive".[41] As Damascius died shortly after 538, it would be strange to suppose that Simplicius, who should be familiar with the entire oeuvre of his master, kept coming back to the theory of 'the whole of time' for, say, ten or fifteen years but failed to be convinced by his master or, for that matter, to convince his master to abandon this idea. It seems more plausible to suppose that Damascius had conceived of his doctrine earlier in Athens but wrote the three treatises at an old age in Syria and send them to Simplicius in Cilicia. We will see in chapter 3 that the core of Damascius' philosophy of time—where the distinction between 'the flowing time' (ὁ ῥέων χρόνος), which manifests itself primarily in the rotation of the heaven, and 'the essential time' (ὁ οὐσιώδης χρόνος), which pertains primarily to the essence of the heaven,[42] lies—is fully present in his commentary on the second hypothesis of the *Parmenides*, which is undoubtedly related to his teaching in Athens. It is telling, however, that Damascius does not use the expression 'the whole of time' (ὁ σύμπας χρόνος) in his commentary on the *Parmenides*.

---

41 Cf. Simplicius, *In Phys.*, 775.31–34.
42 See below, Chapter 3, n. 103.

2 Time as a uniting measure

> When the father that engendered it perceived it in motion and alive, a thing of joy to the eternal gods, he too rejoiced; and being well-pleased he designed to make it resemble its model still more closely. Accordingly, seeing that that model is an eternal living being, he set about making this universe, so far as he could, of a like kind. But inasmuch as the nature of the living being was eternal, this quality it was impossible to attach in its entirety to what is generated; wherefore he planned to make a movable image of eternity, and, as he set in order the heaven, of that Eternity which abides in unity he made an eternal image, moving according to number, even that which we have named time.[1]

Damascius was a Platonist and thus espoused the fundamental conception of time as a "movable image of eternity", as Plato has it in the *Timaeus*. But Damascius' account of time is much richer than Plato's—richer than any Platonist's for that matter. The motion of time "according to number", primarily according to the rotation of the outermost celestial sphere that accomplishes a day and night,[2] is for

---

[1] Plato, *Timaeus*, 37c 6-d 7: Ὡς δὲ κινηθὲν αὐτὸ καὶ ζῶν ἐνόησεν τῶν ἀιδίων θεῶν γεγονὸς ἄγαλμα ὁ γεννήσας πατήρ, ἠγάσθη τε καὶ εὐφρανθεὶς ἔτι δὴ μᾶλλον ὅμοιον πρὸς τὸ παράδειγμα ἐπενόησεν ἀπεργάσασθαι. καθάπερ οὖν αὐτὸ τυγχάνει ζῷον ἀίδιον ὄν, καὶ τόδε τὸ πᾶν οὕτως εἰς δύναμιν ἐπεχείρησε τοιοῦτον ἀποτελεῖν. ἡ μὲν οὖν τοῦ ζῴου φύσις ἐτύγχανεν οὖσα αἰώνιος, καὶ τοῦτο μὲν δὴ τῷ γεννητῷ παντελῶς προσάπτειν οὐκ ἦν δυνατόν· εἰκὼ δ' ἐπενόει κινητόν τινα αἰῶνος ποιῆσαι, καὶ διακοσμῶν ἅμα οὐρανὸν ποιεῖ μένοντος αἰῶνος ἐν ἑνὶ κατ' ἀριθμὸν ἰοῦσαν αἰώνιον εἰκόνα, τοῦτον ὃν δὴ χρόνον ὠνομάκαμεν. (Translation Lamb, slightly modified.)

[2] Plato says later that "with a view to the generation of time, the Sun and Moon and five other stars, which bear the appellation of 'planets', came into existence for the determining and preserving of the numbers of time." (Translation Lamb; *Timaeus*, 38c 4–6: Πρὸς χρόνου γένεσιν, ἵνα γεννηθῇ χρόνος, ἥλιος καὶ σελήνη καὶ πέντε ἄλλα ἄστρα, ἐπίκλην ἔχοντα πλανητά, εἰς διορισμὸν καὶ φυλακὴν ἀριθμῶν χρόνου γέγονεν.) Nonetheless, the heaven came into existence before the planets and it is the heaven, i.e. the outermost celestial sphere, which preserves the primary number of time. Aristotle took over this doctrine, since he says that human souls cognize one rotation of the outermost celestial sphere as the exemplary measure of both other motions and of time; cf. *Phys.*, IV 14, 223b 18–20: "If, then, what is primary is the measure of everything homogeneous with it, regular circular motion is above all else the measure, because the number of this is the best known." (Εἰ οὖν τὸ πρῶτον μέτρον πάντων τῶν συγγενῶν, ἡ κυκλοφορία ἡ ὁμαλὴς μέτρον μάλιστα, ὅτι ὁ ἀριθμὸς ὁ ταύτης γνωριμώτατος. Translation by Hardie, slightly modified.) Alternatively, one can think with Proclus that time is moving according to "the perfect number", i.e. the number that presides over the great or "perfect year" (computed at approximately 36000 solar years), through which all celestial circuits regain their original starting points and a life cycle of the universe is completed; cf. Plato, *Timaeus*, 39d 2–7 and *Republic*, VIII, 546b 3–4: "There is for the divine generated [thing, i.e. the universe] a period that is comprehended by the perfect number." (Ἔστι δὲ θείῳ μὲν γεννητῷ περιόδος ἣν ἀριθμὸς περιλαμβάνει τέλειος.) Cf. Proclus, *In Remp.*, II, 12.8–11: "This is

Damascius a second image of eternity, an image of an image. This "movable image", Damascius contends, must be distinguished from the first image of eternity, namely "the time [that] came into existence along with the heaven", of which Plato speaks a little later in the *Timaeus*.³

We will see in the next chapter that what came into existence along with the heaven was not the flowing time that goes along with the rotation of the heaven, but the whole of time, which pertains not to the activity that proceeds from the essence of the heaven, i.e. to its rotation, but to its very activity of being. The activity of heaven is flowing but its being is not. The heaven, to put it simply, does not grow old. Simplicius found it hard to cope with the idea of a time existing all at once; he thought that the notion of a time non-articulated in past, present, and future is self-contradictory.⁴ At any rate, Damascius was pointing to something

---

why [time] is called 'total' by the Muses [cf. *Republic*, VIII, 546a 3]: it sets before itself the complete number that determines all changes, which by recurring becomes infinite." (Διὸ καὶ ἅπας [scripsi : πᾶς codd. Kroll] κέκληται παρὰ τῶν Μουσῶν, ὡς παντελῆ τὸν ἀριθμὸν προστησάμενος τὸν πασῶν μεταβολῶν ἀφοριστικόν, ὃς ἀνακυκλούμενος ἄπειρος γίνεται.) See Vargas (2021: 202–207), who nevertheless does not properly distinguish in Proclus' passage between the number that is "set before", i.e. the "essential time" (ὁ οὐσιώδης χρόνος), which is called "the true number" (ὁ ἀληθινὸς ἀριθμός) in *Republic*, VII, 529d 2–3, and the recurring "numbered number" (ὁ ἀριθμητὸς ἀριθμός), which is an image of the essential time; cf. Proclus, *In Timaeum*, III, 19.14–28.

3 Cf. Plato, *Timaeus*, 38b 6–7: "Time, then, came into existence along with the Heaven, to the end that having been generated together they might also be dissolved together, if ever a dissolution of them should take place." (Χρόνος δ' οὖν μετ' οὐρανοῦ γέγονεν, ἵνα ἅμα γεννηθέντες ἅμα καὶ λυθῶσιν, ἄν ποτε λύσις τις αὐτῶν γίγνηται. Translation by Lamb.) Proclus also thought that time is somehow a double image of eternity, being unmoved in itself but movable by being participated; cf. Proclus, *In Timaeum*, III, 34.8–10: "[…] the image of Eternity that is simultaneously movable and yet always the same and invariant." ([…] τῆς κινητῆς ἅμα καὶ ἀεὶ κατὰ τὰ αὐτὰ καὶ ὡσαύτως ἐχούσης τοῦ αἰῶνος εἰκόνος. Translation by Baltzly). Cf. also *In Timaeum*, III, 27.13–15: "It would indeed be absurd for time, which is an image of eternity, to be merely a temporal image established within the things that are numbered by it." (Καὶ γὰρ γελοῖον αἰῶνος ὄντα εἰκόνα τοῦτο δὴ εἶναι τὸ ἐν τοῖς ἀριθμουμένοις μόνον ὑφεστὸς χρονικὸν εἴδωλον. Translation by Baltzly.) Damascius' first image, however, is closer to the *Timaeus* in that, unlike Proclus' first image, it is not hypercosmic but pertains to the heaven's activity of being.

4 Cf. Simplicius, *In Phys.*, 777.7–10: "If time has its being in becoming, as does motion, what is there absurd in the whole of time not existing at once? The contrary would indeed be absurd, namely that whatever has its being in becoming exists at once." (Εἰ οὖν ἐν τῷ γίνεσθαι τὸ εἶναι ἔχει ὁ χρόνος ὥσπερ καὶ ἡ κίνησις, πῶς παράλογον τὸ μὴ εἶναι ἅμα τὸν σύμπαντα χρόνον; τοὐναντίον γὰρ ἂν ἦν παράλογον τὸ ἅμα εἶναι πᾶν τὸ ἐν τῷ γίνεσθαι τὸ εἶναι ἔχον.) Simplicius actually espoused Damascius' doctrine of a measuring entity pertaining to the activity of being of the heaven but hesitated as to calling this entity 'time'; cf. Simplicius, *In Phys.*, 632.33–633.6: "In this respect, place resembles time. For one sort of time is perpetual and remains in the same state, and this is the time that has come to be together with the generation of the essence of the heavens, a generation which is in a way ungenerated and has only a suspicion of generation in respect of its bodily

that was previously not perceived. Whereas the activity of being of every sublunary substance necessitates a present, a future and a past, the activity of being of the heaven remains unalterable in time. Past, present and future emerge only as realities related to a thing's growing old in the sublunary world. To be sure, the heaven, unlike an intelligible form, is generated and therefore *is* not but *becomes*; its becoming, however, coincides with its being. Past and future do not pertain to the activity that proceeds from its essence either; as it goes on, the rotation of the heaven runs along with the continuously flowing time, and a single flowing 'now' is coextensive with a single 'leap' of this rotation.

We will see the details of this doctrine later. For the time being, it is important to expand on the distinctions between essence and activity of being, and between activity of being and activity that proceeds from the essence, which are crucial for understanding Damascius' doctrine on time. Although the metaphysics of Damascius (as the metaphysics of any late Platonist) is fundamentally shaped by Plato's *Parmenides*, Damascius is also a subtle interpreter of Aristotle. He articulates and expands his theory on time by building upon Aristotelian conceptions and distinctions: essence and activity, position and order, number and measure, motion and being of motion, and the concept of time as a measure of motion and of being moved. In the next two sections, I will try to elucidate these debts of Damascius to Aristotle by going through the relevant texts.

2.1 Being and activity of being: 2 + 1 measures

Simplicius introduces his digression on time, which 'crowns' his commentary on Aristotle's *Physics* IV 10–14 (and was therefore called "Corollarium de tempore" by Hermann Diels) with a concise presentation of the structure of the intelligible and sensible realms, largely inspired by Damascius. Simplicius' aim was to introduce 'time' as a measure, not merely as a "measure of motion and of being moved",

---

extension and alteration of what kind soever—if, indeed, one is prepared to call this and what measures the essence of the soul time, rather than something between time and eternity). The other sort of time has its whole existence in coming to be and passing away, and this is the time that measures the transitive motion of the heavens and all kinds of change in the things generated." (Καὶ κατὰ τοῦτο ὁ τόπος προσέοικε τῷ χρόνῳ· ὡς γὰρ ἐκείνου ὁ μέν τίς ἐστιν ἀίδιος καὶ ἐν ταὐτῷ μένων ὁ τῇ γενέσει τῆς οὐσίας τῶν οὐρανίων συμπεφυκὼς ἀγενήτῳ πως οὔσῃ καὶ μόνην ὑπόφασιν ἐχούσῃ γενέσεως κατά τε τὴν σωματικὴν διάστασιν καὶ τὴν ὁποιανοῦν ἀλλοίωσιν (εἴπερ ἄρα τις καὶ τοῦτον καὶ τὸν τῆς ψυχικῆς οὐσίας μετρητικὸν χρόνον συγχωρήσοι καλεῖν, ἀλλὰ μὴ μεταξύ τι χρόνου καὶ αἰῶνος), ὁ δέ τις ἐν τῷ γίνεσθαι καὶ φθείρεσθαι τὴν ὅλην ἔχων ὑπόστασιν οὗτος ὁ τήν τε μεταβατικὴν κίνησιν τῶν οὐρανίων καὶ τὴν παντοίαν τῶν ἐν γενέσει μεταβολὴν μετρῶν [...].) Cf. also Simplicius, *In Phys.*, 638.29–34.

as Aristotle himself defined time,[5] but, more generally and rather radically, as a measure which holds together whatever has its being in becoming by ordering the "duration of its being" (παράτασις τοῦ εἶναι).[6] Thus, 'measure' (μέτρον) with regard to time is meant by Simplicius not as a cognitive tool, as is meant by Aristotle (say, a month is our knowledge of the duration of the orbital period of the moon or, roughly, of the motion of the sun from one zodiacal constellation to the next one), but rather, as we already saw in the previous chapter, in the Iamblichean sense of ontological principle of unity. There are, according to Simplicius, four such measures in the sensible realm: number, place, magnitude and time. And, as any Platonist would be ready to affirm, there are four models of these measures in the intelligible realm, which emerge as soon as any kind of formal differentiation appears:

> Certainly, the unitary and the unified nature, which abide in simplicity, rise above all differentiation. The (i) unitary nature is the One (ἕν ἐστιν),[7] whereas (ii) the unified nature has been dominated by the One, having diverged from the One a little towards being the One-which-is (ἕν ὄν);[8] there, the being (τὸ εἶναι) has not been differentiated from that-which-is (τὸ ὄν).[9] But where, to the extent that this occurs in (iii) things unified, differentiation gener-

---

[5] Cf. Aristotle, Phys., IV 12, 220b 32–221a 1: Ἐπεὶ δ' ἐστὶν ὁ χρόνος μέτρον κινήσεως καὶ τοῦ κινεῖσθαι… IV 12, 221b 25–26: Μέτρον μέν ἐστι κινήσεως ὁ χρόνος καθ' αὑτό.

[6] Cf. Simplicius, In Phys., 640.29–30: Τὰ δὲ κατὰ τὴν τοῦ εἶναι παράτασιν ἐξετάθη, ὅσα ἀίδια ἢ κατὰ τοσόνδε χρόνον ἔχειν τὴν ὑπόστασιν λέγομεν. 775.22–23: Πάντων τῶν γενητῶν καὶ πάσης γενέσεως κρατητικὸς ἐν τῷ γίγνεσθαι καὶ συνεκτικὸς ὁ χρόνος.

[7] Cf. Plato, Parm., 137c 4–5: Εἰ ἕν ἐστιν, ἄλλο τι οὐκ ἂν εἴη πολλὰ τό ἕν. This is the One of the first hypothesis put forward by Parmenides (137c 4–142a 8), which, properly speaking, "is not even one"; cf. Parm., 142e 11–12: τὸ ἕν οὔτε ἕν ἐστιν οὔτε ἔστιν. Parmenides' first hypothesis yields negative conclusions for the One with respect both to itself and to the many. On the hypotheses of the Parmenides see Polansky/Cimakasky (2013).

[8] Cf. Plato, Parm., 142d 1–2: Εἰ τὸ ἔστι τοῦ ἑνὸς ὄντος λέγεται καὶ τὸ ἕν τοῦ ὄντος ἑνός […]. Although this phrase introduces the second (positive) conclusion for the One (with respect both to itself and to the many) of the second hypothesis put forward by Parmenides (142b 1–155e 4), the One-which-is, according to the Neoplatonic interpretation after Syrianus and Proclus, refers to the first conclusion (142b 5–c 7) of this hypothesis; it is the ὄν that, as Proclus says paraphrasing Plato's Sophist (245b 7–8): πεπονθός τε γὰρ τὸ ὄν ἕν εἶναί πως οὐ ταὐτὸν ὄν τῷ ἑνὶ φανεῖται), "having the one as an affection, it has the second place after the imparticipable unity" (Plat. Theol., III 8, 31.2–3: τὸ πεπονθὸς τὸ ἕν δευτέραν ἔχει τάξιν μετὰ τὴν ἀμέθεκτον ἕνωσιν).

[9] Siorvanes (1992: 85, n. 2) takes the infinitive τὸ εἶναι to denote 'essence' and the participle τὸ ὄν to denote 'real-existence'. This interpretation, which has a medieval appearance, can find no support in the Neoplatonic literature. Taken stricto sensu, τὸ εἶναι refers not to the essence but to the activity of being, which in the intelligible realm, thanks to eternity, is only formally distinct from the essence, whereas τὸ ὄν refers to the essence that has this activity. See below, Simplicius, In Phys., 773.33: "These are the measures of the differentiation according to the essence (ἡ οὐσία)

ally appeared, there (1) plurality appeared together with the one, and (2) whole and parts came into being, and (3) some preliminary outline of the things in this [i.e. the sensible] realm, which are extended here and there, shone, and (4) the being became other than that-which-is. And where any sort of differentiation appeared, there had at once to be also some measure of the differentiation, in order that the things that depart from the One do not fall into indeterminacy. Therefore, (1) the plurality was measured by the number, in order that it not be innumerable and truly unlimited and indeterminate; (2) the continuous extension was measured by the determination of magnitude, by which something has a determinate quantity of magnitude, and [thus] the continuous came into being like the discrete and stopped the unlimited departure [from the One]; (3) likewise the distinction of parts, one being here and another there, needed to be properly arranged and locally ordered. And these are the measures of the differentiation according to the essence (ἡ οὐσία) and to that-which-is (τὸ ὄν). But (4) since also the being (τὸ εἶναι) was differentiated, to the extent that this occurs in those [i.e. the intelligible] things, from that-which-is, becoming like a sort of extended mode of life (βίος) of that-which-is,[10] but nonetheless abode in the One-that-is, because also the activity (ἡ ἐνέργεια) abode in the essence (for the things there [i.e. the intelligibles] are activities by their essence, as Aristotle too proclaimed it,[11] having seen [those things] with divine insight), it accordingly received as its measure eternity, which assembles the extension of being into the unchanging abiding in the One-that-is. Thus, since the intelligible differentia-

---

and to that-which-is (τὸ ὄν)", which distinguishes the measures according to the ὄν are from the measure according to the εἶναι.

10 Cf. Damascius, *In Parm.*, I, 47.14–17: "Moreover [...] the always is not the same thing as being but is some aspect of being, like a sort of abiding or stationariness [of being] which, as the being proceeds, it [itself] does not proceed; or, [if you prefer,] it is the mode and course of life of the essence; or the way in which the essence exists; or however you can conceive of it." (Ἔτι δὲ [...] τὸ ἀεὶ οὐ ταὐτὸν μὲν τῷ εἶναι, τοῦ δὲ εἶναί τι ἐστίν, οἷον μονή τις ἢ στάσις, τῷ προελθεῖν οὐ προελθοῦσα· ἢ βίος καὶ διαγωγή τις οὐσίας, ἢ τρόπος τῆς ὑποστάσεως αὐτῆς, ἢ ὅπως ἄλλως νοοῖ τις.) *In Parm.*, I, 69.17–18: "The always is like the mode of life of the essence." (Τὸ ἀεὶ οἷον βίος ἐστὶν τῆς οὐσίας.) The word διαγωγή ('course of life') comes from Aristotle, *Metaph.*, XII 7, 1072b 14–16: "[God's] course of life is like the best that we have for a short time; for it is always in that state, whereas we cannot be." (Διαγωγὴ δ'ἐστὶν οἵα ἡ ἀρίστη μικρὸν χρόνον ἡμῖν· οὕτω γὰρ ἀεὶ ἐκεῖνο· ἡμῖν μὲν γὰρ ἀδύνατον.)

11 Cf. Aristotle, *On the Soul*, III 5, 430a 17–18: "And this intelligence is separate and unaffected and unmixed, and it is activity by its essence". (Καὶ οὗτος ὁ νοῦς χωριστὸς καὶ ἀπαθὴς καὶ ἀμιγής, τῇ οὐσίᾳ ὢν ἐνέργεια.) Cf. also *Metaphysics*, XII 7, 1072a 24–26: "Therefore, there is something which moves without being itself moved, [and this is] eternal and an essence and an existing activity [or: activity by essence]. [...] Since there is a mover, which itself is unmoved, being an activity [...]." (Ἔστι τοίνυν τι ὃ οὐ κινούμενον κινεῖ, ἀίδιον καὶ οὐσία καὶ ἐνέργεια οὖσα [an οὐσίᾳ?], and XII 7, 1072b 7–8: ἐπεὶ δὲ ἔστι τι κινοῦν αὐτὸ ἀκίνητον ὄν, ἐνέργεια ὄν.) That there are many things that are activites by their essence is shown in *Metaphysics*, XII 8. The plural, however, appears already in XII 6, 1071b 19–22: "Therefore, there must be such a principle whose essence is activity. Moreover, therefore, these essences must be without matter; for they must be eternal, if there is something else [i.e. the heaven] which is eternal. Therefore, [these essences are] activities." (Δεῖ ἄρα εἶναι ἀρχὴν τοιαύτην ἧς ἡ οὐσία ἐνέργεια. ἔτι τοίνυν ταύτας δεῖ τὰς οὐσίας εἶναι ἄνευ ὕλης· ἀϊδίους γὰρ δεῖ, εἴπερ γε καὶ ἄλλο τι ἀΐδιον. ἐνέργειαι ἄρα.)

tion was fourfold, these four measures appeared: (1) number, (2) magnitude, (3) place and (4) eternity. But **(iv)** the perceptible proceeded from the intelligible, that is, the generated from that-which-is,[12] by some sort of divergence and mutation (for it did not abide in the measures that are put under that-which-is,[13] but it was contaminated with what-is-not; for it was pleased, for the sake of its own existence,[14] with its being tinted in what-is-not, departing from that-which-is; this is why that-which-becomes (τὸ γινόμενον) came into existence as an image of that-which-is); so the perceptible, as is reasonable, did not admit a formal differentiation as [it happens] there, where each [intelligible] is not only unified with all other [intelligibles] but also is what the other [intelligibles] are; rather, as it descended from the indivisible nature to the division, the generation admitted a passive differentiation. This is why (1) what is there discreteness of plurality has become here fragmentation; and (2) the connatural wholeness there has been here continuously distended and has reappeared as enmattered quantity; and (3) what is there a differentiation of parts has become here scattering of different parts here and there. And thus (4) also the extension of being, which is there differentiated formally, whereas in reality it abides in the One-which-is, was here extended in existence, having received its being in the motion that is incident to generation.[15] For that very reason, also the measures themselves of the passive differentiations had a descent into generation: (1) the number has been fragmented through units; (2) the measure of the magnitude has been distended; (3) the place has been shared out into parts; (4) the time both is flowing and has been separated in accordance with the anterior and posterior.[16]

---

12 This echoes Plato's *Timaeus*, 27d 5–28a 4: "Now, first of all we must, in my judgment, make the following distinction. What is that which is always and has no generation? And what is that which is becoming always and never is? The one of these is apprehensible by intellection with the aid of reasoning, since it is always the same; whereas the other is an object of opinion with the aid of unreasoning perception, since it becomes and perishes and is never really." (Ἔστιν οὖν δὴ κατ' ἐμὴν δόξαν πρῶτον διαιρετέον τάδε· τί τὸ ὂν ἀεί, γένεσιν δὲ οὐκ ἔχον, καὶ τί τὸ γιγνόμενον μὲν ἀεί, ὂν δὲ οὐδέποτε; τὸ μὲν δὴ νοήσει μετὰ λόγου περιληπτόν, ἀεὶ κατὰ ταὐτὰ ὄν, τὸ δ' αὖ δόξῃ μετ' αἰσθήσεως ἀλόγου δοξαστόν, γιγνόμενον καὶ ἀπολλύμενον, ὄντως δὲ οὐδέποτε ὄν.)
13 Properly speaking, these measures are under the One-which-is (ἓν ὄν), which itself is in no need of measure.
14 Although Simplicius, following the *Timaeus* (see n. 12), speaks directly of the sensible world, the great departure from the One, which brings about the sensible world, is primarily due to the separately existing souls; cf. Plotinus, *Enneads*, V 1, 1.3–7: "The source of the evil that has overtaken [the souls] is their boldness and their generation, and the fact that they wanted to own themselves. For they were clearly pleased at their freedom and largely indulged their own motion […]." (Ἀρχὴ μὲν αὐταῖς [sc. ταῖς ψυχαῖς] τοῦ κακοῦ ἡ τόλμα καὶ ἡ γένεσις καὶ ἡ πρώτη ἑτερότης, καὶ τὸ βουληθῆναι δὲ ἑαυτῶν εἶναι. τῷ δὴ αὐτεξουσίῳ ἐπειδήπερ ἐφάνησαν ἡσθεῖσαι, πολλῷ τῷ κινεῖσθαι παρ' αὐτῶν κεχρημέναι […].)
15 ἐν κινήσει τῇ γενεσιουργῷ τὸ εἶναι λαχοῦσα: this is, as Damascius says (see n. 38), "the distension that came about through motion in activity or, rather, passivity".
16 Simplicius, *In Phys.*, 773.19–774.24: Ἡ μὲν οὖν ἑνιαία καὶ ⟨ἡ⟩ [addidi] ἡνωμένη φύσις ἐν ἁπλότητι μένουσα πάσης ὑπερανέχει διακρίσεως· καὶ ἡ μὲν ἕν ἐστιν, ἡ δὲ κεκράτηται τῷ ἑνὶ ὀλίγον τι τοῦ ἑνὸς παραλλάξασα πρὸς τὸ ἓν ὂν εἶναι· καὶ οὐδὲ τὸ εἶναι τοῦ ὄντος ἐκεῖ διακέκριται. ὅπου δὲ ὡς ⟨ἓν⟩ [addidi] ἡνωμένοις ὅλως ἀνεφάνη διάκρισις, ἐκεῖ καὶ πλῆθος ἀνεφάνη μετὰ τοῦ ἑνός, καὶ ὅλον καὶ μέρη γέγονε, καὶ τῶν ἐνθάδε ἄλλων ἀλλαχοῦ διαστάντων προϋπογραφή τις ἐξέλαμψε,

There are several Neoplatonic elements in this account of reality, the most conspicuous of which is the conception of the first two principles in accordance with the first two hypotheses of Plato's *Parmenides*.[17] These two principles, namely (i) the One and (ii) the One-which-is, as here conceived, fit Proclus' description of the structure of the Intelligible realm and its relation to the One.

Simplicius distinguishes between (i) the unitary (ἑνιαῖος) and (ii) the unified (ἡνωμένος) nature, which completely transcend differentiation, and (iii) the unified things (τὰ ἡνωμένα, the plural is significant here), in which differentiation appears. 'Unitary' and 'unified' are Proclean terms, which designate respectively the absolute or primal One (αὐτοέν, πρώτιστον ἕν), here simply termed 'One' (ἕν) by Simplicius, and the One-which-is (τὸ ἓν ὄν).[18] According to Proclus, the 'One',

καὶ τὸ εἶναι ἄλλο γέγονε παρὰ τὸ ὄν. ὅπου δὲ διάκρισις ὁπωσοῦν, εὐθὺς ἔδει καὶ μέτρον εἶναι τῆς διακρίσεως, ἵνα μὴ τοῦ ἑνὸς ἐκστάντα πρὸς ἀοριστίαν ὑπενεχθῇ. διὸ τὸ μὲν πλῆθος ἐμετρήθη τῷ ἀριθμῷ, ἵνα μὴ ἀνάριθμον καὶ ὄντως ἄπειρον καὶ ἀόριστον ᾖ, ἡ δὲ κατὰ συνέχειαν διάστασις ἐμετρήθη μεγέθους ὅρῳ, καθ' ὃν τοσόνδε τι, καὶ τὸ συνεχὲς ὥσπερ τὸ διωρισμένον γενόμενον ἔστησε τὴν ἐπ' ἄπειρον ἔκστασιν. ὁμοίως δὲ καὶ ἡ τῶν μερῶν ἄλλου ἀλλαχοῦ διάκρισις εὐθετισμοῦ καὶ τάξεως ἐδεήθη τῆς τοπικῆς. καὶ ταῦτα μὲν τῆς κατὰ τὴν οὐσίαν καὶ τὸ ὂν διακρίσεώς ἐστι τὰ μέτρα· ἐπειδὴ δὲ καὶ τὸ εἶναι τοῦ ὄντος ὡς ἐν ἐκείνοις διεκρίθη οἶον βίος τις τοῦ ὄντος γενόμενον παρατεταμένος, ἔμεινε δὲ ὅμως ἐν τῷ ἑνὶ ὄντι, διότι καὶ ἡ ἐνέργεια ἐν τῇ οὐσίᾳ (τῇ γὰρ οὐσίᾳ ἐστὶν ἐνέργεια τὰ ἐκεῖ, ὡς καὶ Ἀριστοτέλης ἐνθέως θεασάμενος ἀνεφθέγξατο), μέτρον ἔσχε κατὰ τοῦτο τὸν αἰῶνα συνάγοντα τὴν τοῦ εἶναι παράτασιν εἰς τὴν ἀκίνητον ἐν τῷ ἑνὶ ὄντι μονήν. καὶ οὕτως μὲν τῆς νοητῆς τετραχῇ γενομένης διακρίσεως τὰ τέτταρα ταῦτα ἀνεφάνη μέτρα ἀριθμὸς μέγεθος τόπος αἰών· τὸ δὲ αἰσθητὸν ἀπὸ τοῦ νοητοῦ προελθὸν καὶ τὸ γενητὸν ἀπὸ τοῦ ὄντος κατ' ἐκτροπήν τινα καὶ παράλλαξιν (οὐ γὰρ ἔμεινεν ἐν ὑφειμένοις τοῦ ὄντος μέτροις, ἀλλὰ τῷ μὴ ὄντι συνανεφύρη ἀγαπῆσαν πρὸς τὸ ὁπωσοῦν εἶναι τὴν ἀπὸ τοῦ ὄντος ἐν τῷ μὴ εἶναι παράχρωσιν· διὸ καὶ εἰκὼν ὑπέστη τοῦ ὄντος τὸ γινόμενον), εἰκότως οὖν καὶ τὴν διάκρισιν οὐκ εἰδητικὴν ἔσχεν ὥσπερ ἐκεῖ, ἑκάστου μὴ μόνον ἡνωμένου τοῖς ἄλλοις πᾶσιν ἀλλὰ καὶ ὄντος ὅπερ τὰ ἄλλα. παθητικὴν δὲ μᾶλλον τὴν διάκρισιν ἡ γένεσις ἀνεδέξατο ἀπὸ τῆς ἀμερίστου φύσεως εἰς μερισμὸν ὑπελθοῦσα· καὶ διὰ τοῦτο ὁ μὲν τοῦ πλήθους ἐκεῖ διορισμὸς ἐνταῦθα διασπασμὸς γέγονεν, ἡ δὲ ἐκεῖ συμφυὴς ὁλότης ἐνταῦθα διεστῶσα συνεχῶς ποσότης ἔνυλος ἀναπέφανται· καὶ ἡ τῶν μερῶν ἐκεῖ διάκρισις ἐνταῦθα ἄλλων ἀλλαχοῦ διάρριψις ἀπετελέσθη. οὕτω δὲ καὶ ἡ τοῦ εἶναι παράτασις εἰδητικῶς ἐκεῖ διακριθεῖσα τοῦ ὄντος, μείνασα δὲ ἐν τῷ ἑνὶ ὄντι καθ' ὑπόστασιν, ἐνταῦθα παρετάθη καθ' ὕπαρξιν ἐν κινήσει τῇ γενεσιουργῷ τὸ εἶναι λαχοῦσα. τοιγαροῦν καὶ τὰ μέτρα τῶν παθητικῶν διακρίσεων γενητὴν ἔσχε καὶ αὐτὰ τὴν ὑπόβασιν, ἀριθμός τε ταῖς μονάσι διεσπασμένος καὶ μεγεθικὸν μέτρον διεστὼς καὶ τόπος συμμεμερισμένος καὶ χρόνος ῥέων τε καὶ τῷ προτέρῳ καὶ ὑστέρῳ διωρισμένος.
17 See n. 7 and n. 8.
18 Cf. Proclus, *Plat. Theol.*, III 8, 32.8–13: Ὁ μὲν οὖν πρώτιστος καὶ ἑνιαῖος θεὸς ἄνευ προσθήκης ἄλλης θεὸς ὑπ' αὐτοῦ προσείρηται, διότι δὴ τῶν μὲν δευτέρων ἕκαστος θεῶν ὑπὸ τοῦ ὄντος μετέχεται καὶ συνηρτημένον ἔχει τὸ ὄν, ὁ δὲ πρώτιστος μόνος ἀφ' ὅλων τῶν ὄντων ἐξῃρημένος θεός ἐστι, κατ' αὐτὸ τὸ ἄρρητον καὶ ἑνιαῖον μόνον καὶ ὑπερούσιον ἀφωρισμένος. III 9, 36.22–23: [...] ἀπὸ τῶν μετὰ τὸν ἑνιαῖον θεὸν ἀρχῶν, τοῦ ἀπείρου λέγω καὶ τοῦ πέρατος. III 14, 50.24–25 (speaking of the three intelligible triads): Διῃρημένως μὲν τὸ ἑνιαῖον κράτος τοῦ πρώτου παραδεξάμεναι, νοητῶς δὲ τὴν πρὸ τῶν νοητῶν αἰτίαν ἐκφαίνουσαι. III 14, 52.7–11: Μετὰ τὸ ἓν τοίνυν τὸ πρὸ τῶν ὄντων τὸ ἓν

which is the object of the negative conclusions of the first hypothesis of the *Parmenides*,¹⁹ is the "imparticipable, ineffable and most truly supraessential cause, which is separated from all essence, from all power, and from all activity",²⁰ whereas the 'One-which-is', an expression used by Plato in the *Parmenides* and the *Sophist*,²¹ is the first among the three triads of intelligible gods.²² This triad is, as Proclus says,²³ "co-unified with the One" (τῷ ἑνὶ συνηνωμένην)—Simplicius says "having diverged from the One a little towards being the One-which-is"—and precedes both what is being differentiated (διακρινόμενον), i.e. the second intelligible triad, and what has been differentiated (διακεκριμένον), i.e. the third intelligible triad.²⁴ Nonetheless, the second and the third triads of the intelligible gods are also latently present in Simplicius' account.²⁵

The "unified things" (τὰ ἡνωμένα) correspond to the third triad of the intelligible gods, that is, as Proclus says, the "intelligible intelligence" (νοητὸς νοῦς) or the "intelligible plurality" (νοητὸν πλῆθος).²⁶ This is the Paradigm (παράδειγμα) or Liv-

---

πολλὰ κρυφίως καὶ τὸ ἡνωμένον, καὶ μετὰ τοῦτο τὸ διακρινόμενον καὶ προκύπτον ἀπὸ τοῦ ἑνοειδοῦς εἰς τὸ φανόν, ἔσχατον δὲ τῶν νοητῶν τὸ διακεκριμένον καὶ τοῦ νοητοῦ πλήθους περιληπτικόν.

19 Cf. Proclus, *Plat. Theol.*, III 7, 29.22–25: "Parmenides, for his part, names this [cause] 'One' and shows by means of negations that the transcendent and ineffable existence of this One is the cause of everything." (Ὁ δὲ αὖ Παρμενίδης ἓν μὲν αὐτὴν ἐπονομάζει, διὰ δὲ τῶν ἀποφάσεων τὴν ἐξηρημένην τοῦ ἑνὸς τούτου καὶ ἄρρητον ὕπαρξιν αἰτίαν τῶν ὅλων οὖσαν ἐπιδείκνυσιν.)

20 Cf. Proclus, *Plat. Theol.*, III 1, 5.16–6.1: Μετὰ δὲ τὴν ἀμέθεκτον ταύτην καὶ ἄρρητον καὶ ὡς ἀληθῶς ὑπερούσιον αἰτίαν, ἀπὸ πάσης οὐσίας καὶ πάσης δυνάμεως καὶ πάσης ἐνεργείας κεχωρισμένην, συνεχής ἐστιν ὁ περὶ τῶν θεῶν λόγος.

21 Cf. Plato, *Parm.* 142d 1; *Sophist*, 244d 14.

22 Cf. Proclus, *Plat. Theol.*, III 20, 72.19: τὸ δὲ ἓν ὄν, τῇ πρώτῃ. According to Proclus' interpretation, the One-which-is is the intelligible object with which also the first argumentation of the Stranger of Elea in the *Sophist* is concerned.

23 Cf. Proclus, *Plat. Theol.*, III 12, 45.13–15: Μετὰ δὲ τὴν τριάδα ταύτην πρώτην ἀπὸ τοῦ ἑνὸς ὑποστᾶσαν καὶ τῷ ἑνὶ συνηνωμένην, δευτέραν ὑμνήσωμεν ἀπὸ ταύτης προϊοῦσαν.

24 Cf. Proclus, *Plat. Theol.*, III 14, 52.7–11 (quoted above, n. 18).

25 Note that each intelligible triad is characterized by 'the mixed' (τὸ μικτόν, in accordance with Plato's *Philebus*, i.e. its third term (respectively essence, life, and intelligence; cf. Proclus, *Plat. Theol.*, III 14, 51.18–19: καὶ οὗ μὲν οὐσία τὸ μικτόν, οὗ δὲ ζωὴ νοητή, οὗ δὲ νοῦς νοητός), the first and the second term being 'the limit' and 'the unlimitedness' (again in accordance with Plato's *Philebus*) or, as Proclus himself says, 'the (limiting and uniting) existence' and 'the (unlimited) power'. The posterior triad is what the anterior is or are (the intelligence *is* and *lives*), whereas the anterior triad is what the posterior is by way of cause (κατ' αἰτίαν).

26 Cf. Proclus, *Plat. Theol.*, III 21, 77.19–22: "That-which-is exists in the intelligibles in three ways: the first kind is that-which-is primarily and is pre-eternal; the second kind is that-which-is secondarily and is the primal eternity; the third kind is that-which-is lastly and is the intelligence that is intelligible and eternal." (Τριχῶς δὲ τοῦ ὄντος ἐν τοῖς νοητοῖς τὴν ὑπόστασιν ἔχοντος, τὸ μέν ἐστι πρώτως ὂν καὶ προαιώνιον, τὸ δὲ δευτέρως ὂν καὶ αἰὼν ὁ πρώτιστος, τὸ δὲ ἐσχάτως ὂν καὶ νοῦς ὁ

ing-Being-itself (αὐτοζῷον) of the *Timaeus*,[27] which already contains all Forms and is thus distinct both from the intelligible life (νοητὴ ζωή), i.e. the second intelligible triad, which exhibits essentially a dualism that differentiates the being (ὄν, 'that-which-is') from its unity, and the intelligible essence (νοητὴ οὐσία), i.e. the first intelligible triad, in which this difference exists only occultly (κρυφίως): the one is the being and the being is the one, and thus no plurality appears.[28] Similarly,

---

νοητὸς καὶ αἰώνιος.) III 12, 46.9–10: [...] τὸ δὲ ἤδη πᾶν ἐστι τὸ νοητὸν πλῆθος καὶ ὁ τῶν νοητῶν εἰδῶν διάκοσμος (quoted n. 28).

27 Cf. Proclus, *Plat. Theol.*, III 15, 53.22–54.9: "Therefore, the Living-Being-itself is transcends the Demiurge and is, as Timaeus everywhere designates it, intelligible; and since the forms have been first differentiated in it and since it is complete, it comes into existence in the third order of the intelligibles. In fact, neither that-which-is primarily nor that-which-is secondarily are complete; for the first is beyond all differentiation, the other generates and labours the intelligibles but is not yet a multiplicity of beings. If then none of them is multiplicity, how could they be a complete multiplicity? And if this [multiplicity] appeared in the third triad of the intelligibles [...] and the Living-Being-itself is the primal Paradigm [...], it is necessary that the Living-Being-itself be established in this triad." (Διὰ ταῦτα μὲν οὖν [...] ἐξῃρημένον ἐστὶ τοῦ δημιουργοῦ τὸ αὐτοζῷον καί, ὥσπερ ὁ Τίμαιος αὐτὸ πανταχοῦ προσείρηκε, νοητόν· διότι γε μὴν τὰ εἴδη πρῶτον ἐν αὐτῷ διακέκριται καὶ διότι παντελές ἐστιν, ἐν τῇ τρίτῃ τάξει τῶν νοητῶν ὑφέστηκεν. οὔτε γὰρ τὸ πρώτως ὂν οὔτε τὸ δευτέρως παντελές· τὸ μὲν γὰρ ἐπέκεινα πάσης διακρίσεως, τὸ δὲ γεννᾷ μὲν καὶ ὠδίνει τὰ νοητά, πλῆθος δὲ οὔπω τῶν ὄντων ἐστίν. εἰ τοίνυν μηδέτερόν ἐστι πλῆθος, πῶς ἂν εἴη πλῆθος παντελές; εἰ δὲ κατὰ τὴν τρίτην ἐξεφάνη τριάδα τῶν νοητῶν [...], τὸ δὲ αὐτοζῷον πρώτιστόν ἐστι παράδειγμα [...], ἀνάγκη δήπου κατὰ ταύτην τὴν τάξιν ἱδρῦσθαι τὸ αὐτοζῷον.) Cf. also *Plat. Theol.*, III 14, 51.27–52.6: "What the forms bring into existence in a divided way, this has as its transcendent cause 'that-which-is', and what 'that-which-is' produces collectively, this has as its cause of its being divided the forms; for the forms are called paradigms of beings, whereas 'that-which-is' is the cause and not the paradigm of everything that comes after it; for the paradigms are causes of the things that are differentiated in their being and whose essences are characterized differently." (Ὧν γὰρ ὑποστατικὰ τὰ εἴδη μεμερισμένως, τούτων ἐστὶν αἴτιον ἐξῃρημένον τὸ ὄν, καὶ ὧν ἀθρόως τὸ ὂν παρακτικόν, τούτων τὰ εἴδη διακεκριμένως ἐστὶν αἴτια, διότι τὰ μὲν εἴδη παραδείγματα καλεῖται τῶν ὄντων, τὸ δὲ ὂν αἴτιον τῶν μετ' αὐτὸ πάντων, ἀλλ' οὐ παράδειγμα· τῶν γὰρ διῃρημένων κατὰ τὸ εἶναι καὶ διαφόρους τῆς οὐσίας ἐχόντων τοὺς χαρακτῆρας αἴτια τὰ παραδείγματα.)

28 Cf. Proclus, *Plat. Theol.*, III 12, 46.5–10: "In the Intelligible there exist all things [...]: being, living, cognizing. Being is all things by way of cause and, as we have said several times, occultly; living makes multiplicity appear and proceeds from the unity of being to the manifestation of this multiplicity; finally, cognizing is already the totality of the intelligible multiplicity and the realm of the intelligible forms." (Πάντα γάρ ἐστιν ἐν τῷ νοητῷ [...], τὸ εἶναι, τὸ ζῆν, τὸ νοεῖν. καὶ τὸ μὲν κατ' αἰτίαν ἐστὶ πάντα καὶ ὡς πολλάκις εἴπομεν κρυφίως, τὸ δὲ προφαίνει τὸ πλῆθος καὶ πρόεισιν ἀπὸ τῆς ἑνώσεως τοῦ ὄντος εἰς ἔκφανσιν, τὸ δὲ ἤδη πᾶν ἐστι τὸ νοητὸν πλῆθος καὶ ὁ τῶν νοητῶν εἰδῶν διάκοσμος.) III 26, 89.4–11: "After the occult unity of the first triad and the dyadic differentiation of the second [triad], the procession of the third [triad] is produced, which has its existence in parts, but parts that are numerous and whose multiplicity is laboured by the preceding triad." (Μετὰ γὰρ τὴν κρύφιον ἕνωσιν τῆς πρώτης καὶ τὴν τῆς δευτέρας δυαδικὴν διάκρισιν ἡ τῆς τρίτης

the measure of the extension of being (εἶναι), i.e. eternity (αἰών) itself, corresponds to the second triad of the intelligible gods,[29] in which the third triad participates, so as to be eternal.[30] Eternity becomes the 'mode of life' (βίος)—a property that is similar but not identical to 'life' (ζωή)—of the intelligible plurality ("the unified things"), in virtue of which the activity of this plurality, which is essential to its being an αὐτοζῷον in itself and a paradigm for the Demiurge ('being a paradigm for' is its external activity), is maintained in the One-which-is, i.e. the first triad of intelligible gods or intelligible essence.[31] Thus, "that-which-is lastly", i.e. the Living-Being-itself, participates in eternity and its activity eternally abides in the intelligible essence.[32] It is thanks to the first and the second intelligible triads that τὰ ἡνωμένα, the unified intelligibles, which constitute the Living-Being-itself, are, as Aristotle puts it, "activities by their essence".[33] As we can see, the Proclean scheme of the One and the intelligible gods, as distinct from the intelligible-intellective gods

---

ἀπογεννᾶται πρόοδος, ἐκ μερῶν μὲν ἔχουσα τὴν ὑπόστασιν, πλειόνων δὲ μερῶν, ὧν τὸ πλῆθος ὡδίνει ἡ πρὸ αὐτῆς.)

29 Cf. Proclus, *Plat. Theol.*, III 16, 56.6–7: "Therefore, eternity will have its existence in life and will be established in the middle of the intelligible." (Ἐν ζωῇ ἄρα ὁ αἰὼν τὴν ὑπόστασιν ἕξει καὶ ἔσται κατὰ τὴν μεσότητα τὴν νοητὴν ἱδρυμένος.)

30 Note that the model of time is not the first Eternity (i.e. the second intelligible triad) but the (second) eternity that coexists with the third intelligible triad, i.e. the Living-Being-itself; cf. Damascius, *In Parm.*, III, 181.22–23: Τὸ τοῦ χρόνου παράδειγμα οὐκ ἔστιν ὁ πρῶτος αἰών, ἀλλ' ὁ συνὼν τῷ αὐτοζῴῳ.

31 Cf. Proclus, *Plat. Theol.*, III 17, 58.6–9: "If then eternity cannot abide either in itself or in the primal One, it is clear that, since, according to Timaeus, it 'abides in a one', it is established in the one of the first triad [i.e. the first of the three terms] or, more precisely, in this entire triad." (Εἰ τοίνυν ὁ αἰὼν μήτε ἐν ἑαυτῷ δύναται μένειν μήτε ἐν τῷ πρωτίστῳ ἑνί, δῆλον ὅτι κατὰ τὸν Τίμαιον ἐν ἑνὶ μένων ἐν τῷ τῆς πρώτης ἵδρυται τριάδος ἑνί, μᾶλλον δὲ ἐν τῇ πάσῃ τριάδι.)

32 Cf. Proclus, *Plat. Theol.*, III 16, 54.22–55.6: "But, of course, the Living-Being-itself is eternal, as Timaeus himself says: 'The nature of the Living-Being was found to be eternal', and again elsewhere he says: 'The Paradigm exists for all eternity'. If, therefore, the Living-Being-itself is eternal, it participates in eternity; and if what participates is in any case inferior to what is participated, then the Living-Being-itself is also inferior to eternity. And if it exists for all eternity, it is filled with all the power of eternity; if this is so, it comes immediately after eternity; for to enjoy one's cause in its entirety is proper to that which is ranked immediately after this cause." (Ἀλλὰ μὴν τὸ αὐτοζῷον αἰώνιόν ἐστιν, ὡς αὐτός φησιν ὁ Τίμαιος· "Ἡ μὲν ζῴου φύσις ἐτύγχανεν οὖσα αἰώνιος" [37d 3]· καὶ πάλιν ἐν ἄλλοις [cf. 38c 1–2], ὅτι "τὸ παράδειγμα τὸν πάντα αἰῶνά ἐστιν ὄν". Εἰ τοίνυν αἰώνιόν ἐστι, μετέχει τοῦ αἰῶνος· εἰ δὲ τὸ μετέχον πανταχοῦ τοῦ μετεχομένου δεύτερον, καὶ τὸ αὐτοζῷον τοῦ αἰῶνος δεύτερον. Καὶ εἰ "τὸν πάντα αἰῶνά ἐστιν ὄν", ὅλης πεπλήρωται τῆς τοῦ αἰῶνος δυνάμεως· εἰ δὲ τοῦτο, προσεχῶς ἐστι μετὰ τὸν αἰῶνα· τὸ γὰρ ὅλων ἀπολαύειν τῶν αἰτίων τῶν προσεχῶς ἐστι τεταγμένων μετὰ ταῦτα.)

33 See n. 11.

and the intellective gods,[34] lies in the background of Simplicius' account, which is nevertheless inspired by Damascius.

Still, Proclus' considerations are far from being sufficient to account for all that is recounted in Simplicius' introduction of his digression on time. Whereas Simplicius speaks of four intelligible and four sensible measures, Proclus explicitly recognized only one intelligible measure, namely eternity, as well as one sensible measure, namely time, which is the image of eternity. Eternity measures the abiding of the intelligible beings which receive unity, whereas time measures the duration of the perceptible beings which receive a number.[35] This implies that Proclus linked the concept of measure as a principle of unity solely to the idea of 'being' (τὸ εἶναι) and, derivatively, to a perceptible thing's becoming (τὸ γίγνεσθαι), and remained ignorant of or, rather, indifferent to the measures of 'that-which-is' (τὸ ὄν). Nonetheless, the distinction between ὄν and εἶναι, in Aristotelian terminology between essence (οὐσία) and activity (ἐνέργεια), is crucial for Simplicius' account of the measures of the sensible realm and, since a passive measure cannot exist without its formal counterpart that causes it, this distinction is also crucial for determining the measures of the intelligible realm.[36]

According to Simplicius, it is not enough for 'that-which-becomes' (τὸ γιγνόμενον) to have only the duration of its being measured in order to exist well. Its original fragmentation, in addition, could not be left innumerable but also had to be measured in order to become (passive) plurality, its enmattered quantity could not be left unlimited but had also to be measured in order to become (passive)

---

34 Proclus discusses these further triads of gods in books IV and VI of his *Platonic Theology*; see Westerink/Saffrey (1981) and Westerink/Saffrey (1987).
35 Cf., most characteristically, Proclus, *In Timaeum*, III, 17.22–30: "Hence it is surely better to say that the god has introduced these two—I mean Eternity and time—forth as measures of different things; the one of beings that exist intelligibly, the other of encosmic beings. Therefore, just as the cosmos has been said to be an image of the intelligible, so too the cosmic measure has been denominated an image of the measure of the intelligible. Eternity, however, is a measure in the way the one, while time is a measure in the way that number is. Each of these two performs measuring, but while the first measures those things that are made one, as well as the abiding of the things that are, the other measures those things that are numbered and the duration of the things that come to be." (Βέλτιον οὖν λέγειν, ὅτι δὴ δύο μέτρα ταῦτα τῶν ὄντων ὁ θεὸς παρήγαγε, τὸν αἰῶνά φημι καὶ τὸν χρόνον, τὸν μὲν τῶν νοητῶς ὄντων, τὸν δὲ τῶν ἐγκοσμίων. καθάπερ οὖν ὁ κόσμος εἰκὼν εἴρηται τοῦ νοητοῦ, καὶ τὸ κοσμικὸν μέτρον εἰκὼν τοῦ μέτρου τοῦ νοητοῦ κατωνόμασται. ἀλλ' ὁ μὲν αἰὼν μέτρον ὡς τὸ ἕν, ὁ δὲ χρόνος ὡς ὁ ἀριθμός· μετρεῖ γὰρ ἑκάτερος, ὁ μὲν τὰ ἑνιζόμενα, ὁ δὲ τὰ ἀριθμούμενα, καὶ ὁ μὲν τὴν διαμονὴν τῶν ὄντων, ὁ δὲ τὴν παράτασιν τῶν γινομένων. Translation by Baltzly, slightly modified.)
36 Although this is not explicitly said in any source, the intelligible measures, as they relate to plurality, totality and activity, must have their first existence in the intelligible life (i.e. the second intelligible triad).

wholeness, its parts could not be scattered here and there but also had to be measured in order to become well positioned and arranged. Arrangement, wholeness and plurality, however, pertain not to (the activity of) being but to essence. Thus, next to eternity and time, which are respectively the measures of being and of becoming, number, magnitude and place appear in Simplicius' account as the formal and passive measures of 'that-which-is' and of 'that-which-becomes'. All these measures prevent all the things that depart from the One, that is, the unified things and the perceptible things, from falling into indeterminacy. Had it not been because of these measures, the reality would be deprived of every kind of unity and order. This doctrine, which we may call 'the doctrine of the uniting measures' (μέτρα συναγωγά),[37] does not relate to Proclus but comes directly from Damascius.

In his digression on place, which 'crowns' his commentary on Aristotle's *Physics* IV 1–5 (and was therefore called "Corollarium de loco" by Hermann Diels), Simplicius quotes *verbatim* from Damascius' treatise *On Place*. In this crucial text, Damascius unfolds the basic structure of the sensible realm, as it proceeds from the intelligible realm, through a series of twofold existent distinctions, initially between essence and activity, which comes along with motion or change, then between activity *of* the essence and activity *from* the essence, then between plurality (i.e. the state of being plural) of essence and magnitude of essence, which comes along with position, and, finally, between position (i.e. disposition) of essence and positioning (i.e. position) of essence:

> Everything in generation, having fallen away from the indivisible and undistended nature in both essence and activity, suffered a double distension, one in essence and the other in activity or, rather, passivity. The distension in activity was also twofold, one that is connatural to the essence, through which the essence is in continuous flux, the other proceeding from the essence, through which it acts in different ways at different times, having its activities extended and not all at once. The distension of the activity immediately demanded motion,[38] and motion came into being with it, and its distension came about through motion in activity or, rather, passivity.[39] The distension in essence was also twofold: one descended into becoming fragmentation of plurality, the other into becoming acquisition of bulk. The distension in magnitude and bulk came about immediately in position because of the scattering of the parts here and there. This, too, was twofold: one connatural to the essence, such as in my body the head being above and the feet below, the other adventitious, such as my being positioned sometimes at home, sometimes in the marketplace. Of these, the first clearly continues the same so long as the thing lasts, whereas the other is different at different times. And those

---

37 Cf. Simplicius, *In Phys.*, 625.28.
38 This can be traced back to Aristotle; cf. *Phys.*, IV 13, 222b 21: "Change in itself makes things depart [from what they were]." (Ἐκστατικὸν γὰρ ἡ μεταβολὴ καθ' αὑτήν.)
39 Cf. Simplicius, *In Phys.*, 774.19–20 (quoted n. 15): ἐν κινήσει τῇ γενεσιουργῷ τὸ εἶναι λαχοῦσα.

things are properly said to have a position that have extended parts, which are distended from each other. This is why position seems properly to belong to magnitudes and to their limits, because they are continuously distended. At any rate, numbers, although they are discrete from each other, do not seem to have a position, because they are not extended and distended, unless they too acquire at some level magnitude and distension. For everything distended, having lost its unified contraction, exchanged its being in itself for becoming in something else, in which it is said to be positioned, having, as it were, been let fall and having lost its self-government;[40] similarly in its activities, having departed from itself, it is said to be moved and change.[41]

According to Damascius, distension (διάστασις) principally emerges according to two modalities: (i) the positioning in something else (ἐν ἄλλῳ), which is the consequence of the loss of unified contraction in itself (ἐν αὐτῷ), and (ii) the departure from oneself (ἔκστασις ἀφ' ἑαυτοῦ), which is the consequence of not having *the activity of being* abiding *in* the being. ἐν ἄλλῳ and ἀφ' ἑαυτοῦ are the two modes of distension, which necessitate the conceptual distinction between measures of ὄν and measure of εἶναι: (i) for a thing to be *in* something else, it has to be a being (ὄν) discrete in number—discrete from the thing in which it is—and it has to be an extended being (a point is not *in* a line); and (ii) for a thing to depart from itself, it has to have its activity of being (εἶναι) extended. According to Damascius, there

---

40 Cf. Damascius, *In Parm.*, III, 189.18–20: γένεσις οὐδεμία αὐτοκρατής ἐστιν εἰ μὴ ἔχοι τι ὄν, τὸ διακρατοῦν αὐτῆς τὸν σκορπισμόν, ὥσπερ καὶ τὸ τοῦ χρόνου συνεχὲς τὸ νῦν, ὅ ἐστιν ἴχνος αἰώνιον.
41 Damascius *apud Simplicium, In Phys.*, 625.4–27: Τὰ ἐν γενέσει πάντα τῆς ἀμερίστου καὶ ἀδιαστάτου φύσεως ἐκπεσόντα κατά τε οὐσίαν καὶ κατ' ἐνέργειαν διττὴν ἔσχε τὴν διάστασιν τὴν μὲν κατ' οὐσίαν τὴν δὲ κατ' ἐνέργειαν ἢ πάθος, καὶ τὴν κατ' ἐνέργειαν διττὴν τὴν μὲν τῇ οὐσίᾳ σύμφυτον, καθ' ἣν ἐν συνεχεῖ ῥοῇ ἐστιν ἡ οὐσία, τὴν δὲ ἀπὸ τῆς οὐσίας προϊοῦσαν, καθ' ἣν ἄλλοτε ἄλλα ἐνεργεῖ παρατεταμένας ἔχοντα καὶ οὐκ ἀθρόας τὰς ἐνεργείας. καὶ ἡ μὲν τῆς ἐνεργείας διάστασις κινήσεως εὐθὺς ἐδεήθη, καὶ συνυπῆρξεν αὐτῇ κίνησις, καὶ ἐγένετο κατὰ κίνησιν ἡ διάστασις τὴν ἐνεργητικὴν ἤτοι παθητικήν. ἡ δέ γε τῆς οὐσίας διάστασις διττὴ καὶ αὐτὴ γέγονεν, ἡ μὲν εἰς πλήθους διασπασμὸν ἡ δὲ εἰς ὄγκον ὑπελθοῦσα. ἡ δὲ κατὰ μέγεθος καὶ ὄγκον ἐν θέσει γέγονεν εὐθὺς διὰ τὴν ἄλλου ἀλλαχοῦ τῶν μορίων διάρριψιν. διττὴ δὲ καὶ αὐτή· ἡ μὲν σύμφυτος τῇ οὐσίᾳ, ὥσπερ τοῦ ἐμοῦ σώματος τὸ τὴν κεφαλὴν ἄνω εἶναι τοὺς δὲ πόδας κάτω, ἡ δὲ ἐπείσακτος, ὡς ποτὲ μὲν ἐν τῇ οἰκίᾳ ποτὲ δὲ ἐν τῇ ἀγορᾷ τὴν θέσιν ἔχω. καὶ δῆλον ὅτι ἡ μέν ἐστι διηνεκὴς ἡ αὐτή, ἕως ἂν ᾖ τὸ πρᾶγμα, ἡ δὲ ἄλλοτε ἄλλη γίνεται. κεῖσθαι δὲ λέγομεν ἐκεῖνα κυρίως, ὧν τὰ μόρια παρατέταται καὶ διέστηκεν ἀπ' ἀλλήλων. διὸ καὶ τῶν μεγεθῶν καὶ τῶν ἐν αὐτοῖς περάτων ἡ θέσις εἶναι κυρίως δοκεῖ, ὅτι διέστη ταῦτα κατὰ συνέχειαν. οἱ δέ γε ἀριθμοὶ καίτοι διακριθέντες ὅμως οὐ δοκοῦσι θέσιν ἔχειν διὰ τὸ μὴ διεστάναι καὶ παρατετάσθαι, πλὴν εἴ που καὶ οὗτοι μέγεθος προσλάβωσι καὶ διάστασιν. τὰ γὰρ διαστάντα πάντα τὴν ἡνωμένην συναίρεσιν ἀπολέσαντα τὸ ἐν αὑτοῖς εἶναι εἰς τὸ ἐν ἄλλῳ γίνεσθαι μετέβαλεν, ἐν ᾧ καὶ κεῖσθαι λέγεται οἷον παρεθέντα καὶ τὸ αὐτοκρατὲς ἀπολέσαντα, ὥσπερ καὶ ἐν ταῖς ἐνεργείαις ἀφ' ἑαυτῶν ἐκστάντα κινεῖσθαι λέγεται καὶ μεταβάλλειν.

are three uniting measures that exercise their salvaging function in accordance with these modes of distension.

Thus, (1) number is the measure that prevents a generated thing from being a fragment and turns it into a singular essence within a plurality of essences of generated things; (2) place is the measure that prevents a generated thing from being confused with other generated things and turns it into an essence of a delimited magnitude, which is both a whole with its own parts and itself a part of a larger whole; (3) time is the measure that enables the essence of a generated thing to have its being in becoming. It is in virtue of time that a generated thing is in constant flux until it perishes. We saw that Simplicius added a fourth measure, namely magnitude, considering that it is one thing for a sensible thing to be, say, of two or three cubits and another thing for it to have parts that are ordered in this whole of two or three cubits.[42] His master, however, apparently found it hard to see how bulk and magnitude could correspond to a differentiation in the intelligible realm other than the differentiation of the unified things in whole and parts.[43] At any rate, Damascius thought that there was an analogy between the extension of essence and the activity of being of a generated thing: (a) the activity of being comes about together with change (κίνησις), the extension of essence occurs immediately in (dis)position (θέσις): there is no activity of being without change,[44] as there is no generated essence without position; (b) the activity of being lasts so

---

[42] Cf. Simplicius, In Phys., 774.28–35: "At this point, I beg the pardon of my teacher Damascius, who wants that the measures be not four but three, i.e. number, place and time, in the treatises that he wrote on number, place and time. "As number is the measure of plurality", he says, "so place is the measure of magnitude". I think, however, that it is evidently clear that there is one measure and delimitation when we say that something is of two or three cubits, and another when we say [that something is measured] in the sense of having the right disposition, according to which one part is above, one below, one to the right, one to the left." (Παραιτοῦμαι δὲ ἐνταῦθα τὸν ἐμαυτοῦ καθηγεμόνα Δαμάσκιον οὐ τέτταρα βουλόμενον εἶναι τὰ μέτρα ἀλλὰ τρία ἀριθμὸν καὶ τόπον καὶ χρόνον ἐν τοῖς περὶ ἀριθμοῦ καὶ τόπου καὶ χρόνου γεγραμμένοις αὐτῷ συγγράμμασιν· "ὥσπερ γὰρ τοῦ πλήθους ὁ ἀριθμὸς μέτρον, οὕτως τοῦ μεγέθους", φησίν, "ὁ τόπος". καίτοι ἐναργῶς οἶμαι δῆλόν ἐστιν, ὅτι ἄλλο μὲν τὸ μέτρον καὶ ὁ ὅρος ἐστί, καθ' ὃ δίπηχυ ἢ τρίπηχυ λέγομεν εἶναί τι, καὶ ἄλλο τὸ κατὰ τὸν εὐθετισμόν, καθ' ὃ τὸ μὲν ἄνω τῶν μορίων τὸ δὲ κάτω καὶ τὸ μὲν δεξιὰ τὸ δὲ ἀριστερά.)

[43] It is indeed hard to attribute 'magnitude' to any intelligible form. Simplicius' own words, when speaking of the intelligible measure of magnitude reveal this sort of difficulty; cf. Simplicius, In Phys., 773.29–31: "The distension in continuity was measured by the delimitation of magnitude, according to which something is of such magnitude, and [thus] the continuous, becoming like the discrete, stopped the extension into the unlimited." (Ἡ δὲ κατὰ συνέχειαν διάστασις ἐμετρήθη μεγέθους ὅρῳ, καθ' ὃν τοσόνδε τι, καὶ τὸ συνεχὲς ὥσπερ τὸ διωρισμένον γενόμενον ἔστησε τὴν ἐπ' ἄπειρον ἔκστασιν.)

[44] Simplicius criticizes Damascius' doctrine of 'the whole of time' along this premise; see n. 4.

long as the generated thing lasts (and, therefore, it necessitates a duration formed by the past, present and future, which are arranged in accordance with the sequence of the anterior and posterior). In other words, it is connatural and coextensive to its essence, as connatural and coextensive to its essence is also its (dis)position, i.e. its intrinsic arrangement in whole and parts. On the contrary, the various activities that proceed from the essence of the generated thing, say, its various mental acts and/or psychocorporeal activities, are different at different times, as different at different times are also its extrinsic positions.

This theory exhibits some novelty with regard to the previous Neoplatonic tradition. As in many other cases, however, Damascius develops distinctions that are latent, or vaguely conceived, in Proclus' thought. As we have seen, Proclus identified the measure of the being of the Living-Being-itself, that is, eternity, as the only intelligible measure,[45] and this in accordance with the *Timaeus*.[46] Nevertheless, when he follows the *Parmenides*,[47] Proclus speaks once of the 'totality' (ὁλότης), which "co-subsists with eternity", as "the measure of parts and of plurality".[48] It seems that Damascius separated Proclus' 'totality' into 'number' and 'magnitude' and posited them as further formal measures, next to eternity: magnitude (which, as we have seen, Damascius takes as equivalent to place) both determines the essence as a whole and arranges its parts, whereas number delimits its plurality. But we should now ask how Damascius arrived at such a division and thus enriched the Neoplatonic discourse on measures. The answer is twofold: (i) Damascius focused more than Proclus on the way of being of a generated thing and thus

---

45 Cf. Proclus, *Plat. Theol.*, III 8, 33.4–7: "In fact, eternity itself participates both in the limit and the unlimitedness: insofar as it is an intelligible measure, it participates in the limit, but insofar as it is the cause of inexhaustible power of being, it participates in the unlimitedness." (Καὶ γὰρ ὁ αἰὼν αὐτὸς ἅμα καὶ πέρατος μετέχει καὶ ἀπειρίας, ὡς μὲν νοητὸν μέτρον ὑπάρχων, τοῦ πέρατος, ὡς δὲ τῆς ἀνεκλείπτου κατὰ τὸ εἶναι δυνάμεως αἴτιος, τῆς ἀπειρίας.) III 16, 55.11–14: "Eternity, therefore, is beyond the first Paradigm; in fact, eternity measures the being of the Living-Being-itself, and this is measured filled with the everlastingness that comes from eternity." (Ἐπέκεινα οὖν ἐστι τοῦ πρώτου παραδείγματος ὁ αἰών· καὶ γὰρ μετρεῖ μὲν ὁ αἰὼν τὸ εἶναι τοῦ αὐτοζῴου, μετρεῖται δὲ τοῦτο καὶ πληροῦται τῆς ἀιδιότητος ἀπ' αὐτοῦ.) Cf. also *Plat. Theol.*, III 20, 72.17–18: "Eternity is the measure of all the intelligible plurality." (Μέτρον γάρ ἐστιν ὁ αἰὼν παντὸς τοῦ νοητοῦ πλήθους.) Strictly speaking, however, eternity is the measure of the being of the Living-Being-itself, whereas the measure of plurality is totality, which co-subsists with eternity; see n. 48.
46 Cf. Plato, *Timaeus*, 37d 6: μένοντος αἰῶνος ἐν ἑνί.
47 Cf. Plato, *Parm.*, 142c 7-d 9.
48 Cf. Proclus, *Plat. Theol.*, III 27, 94.21–24: "Therefore, eternity exists in conjunction with totality, and totality and eternity are identical; each of them is a measure: eternity is the measure of all eternal and everlasting beings, whereas totality is the measure of the parts and of all plurality." (Συνυφέστηκεν οὖν ὁ αἰὼν τῇ ὁλότητι καὶ ταὐτόν ἐστιν ὁλότης καὶ αἰών, καὶ μέτρον ἑκάτερον, τὸ μὲν τῶν αἰωνίων καὶ τῶν ἀιδίων πάντων, τὸ δὲ τῶν μερῶν καὶ τοῦ πλήθους παντός.)

adopted a bottom-up approach in its elucidation of the structure of the intelligible realm; (ii) in doing so, he drew more than Proclus on Aristotle: he brought into his discourse Aristotelian distinctions that were more apt to describe the image-model relation between the sensible and the intelligible realms.

2.2 Time as a measure of the duration of being: transforming the Aristotelian conception of time as a measure of the being of motion

In chapter 6 of the *Categories*, in which the category of quantity is elucidated, Aristotle distinguishes between discrete quantities, i.e. number and uttered speech, and continuous quantities, which, unlike discrete quantities, are constituted by parts whose boundaries are common; the magnitudes (line, surface and body), as well as time and place, are said by Aristotle to belong to continuous quantities.⁴⁹ Time, however, Aristotle further explains, unlike place, is not constituted by parts that have "a relative position to each other" (θέσις πρὸς ἄλληλα) and are thus "co-existent" (ὑπομένει), but by parts that are ordered, that is, parts that do not abide but partake in existence according to a τάξις. Time in this respect is like a number, which is prior to one and posterior to another.⁵⁰ Damascius' concepts of place as an active power of *positioning* and his concept of time as active power of *ordering* ultimately go back to the Aristotelian distinction between position and order.

The Platonic successor, of course, went much further than Aristotle. Whereas Aristotle was interested in clarifying the differentiating properties of the various kinds of quantity, Damascius transformed the property 'simultaneous existence of parts' and the property 'successive existence of parts' into some kind of hypostases, namely place and time as uniting measures. The parts of a an extended being exist simultaneously within an arranged whole because of place and the parts of its extended (durative) activity of being exist successively in an ordered way because of time and, of course, this being and its activity of being are different from another being and its own activity of being because of number. This transformative operation of Aristotle's concepts of place and time necessitated a strict distinction between a thing and the being of a thing, in other words between essence and activity of being. This distinction can also be traced back to Aristotle.

As is known, the concepts of essence (οὐσία) and activity (ἐνέργεια) are highly effectual in book III of Aristotle's *On the Soul* and in book XII (*Lambda*) of Aristo-

---

49 See chapter 1, n. 38.
50 Cf. Aristotle, *Cat.*, 6, 4b 20–5a 37.

tle's *Metaphysics*.⁵¹ Aristotle defines the separately existing, eternal and unmoved substances, that are the intelligible movers of the concentric celestial spheres, as immaterial entities whose essence is their very activity, and the efficient or productive intelligence (ποιητικὸς νοῦς) is said to be the entity whose essence *is* its activity. Nevertheless, from Damascius' point of view, the most crucial text for distinguishing between being and the activity of being was part of Aristotle's treatment of time in book IV of the *Physics*, especially in our chapter 12, where the being of motion is distinguished from motion itself. Aristotle sets out there his thought by making, first, the distinction between discrete and continuous quantity, in other words between plurality (πλῆθος) and magnitude (μέγεθος):

> The smallest number, taken abstractly, is the number two. But of number as concrete, sometimes there is a minimum, sometimes there is not: e.g. of a line, the smallest number in respect of plurality is two [lines] or, if you like, one [line], but in respect of magnitude there is no smallest number; for every line is divided infinitely. Hence it is so with time. In respect of number the smallest is one [time] or two [times]; in respect of magnitude, however, there is no smallest number.⁵²

Aristotle is here interested in distinguishing between quantification by numbering (ἀριθμεῖν), for which there is a smallest number, and quantification by measuring (μετρεῖν), for which there is no smallest number.⁵³ For Aristotle, this distinction yields two different cognitions of time on the part of the human soul: (i) time as a number of motion according to the anterior and posterior,⁵⁴ which counts *motion(s)* and results in a conception of time as an infinite set of time intervals (days, months, seasons, years, four-year cycles or "Olympiads") in terms of ordinal numbers;⁵⁵ and (ii) time as a measure of motion,⁵⁶ which measures the *being of motion*, that is, to put it simply, time as duration,⁵⁷ which, like motion itself, is continuous and infinitely divisible. Whereas Aristotle's first conception grasps time in

---

51 See n. 11.
52 Cf. Aristotle, *Phys.*, IV 12, 220a 27–32: Ἐλάχιστος δὲ ἀριθμὸς ὁ μὲν ἁπλῶς ἐστὶν ἡ δυάς· τὶς δὲ ἀριθμὸς ἔστι μὲν ὡς ἔστιν, ἔστι δ' ὡς οὐκ ἔστιν, οἷον γραμμῆς ἐλάχιστος πλήθει μέν ἐστιν αἱ δύο ἢ ἡ μία, μεγέθει δ' οὐκ ἔστιν ἐλάχιστος· ἀεὶ γὰρ διαιρεῖται πᾶσα γραμμή. ὥστε ὁμοίως καὶ χρόνος· ἐλάχιστος γὰρ κατὰ μὲν ἀριθμὸν ἐστιν ὁ εἷς ἢ οἱ δύο, κατὰ μέγεθος δ' οὐκ ἔστιν.
53 See further Roark (2011: 109–112).
54 Cf. Aristotle, *Phys.*, IV 11, 219b 1–2: Τοῦτο γάρ ἐστιν ὁ χρόνος, ἀριθμὸς κινήσεως κατὰ τὸ πρότερον καὶ ὕστερον.
55 See further Detel (2021).
56 Cf. Aristotle, *Phys.*, IV 12, 220b 32–221a 1: Ἐπεὶ δ' ἐστὶν ὁ χρόνος μέτρον κινήσεως καὶ τοῦ κινεῖσθαι [...]; IV 12, 221b 25–26: μέτρον μέν ἐστι κινήσεως ὁ χρόνος καθ' αὑτό.
57 Note that there was no proper word for 'duration' in Aristotle's time, as there was 'παράτασις' for Greek philosophers of Late antiquity. See Stevens (2021: 21–23).

its perfect aspect, i.e. as completed, his second conception considers time in its progressive aspect. The Damascian concept of the activity of being, which is continuously ordered by time, arises from the second conception:

> Time is the measure of the flow of being, and by 'being' I mean not only the being according to essence but also the being according to activity. Aristotle admirably saw the nature of time and made it clear, saying that both for motion and "for other things this is to be in time, that their being is measured by time".[58] Just as motion does not take place according to the indivisibles (for it is not composed of divisions of changes; for neither the line is composed of points, but the limits of both the line and the motion are indivisible, whereas the parts of them of which they are composed, being continuous, are not indivisible but divisible), so in the same way the limits of time, the 'nows', are indivisible, whereas its parts are not. For, since time is continuous, it, too, has parts that are infinitely divisible.[59] So that, even if motion and time are in continuous flux, they are not unreal, but have their being in becoming. But becoming is not simply non-being, but is to exist at different times in different part of being.[60] For just as eternity is the cause, to that which undergoes the intelligible differentiation from the proper One-which-is,[61] of its abiding in its own One-which-is[62] in respect with its being, so time is the cause, to what descended from there into perception, of its dancing around the one intelligible radiance of the form and of its having the continuity of this dance in order. For just as because of place the parts of distended things do not merge together, so because of time the being of the Trojan war is not confounded with the being of the Peloponnesian war, nor in each person the being of the baby with the being of the adolescent. And it is clear that everywhere time coexists with motion and change, holding together in becoming those things which have their being therein, which is the same thing as to make that-which-becomes dance around that-which-is.[63]

---

58 Aristotle, *Phys.*, IV 12, 221a 8.
59 Cf. Aristotle, *Phys.*, VI 2, 232b 24–25: "By continuous I mean that which is divisible into divisibles that are infinitely divisible." (Λέγω δὲ συνεχὲς τὸ διαιρετὸν εἰς ἀεὶ διαιρετά. Translation by Hardie.)
60 This idea comes from Iamblichus. But Iamblichus attributes it not to time itself, as Damascius does here, but to the things that participate in time; cf. Iamblichus *apud Simplicium, In Phys.*, 787.17–21 (quoted Chapter 3, n. 77).
61 τὸ οἰκεῖον: that is, the first intelligible triad.
62 τὸ ἑαυτοῦ: that is, the one-which-is of each intelligible within the intelligible plurality that emerges in the third intelligible triad.
63 Damascius *apud Simplicium, In Phys.*, 774.35–775.21: Ἔστιν οὖν ὁ χρόνος μέτρον τῆς τοῦ εἶναι ῥοῆς, εἶναι δὲ λέγω οὐ τοῦ κατὰ τὴν οὐσίαν μόνον ἀλλὰ καὶ τοῦ κατὰ τὴν ἐνέργειαν. καὶ θαυμαστῶς ὁ Ἀριστοτέλης εἶδέ τε τοῦ χρόνου τὴν φύσιν καὶ ἐξέφηνεν, εἰπὼν ὅτι καὶ τῇ κινήσει "καὶ τοῖς ἄλλοις τοῦτό ἐστι τὸ ἐν χρόνῳ εἶναι τὸ μετρεῖσθαι αὐτῶν τὸ εἶναι ὑπὸ τοῦ χρόνου". ὥσπερ δὲ ἡ κίνησις οὐ κατὰ τὰ ἀμερῆ γίνεται (οὐδὲ γὰρ σύγκειται ἐκ κινημάτων· οὐδὲ γὰρ ἡ γραμμὴ ἐκ στιγμῶν, ἀλλὰ τὰ μὲν πέρατα καὶ τῆς γραμμῆς καὶ τῆς κινήσεως ἀμερῆ ἐστι, τὰ δὲ μέρη αὐτῶν ἐξ ὧν σύγκειται συνεχῆ ὄντα οὐκ ἔστιν ἀμερῆ ἀλλὰ μεριστά), οὕτω δὲ καὶ τοῦ χρόνου τὰ μὲν ὡς πέρατα τὰ νῦν ἀμερῆ ἐστι, τὰ δὲ ὡς μέρη οὐκέτι· συνεχὴς γὰρ ὢν ὁ χρόνος διαιρούμενα ἔχει καὶ αὐτὸς τὰ μέρη εἰς ἀεὶ διαιρετά. ὥστε κἂν ἐν συνεχεῖ ῥοῇ ᾖ ἥ τε κίνησις καὶ ὁ χρόνος, οὐκ ἔστιν ἀνυπόστατα

Now, if we look at the Aristotelian passage quoted by Damascius, we will see that the distinction between time as number and time as measure was important to Aristotle for determining the things that are in time. Properly speaking, it is not 'numbering' but 'measuring'—which occurs by giving the number of the multiples of some conventionally defined segment of the continuum that exhausts the measured whole—that allows for expandability as a fundamental property of time. Aristotle firmly believed that whatever period of time one takes, there would always be a period of time greater than it:

> Since what is in time is so in the same sense as what is in number is so,[64] a time greater than everything [that is] in time can be found. So it is necessary that all the things [that are] in time should be contained by time, just like all other things that are in something; for instance, the things [that are] in place [are contained] by place.[65]

According to Aristotle, things in time are things whose being, like the exemplary case of the being of motion, is measured by time, and which are therefore contained by (a greater) time. Here is the Aristotelian passage quoted by Damascius:

> Since time is a measure of motion and of being moved, and since it measures the motion by determining a motion which will measure exactly the whole motion (as the cubit measures the length by determining an amount which will measure out the whole) and to be in time means for motion that both it and its being are measured by time (for simultaneously it measures both the motion and the being of motion,[66] and this is what being in time means for

---

ἀλλ' ἐν τῷ γίνεσθαι τὸ εἶναι ἔχει· τὸ δὲ γίνεσθαι οὐ τὸ μὴ εἶναι ἁπλῶς ἐστιν, ἀλλὰ τὸ ἄλλοτε ἐν ἄλλῳ μέρει τοῦ εἶναι ὑφίστασθαι. ὥσπερ γὰρ ὁ αἰὼν αἴτιός ἐστι τοῦ κατὰ τὸ εἶναι μένειν ἐν τῷ ἑαυτοῦ ἑνὶ ὄντι τὸ τὴν νοητὴν διάκρισιν ὑπομεῖναν ἀπὸ τοῦ οἰκείου ἑνὸς ὄντος, οὕτως ὁ χρόνος αἴτιος τοῦ χορεύειν περὶ τὸ νοητὸν ἓν τοῦ εἴδους ἀπαύγασμα τὸ εἰς αἴσθησιν ἐκεῖθεν ὑπελθὸν καὶ τεταγμένην ἔχειν τὴν τῆς χορείας συνέχειαν. ὡς γὰρ διὰ τὸν τόπον οὐ σύγκειται τὰ μέρη τῶν διεστώτων, οὕτω διὰ τὸν χρόνον οὐ συγχεῖται τὸ εἶναι τῶν Τρωικῶν τῷ τῶν Πελοποννησιακῶν εἶναι, οὐδὲ ἐν ἑκάστῳ τὸ εἶναι τοῦ βρέφους τῷ εἶναι τοῦ νεανίσκου. καὶ δῆλον ὅτι πανταχοῦ κινήσει σύνεστιν ὁ χρόνος καὶ μεταβολῇ, συνέχων ἐν τῷ γίνεσθαι τὰ ἐν τούτῳ τὴν ὕπαρξιν ἔχοντα, ὅπερ ταὐτόν ἐστι τῷ χορεύειν ποιῶν περὶ τὸ ὂν τὸ γινόμενον.

64 "In number", not in the sense of belonging to number (as a part or as a mode of number), but in the sense of having a number; cf. Aristotle, *Phys.*, IV 12, 221a 13: ὅτι ἔστιν αὐτοῦ ἀριθμός. For a thing to be in number is tantamount to there being a number that pertains to it, a number *of* it; for a thing to be in time is tantamount to there being a number that measures its motion, a number *of* the being (the duration) of its motion.

65 Cf. Aristotle, *Phys.*, IV 12, 221a 26–30: Ἐπεὶ δέ ἐστιν ὡς ἐν ἀριθμῷ τὸ ἐν χρόνῳ, ληφθήσεταί τις πλείων χρόνος παντὸς τοῦ ἐν χρόνῳ ὄντος· διὸ ἀνάγκη πάντα τὰ ἐν χρόνῳ ὄντα περιέχεσθαι ὑπὸ χρόνου, ὥσπερ καὶ τἆλλα ὅσα ἔν τινί ἐστιν, οἷον τὰ ἐν τόπῳ ὑπὸ τοῦ τόπου. Translation by Hardie, slightly modified.

66 One could say more accurately: it numbers the motion and measures the being of motion.

motion, that its being is measured), it is clear that this is to be in time for other things too, namely that their being is measured by time.[67]

Aristotle thus excluded the eternal celestial beings, insofar as they always exist (and not insofar as they accomplish circular motions), from being in time.[68] Their being is not measured by time, since it is not contained by time. There is a number greater than the number that counts a celestial being's accomplished motion—say, two as pertaining to the outermost celestial sphere's motion in a day is greater than one as pertaining to the outermost celestial sphere's motion in a day and, in general, if n is the number of the accomplished motions of an eter-

---

[67] Aristotle, *Phys.*, IV 12, 220b 32–221a 9: Ἐπεὶ δ' ἐστὶν ὁ χρόνος μέτρον κινήσεως καὶ τοῦ κινεῖσθαι, μετρεῖ δ' οὗτος τὴν κίνησιν τῷ ὁρίσαι τινὰ κίνησιν ἣ καταμετρήσει τὴν ὅλην (ὥσπερ καὶ τὸ μῆκος ὁ πῆχυς τῷ ὁρίσαι τι μέγεθος ὃ ἀναμετρήσει τὸ ὅλον), καὶ ἔστιν τῇ κινήσει τὸ ἐν χρόνῳ εἶναι τὸ μετρεῖσθαι τῷ χρόνῳ καὶ αὐτὴν καὶ τὸ εἶναι αὐτῆς (ἅμα γὰρ τὴν κίνησιν καὶ τὸ εἶναι τῆς κινήσεως μετρεῖ, καὶ τοῦτ' ἔστιν αὐτῇ τὸ ἐν χρόνῳ εἶναι, τὸ μετρεῖσθαι αὐτῆς τὸ εἶναι), δῆλον ὅτι καὶ τοῖς ἄλλοις τοῦτ' ἔστι τὸ ἐν χρόνῳ εἶναι, τὸ μετρεῖσθαι αὐτῶν τὸ εἶναι ὑπὸ τοῦ χρόνου. Cf. also *Phys.*, IV 12, 221b 25–31: "Generally, if time is *per se* the measure of motion and *per accidens* of other things, it is clear that a thing whose existence is measured by it will have its existence in rest or motion. Those things therefore which are subject to perishing and becoming—generally, those which at one time exist, at another do not—are necessarily in time: for there is a greater time which will extend both beyond their existence and beyond the time which measures their existence." (Ὅλως γάρ, εἰ μέτρον μέν ἐστι κινήσεως ὁ χρόνος καθ' αὑτό, τῶν δ' ἄλλων κατὰ συμβεβηκός, δῆλον ὅτι ὧν τὸ εἶναι μετρεῖ, τούτοις ἅπασιν ἔσται τὸ εἶναι ἐν τῷ ἠρεμεῖν ἢ κινεῖσθαι. ὅσα μὲν οὖν φθαρτὰ καὶ γενητὰ καὶ ὅλως ὁτὲ μὲν ὄντα ὁτὲ δὲ μή, ἀνάγκη ἐν χρόνῳ εἶναι· ἔστιν γὰρ χρόνος τις πλείων, ὃς ὑπερέξει τοῦ τε εἶναι αὐτῶν καὶ τοῦ μετροῦντος τὴν οὐσίαν αὐτῶν. Translation by Hardie, slightly modified.) The idea that both the motion and the being of a thing are in time is overtaken by Chrysippus; cf. *SVF* II, 509 (p. 164.17–18): "[…] each thing moves and exists in accordance with time." ([…] καὶ κατὰ μὲν τὸν χρόνον κινεῖσθαί τε ἕκαστα καὶ εἶναι.)

[68] Cf. Aristotle, *Phys.*, IV 12, 221b 3–7: "Hence, it is clear that the eternal things, insofar as they are eternal, are not in time; for they are not contained by time, nor is their being measured by time. An indication of this is that none of them is affected by time, because they are not in time." (Ὥστε φανερὸν ὅτι τὰ αἰεὶ ὄντα, ᾗ αἰεὶ ὄντα, οὐκ ἔστιν ἐν χρόνῳ· οὐ γὰρ περιέχεται ὑπὸ χρόνου, οὐδὲ μετρεῖται τὸ εἶναι αὐτῶν ὑπὸ τοῦ χρόνου· σημεῖον δὲ τούτου ὅτι οὐδὲ πάσχει οὐδὲν ὑπὸ τοῦ χρόνου ὡς οὐκ ὄντα ἐν χρόνῳ.) In other words, celestial beings are not in time insofar as they always exist, but they are related to time insofar as they are in motion: their motions *qua* measured and numbered by time are in time and, in their turn, since also time may be delimited through motion (cf. IV 12, 220b 15–19), measure time; cf. *Phys.*, IV 14, 223b 15–18: "As we said, time is measured by motion as well as motion by time; this is so because by a motion delimited by time the quantity both of the motion and of the time is measured." (Μετρεῖται δ', ὥσπερ εἴπομεν, ὅ τε χρόνος κινήσει καὶ ἡ κίνησις χρόνῳ· τοῦτο δ' ἐστίν, ὅτι ὑπὸ τῆς ὡρισμένης κινήσεως χρόνῳ μετρεῖται τῆς τε κινήσεως τὸ ποσὸν καὶ τοῦ χρόνου.) We will see in the following chapter that the exclusion of the eternal celestial beings from being in time was formative of Damascius' doctrine of 'the whole of time', that is, a still time that pertains to the essence of the heaven.

nal celestial being, there is always 1>*n*—but there is no time greater than the time that pertains to a celestial being's being (and to the being of its single continuous motion). Damascius, however, was not interested in determining the things that are in time through the Aristotelian criterion of the expandability of time. As a follower of the *Timaeus*, he presumed that time was generated by the Demiurge together with the heaven. As a Platonist, he contended that 'generated' (γενητόν) is not what has come into being *in* time, so that its being is contained by (a greater) time, but whatever has a cause of its existence other than itself;[69] and eternal celestial beings certainly had such a cause. For Damascius, it was enough to know, following Aristotle, that for a thing to be in time is tantamount to having not merely its motion but also the being of its motion measured by time. And motion, as we know, came into being together with the distension of the activity of being.[70]

To put it differently, Damascius accepted Aristotle's postulate 'if in time, then (measured) by time',[71] but tacitly rejected the idea of time as being only extrinsically related, as a concomitant of the human soul, to things in time. Things are measured by time not merely to the extent that they are simply cognized by the human soul to grow old and therefore to be eventually destroyed by time,[72] or to be posterior, simultaneous or anterior to other things, but primarily to the extent that they are ordered by time. In other words, they exist as having their activity of being in *orderly* becoming because of an inherent time, a time that runs along with their generated essence. The essence of a generated human being, for instance, i.e. her humanity, is to exercise, as separate from the essence, the ordered activity of being an embryo, of being a small child, of being a child, of being a youth, of being a young man etc. The activity of being of a generated es-

---

69 See Chapter 1, n. 2.
70 Cf. Damascius, *apud Simplicium, In Phys.*, 625.9–11 (quoted n. 41): "The distension of the activity immediately demanded motion, and motion came into being with it, and its distension came about through motion in activity or, rather, passivity."
71 Cf. Aristotle, *Phys.*, IV 12, 221b 14–16: "To be in number means that there is a number of the thing, and that its being is measured by the number in which it is; hence, if a thing is in times, it will be measured by time." (Τὸ δ' εἶναι ἐν ἀριθμῷ ἐστιν τὸ εἶναί τινα ἀριθμὸν τοῦ πράγματος, καὶ μετρεῖσθαι τὸ εἶναι αὐτοῦ τῷ ἀριθμῷ ἐν ᾧ ἐστιν, ὥστ' εἰ ἐν χρόνῳ, ὑπὸ χρόνου. Translation by Hardie.)
72 Aristotle thinks that, properly speaking, it is not time that destroys things, but their destruction takes place incidentally in time; cf. *Phys.*, IV 13, 222b 24–27: "And this is what we are accustomed to mean by a thing's being destroyed by time. Still, time does not work even this change; even this sort of change takes place incidentally in time." (Καὶ ταύτην μάλιστα λέγειν εἰώθαμεν ὑπὸ τοῦ χρόνου φθοράν. οὐ μὴν ἀλλ' οὐδὲ ταύτην ὁ χρόνος ποιεῖ, ἀλλὰ συμβαίνει ἐν χρόνῳ γίγνεσθαι καὶ ταύτην τὴν μεταβολήν. Translation by Hardie, slightly modified.)

sence is not one with its essence; it does not "abide" in the essence, as it does in the intelligible realm, but is extended.

Thus, Damascius transformed Aristotle's merely epistemological distinction between a motion and the being of a motion, say, between the diurnal motion of the outermost celestial sphere as a "counted number" (i.e. a multiple with which an amount of days is counted) and the motion of the outermost celestial sphere in a day (which is not counted but measured), to an ontological differentiation between being (or essence) and the activity of being. Damascius was thinking about the world within the Platonic dualism of model and image. But by reflecting, on the basis of Aristotelian distinctions, upon the structure of the image, he deepened his understanding of the model. He distinguished between the activities that proceed from the essence of a generated thing (for a human being, his various mental acts and psychocorporeal activities) and his very activity of being, through which his very essence or being, i.e. his humanity, exists continuously in becoming —and therefore has a duration—until he perishes. Thus, the *real* (and passive) distinction between being and the activity of being is what characterizes, most fundamentally, the sensible realm and, at the same time, what defines it as an image of the intelligible realm. In the intelligible realm the activity of being of the intelligible forms remains in their being thanks to eternity; in the sensible realm each generated being has an activity of being that is separate from its essence and extended along with it thanks to time.

2.3 Time as a uniting measure from a contemporary point of view: McTaggart's B and C series and an ancient case for presentism

Damascius teaches that the inhabitants of the sensible realm, that is, the forms that are mixed with matter, like the forms of individual human beings, animals and plants, are different from each other thanks to their number, and that their bodies have the right disposition within themselves (say, the head is at the top of the human body and the feet at the bottom, the eyes are on the front of the head and not on its back etc.), as well as the right position within the sensible realm itself (human beings live on earth, and fish in the water, and earth occupies the center of the living cosmos, and the celestial element its periphery), thanks to their place. But the compounds of form and matter also have their being in flux, which has to be ordered, so that they may live and live well. Just as eternity secures the unextended mode of life of the intelligible forms, so time secures the durative mode of life of the forms mixed with matter. Thus, time, according to Damascius, emerges as an inherent principle of order, which prevents confusion of stages and events. Time regulates, for instance, the formation of the different parts of the embryo and, subsequently, the progression of the ages of individual human life from small child to old age in a fixed sequence, just as it separates the existence of the War of Troy from the existence of the Peloponnesian War as external events that occur in the life of the cosmos.[73] It is time that enables the different stages of the durative life of an individual living being and of the cosmos as a whole to occur exactly when they should and thus to be 'timely' or 'opportune' (εὔκαιρα)—similarly to place, which secures the 'right positioning' (εὐθετισμός) of all spatial parts and wholes:

> We say that each thing has a posture, however disordered this may be, but a thing is said to be rightly positioned when it gains its proper place, just as a thing comes to be at whatever time, but has its proper opportunity when it comes to be at the right time. So, because place properly positions each part, the head is at the top of my body and my feet are at the bottom, and my liver is to the right and my heart in the centre; also the eyes, through which we see as we move forward, are in front, but the back on which we carry burdens is behind. These differences are because of place, just as because of time the parts of the embryo are created one after the other, and one age precedes another in proper order, and the Trojan War is not confused with the Peloponnesian War; for the earlier and later are differences of time, just as up and down and the other four dimensions are differences of place, as Aristotle grants.[74] Therefore, the parts of the cosmos too have their proper right positioning within the whole because of place.[75]

---

73 Cf. Damascius *apud Simplicium, In Phys.*, 775.17–19. See also next note.
74 Cf. Aristotle, *On the Progression of Animals*, 2, 704b 19–22: "There are indeed six dimensions and three pairs: the first is the up and down, the second is the front and the back, and the third is the right and the left." (Εἰσὶ γὰρ διαστάσεις μὲν ἕξ, συζυγίαι δὲ τρεῖς, μία μὲν τὸ ἄνω καὶ τὸ κάτω, δευτέρα δὲ τὸ ἔμπροσθεν καὶ τὸ ὄπισθεν, τρίτη δὲ τὸ δεξιὸν καὶ τὸ ἀριστερόν. Translation by Falcon.)
75 Simplicius, *In Phys.*, 626.4–17: Κεῖσθαι μὲν ἕκαστόν φαμεν κἂν ὁπωσοῦν ἀτάκτως κέηται, τὸν δὲ εὐθετισμὸν τὸν οἰκεῖον ἕκαστον τότε λέγεται ἔχειν, ὅταν τὸν οἰκεῖον ἀπολάβῃ τόπον, ὥσπερ γίνεται μὲν ἕκαστον ὁτεοῦν εἰς τὸ εἶναι παρελθόν, τὸ δὲ εὔκαιρον ἔχει τὸ οἰκεῖον, ὅταν ἐν τῷ δέοντι γένηται χρόνῳ. διὰ τὸν τόπον οὖν τῶν μορίων ἕκαστον εὐθετίζοντα ἡ μὲν κεφαλὴ τοῦ ἐμοῦ σώματος γέγονεν ἄνω, οἱ δὲ πόδες κάτω· καὶ τὸ μὲν ἧπαρ ἐν τοῖς δεξιοῖς, ἡ δὲ καρδία ἐν τῷ μέσῳ. καὶ οἱ μὲν ὀφθαλμοὶ δι' ὧν ὁρῶντες πρόιμεν ἔμπροσθεν, τὸ δὲ μετάφρενον ᾧ ἀχθοφοροῦμεν ὄπισθεν. καὶ εἰσὶν αὗται διὰ τὸν τόπον αἱ διαφοραί, ὥσπερ διὰ τὸν χρόνον ἄλλο τι πρὸ ἄλλου δημιουργεῖται τῶν τοῦ ἐμβρύου μερῶν, καὶ ἄλλη πρὸ ἄλλης ἡλικία πρόεισι τεταγμένως, καὶ οὐκ ἐπισυγχεῖται τὰ Τρωϊκὰ τοῖς Πελοποννησιακοῖς· τὸ γὰρ πρότερον καὶ ὕστερον χρόνου διαφοραί εἰσιν, ὡς τὸ ἄνω καὶ κάτω καὶ αἱ λοιπαὶ τέτταρες διαστάσεις τοῦ τόπου, καθάπερ καὶ Ἀριστοτέλης ὁμολογεῖ. καὶ τοῦ κόσμου ἄρα τὰ μόρια διὰ τὸν τόπον ἔχει τὸν οἰκεῖον εὐθετισμὸν ἐν τῷ ὅλῳ.

2 Time as a uniting measure

The comparison of time with place as a "perfecting element" can help us understand better the nature of time as an inborn measure. In a further passage from the digression on place, largely inspired by Damascius, Simplicius writes:

> So place seems to be the measure of the position of things positioned, just as time is said to be the number of the motion of the things moved. But since position is of two kinds, one essential, the other adventitious, so place will be of two sorts, one being an element perfecting that which has a position, the other contingent. There is a further difference within the essential position, insofar as either the wholes themselves have the proper position of their proper parts in relation to each other and in relation to the whole, or else they as parts have [their proper position] in relation to the whole and in relation to other parts. In this way place comes to be of two kinds, one suited properly to each thing, the other determined in accordance with the position [of this thing] in the whole. For just as the whole is of two kinds, one suited to each of the parts in accordance with its determined and distinct existence (in this way the earth is said to be a whole, but not only the earth, but also [each] animal and plant and each one of their parts), the other more surrounding (as we say that the universe is a whole, the earth a whole and the air a whole), and there are proper parts of each wholeness, in the same way we say that place of one kind is the right positioning of the parts of each thing, as the right positioning of my parts within my body as a whole, of the other kind is the right positioning of this whole too as a part in the place of the more surrounding whole, in accordance with which the place of the terrestrial animals is the place of the earth and the earth occupies the middle of the universe. For even if one removed the earth from its position around the middle of the universe [by force], it would retain the right positioning of its proper parts in its proper whole, but will no longer have its [proper] position as a part of the whole; this is the reason for which the whole earth, if it were [then] set free, would bear towards the middle, despite the fact that its parts retained their relative disposition, even when it happened to be outside the middle [of the universe]. In the same way, a human being up in the air will retain the good arrangement of his proper parts, but will have lost his good arrangement as a part in relation to the whole.[76]

---

76 Simplicius, *In Phys.*, 627.16–628.2: Ἔοικεν οὖν ὁ τόπος μέτρον εἶναι τῆς τῶν κειμένων θέσεως, ὥσπερ ὁ χρόνος ἀριθμὸς λέγεται τῆς τῶν κινουμένων κινήσεως. ἐπεὶ δὲ ἡ θέσις διττή, ἡ μὲν οὐσιώδης ἡ δὲ ἐπείσακτος, καὶ ὁ τόπος ἂν εἴη διττός, ὁ μὲν στοιχεῖον τελειωτικὸν τοῦ θέσιν ἔχοντος γινόμενος, ὁ δὲ κατὰ συμβεβηκὸς ὑπάρχων. ἔστι δέ τις καὶ τῆς οὐσιώδους θέσεως διαφορά, καθόσον ἢ ὡς αὐτὰ ὅλα τὴν οἰκείαν ἔχει θέσιν τῶν οἰκείων μερῶν πρός τε ἄλληλα καὶ πρὸς τὸ ὅλον ἢ ὡς μέρη τὴν πρὸς τὸ ὅλον τε καὶ τὰ λοιπὰ μέρη. καὶ ταύτῃ διττὸς ὁ τόπος γίνεται, ὁ μὲν ἰδίᾳ ἑκάστοις ἐπιβάλλων, ὁ δὲ κατὰ τὴν ἐν τῷ ὅλῳ θέσιν ἀφοριζόμενος. ὥσπερ γὰρ τὸ ὅλον διττόν, τὸ μὲν ἑκάστῳ τῶν μερῶν ἐπιβάλλον κατὰ τὴν ἀφωρισμένην αὐτοῦ καὶ διακεκριμένην ὑπόστασιν (καθὸ καὶ τὴν γῆν ὅλον τι εἶναί φαμεν, καὶ οὐ τὴν γῆν μόνον, ἀλλὰ καὶ ζῷον καὶ φυτὸν καὶ τῶν ἐν τούτοις μορίων ἕκαστον), τὸ δὲ καὶ περιεκτικώτερον (ὡς τὸν κόσμον ὅλον καὶ τὴν γῆν ὅλην καὶ τὸν ἀέρα ὅλον λέγομεν), καὶ ἔστιν ἑκάστης ὁλότητος οἰκεῖα μέρη, οὕτως οὖν καὶ τόπον ἄλλον μὲν τὸν τῶν οἰκείων ἑκάστου μορίων εὐθετισμόν φαμεν οἷον τῶν ἐμῶν ἐν τῷ ἐμῷ ὅλῳ σώματι, ἄλλον δὲ τὸν καὶ τοῦ ὅλου τούτου ὡς μέρους ἐν τόπῳ τῆς περιεκτικωτέρας ὁλότητος, καθὸ τόπος τῶν χερσαίων ἐστὶν ὁ τῆς γῆς τόπος, καὶ καθὸ ἡ γῆ τὸ μέσον ἐπέχει τοῦ παντός· κἂν γὰρ ἐκστήσῃ τις τὴν γῆν τῆς περὶ τὸ μέσον τοῦ παντὸς θέσεως, τῶν μὲν οἰκείων μερῶν τὸν εὐθετισμὸν ἐν τῷ οἰκείῳ ὅλῳ κα-

Place primarily is "the measure of the (essential) position of the things positioned", which is twofold: essential is (a) the position of the parts of a body within the whole that this body is, i.e. its disposition, and (b) the right position that this whole has within a greater surrounding whole. Thus, place as an inherent measure is a power of spatial organization or, more precisely, a power of both intrinsic *spatialization* (in other words, it arranges the parts in a whole) and extrinsic *localization* (in other words, it positions a body as a whole in respect of another, more inclusive whole). In the same vein, time as an inherent measure is "the number of the motion of the things moved", that is, a power of temporal organization in two respects: (a) it arranges the existence of a matter-form compound that cannot have all of its activity of being at once, because it *is* not but *comes to be* continuously until it perishes; (b) it enables its activities (including its very activity of being) to be situated in time, that is, to be events that happen before, after or simultaneously with other events. Thus, time secures both the *temporality* of a matter-form compound, which we may call its biological time, and the *temporalization* of its activities, which we may call its historical time.[77] Temporality is intrinsic and necessarily the same in order for all individuals belonging to the same species,[78] whereas temporalization occurs extrinsically through the temporality of the sublunary world whose activity of being runs along with the flowing 'now',[79] which inheres to the activity that proceeds from the essence of the heaven. We can observe that through this double inherence both the biological time(s) and the historical time do not alter. This observation brings forth Damascius' doctrine of time as a uniting measure as anticipating McTaggart's conception of the B series.

As is well known, the British Idealist philosopher J. M. E. McTaggart denied the very existence of time by distinguishing between two series (A, B) in which things are generally thought to be in time.[80] The unreality of time, according to McTaggart,[81] emerges from the A series, which, unlike the B series, is essential to the

---

θέξει, τὴν δὲ ὡς μέρος τοῦ παντὸς οὐκ ἔχει τότε· διὸ καὶ αὐτὴ ὅλη ἀφεθεῖσα ἂν ἐπὶ τὸ μέσον οἰσθείη, καίτοι τῶν ἐν αὐτῇ μερῶν φυλαττόντων τὴν πρὸς ἄλληλα διατύπωσιν, καὶ ὅταν αὕτη ἔξω τοῦ μέσου τυγχάνῃ. οὕτω δὲ καὶ ὁ ἐν τῷ ἀέρι μετέωρος ἄνθρωπος τῶν μὲν οἰκείων μερῶν ἕξει τὴν εὐταξίαν, τὴν δὲ ὡς μέρους πρὸς τὸ ὅλον οὐκέτι.

77 See also Hoffmann (1983: 17).
78 We will see in the following chapter that this necessity is related to the enmattered form (τὸ ἔνυλον εἶδος), which has to be carefully distinguished from the mixed form of the compound, also called "the common form" (τὸ κοινὸν εἶδος).
79 See below, Chapter 3.
80 See McTaggart (1908); McTaggart (1927).
81 Cf. McTaggart (1908: 470): "Whenever we judge anything to exist in time, we are in error. And whenever we perceive anything as existing in time—which is the only way in which we ever do perceive things—we are perceiving it more or less as it really is not."

idea of temporality; in order to count as being in time, an event must belong to the A series, that is, it must have a place as future, present and past. It turns out, however, that events only appear to have the properties of being future, present and past *successively*. In substance, they must have them *simultaneously* and, hence, the A series is logically incoherent and thus unreal.[82] On the other hand, the B series, in which the events are tenselessly ordered as earlier and later, is grounded on the A series: the Fall of Rome will always be earlier than the Fall of Constantinople because these two Falls are situated in time as events in the A series, insofar as they once were going to be, once were, and no longer are but become further and further past. If the A series, i.e. the distinction between past, present and future, is removed, there remains a changeless, and thus timeless,[83] C series, which involves only order, say the order M, N, O and not the order M, O, N or O, N, M or any other possible order. But we cannot know that M, e.g. the Trojan War, is earlier than N, e.g. the Persian War, and O, e.g. the Peloponnesian War, later than N, unless this series is combined with the A series. The time direction ..., M, N, O, ... (instead of ..., O, N, M, ...) emerges insofar as each one position in this series was once present to the exclusion of all others and presentness passed along this series in such a way that all positions on the left side, say, of N had been present, and all positions on the right side of N were going to be present. So McTaggart concludes that the series of earlier and later is constituted by an atemporal order that becomes temporal once it is combined with the series of past, present and future.

Anticipating but also reversing McTaggart's analysis of time, Damascius at first looks at, we would say, the ordering in the B series as the basic function of time. Temporality, to put it otherwise, precedes temporalization. Things are primarily in time not insofar as they are variously situated in future, present and past, but insofar as they are changelessly earlier and later. The formation of the heart in the embryo, for instance, is in time because it is always earlier than the formation of

---

[82] To have the properties of being future, present and past successively can only mean, so McTaggart argues, that there is a moment at which the event is future, a moment at which the event is present, and a moment at which the event is past. Thus we find ourselves in a vicious circle. Whereas the A series was posited in order to explain the reality of time, now time (a further A series) is posited in order to explain the A series; for these moments are themselves positions in time and hence they, too, must have the properties of being past, present and future. If we argue anew that these moments have these properties not simultaneously but successively, we are led to an infinite regress. In the same vein, McTaggart further argues that the properties of being past, present and future are relational properties; but as the relations of terms of the time-series to one another do not change, only one term of each relation can be in the A series; it is, however, hard to conceive of the other term of the relation, which has to be outside time.
[83] That time is intimately related to change is considered by McTaggart (1908: 459) as a universal truth.

the liver, and the Peloponnesian War is in time because, once it occurred as an event external to the life of the sublunary world, it is always later than the War of Troy. This is so in virtue of the flowing time, which is generated by the continuously flowing present that pertains primarily to the everlasting activity that proceeds from the essence of the heaven, i.e. its rotation. This activity always runs along with the flowing present and is not really connected to a past or a future. Past, present and future appear together with a properly durative activity of being. And such an activity of being pertains only to sublunary substances (and, thus, also to the sublunary time):

> All time exists in becoming but not in being [...] and preserves in this respect its continuity, which *in respect to us* and the time which is present *for us* is divided into three [i.e. present, past and future]. Assuredly, the present time is different for different people, whereas in itself time is one and continuous,[84] indivisible but infinitely divisible [i.e. in thought] *qua* continuous.[85]

---

[84] The expression "in itself time is one and continuous" is taken from Alexander's *On Time*, a treatise lost in Greek but surviving in an Arabic and a Latin translation. See Sharples 1982: 97.5.

[85] Damascius *apud* Simplicium, *In Phys.*, 798.4–9: [...] τὸν σύμπαντα χρόνον ὑφεστάναι γινόμενον ἀλλ' οὐκ ὄντα [...] καὶ τὴν συνέχειαν κατὰ τοῦτο σῴζειν τριχῆ ταύτην διαιρουμένην ὡς πρὸς ἡμᾶς καὶ τὸν καθ' ἡμᾶς ἐνεστῶτα χρόνον. ἄλλοις γοῦν ἄλλος ὁ ἐνεστώς, ἐπεὶ καθ' ἑαυτόν γε ὁ χρόνος εἷς συνεχής, ἀδιαίρετος μὲν διαιρετὸς δὲ ἐπ' ἄπειρον οἷα συνεχής. Note that the expression τὸν σύμπαντα χρόνον in this passage does not have the technical meaning (i.e. "the whole of time", "all time at once") that has at a higher level of Damascius' philosophy of time but is meant as in Plato's *Timaeus*, 36e 4–5: θείαν ἀρχὴν ἤρξατο [sc. ἡ ψυχὴ] ἀπαύστου καὶ ἔμφρονος βίου πρὸς τὸν σύμπαντα χρόνον. Indeed, a σύμπας χρόνος can be spotted at more than one level. Proclus, for instance, calls σύμπας χρόνος the totality of time (i.e. all 'was', 'is', and 'will be'; cf. *In Timaeum*, III, 50.28–51.1: "[...] the cosmos has admitted the entire circling motion of time in a manner that is separate and divided. Due to this, the cosmos "was, and is, and will be". It does not have [all] three [tenses] in *the whole of time*, and has each one in a portion of time, but also has each of the three in *the whole of time* due to the period that is past, ⟨the period that is present⟩ and the period that is future. [Οὕτω καὶ ὁ κόσμος τὴν σύμπασαν τοῦ χρόνου χορείαν μεριστῶς καὶ διῃρημένως ὑπομεμένηκε, δι' ἣν "καὶ γεγονὼς καὶ ὢν καὶ ἐσόμενός" [*Timaeus*, 38c 3] ἐστιν, οὐκ ἐν τῷ σύμπαντι χρόνῳ τὰ τρία ἔχων, ἕκαστον δὲ ἐν μορίῳ χρόνου, ἀλλὰ καὶ ἕκαστον τῶν τριῶν ἐν τῷ σύμπαντι χρόνῳ διά τε τὴν φθάσασαν καὶ ⟨τὴν παροῦσαν καὶ⟩ τὴν μέλλουσαν περίοδον. Translation by Baltzly.]) but also the primary or intellectual time; cf. *In Timaeum*, III, 40.8–13: [...] the one time that proceeds from the Demiurge and his will remains one, whole and undifferentiated, even though by dint of the motions of these [heavenly bodies] it comes to be plural in number and appears as if it were divided and differentiated, so that the measure that is appropriate to each one is, as it were, separated from *the whole of time* and always preserved by virtue of the regular and orderly movement [of each heavenly body]. ([...] μένοντα ἕνα καὶ ὅλον καὶ ἀδιάφορον ὑπὸ τῆς τούτων κινήσεως πολὺν κατ' ἀριθμὸν γίγνεσθαι καὶ οἱονεὶ τέμνεσθαι καὶ διορίζεσθαι,, ἑκάστου τὸ πρόσφορον ἑαυτῷ μέτρον ἀπὸ τοῦ χρόνου τοῦ σύμπαντος οἷον ἀποτεμνομένου καὶ τοῦτο φρουροῦντος ἀεὶ διὰ τῆς ὁμαλῆς καὶ τεταγμένης κινήσεως. Translation by Baltzly.)

2 Time as a uniting measure

Human beings experience a different present, which separates their past from their future, in virtue of their durative (and limited) activity of being. The heaven itself, however, through its rotation has only a flowing present, which actualizes in the sublunary world a "leap of generation",[86] through which the B series is created. The differences of time, i.e. the earlier and later, emerge from the actualized ordering of the stages that make up a properly durative activity of being, and their being past and future is in reality secondary. It depends on the present activity of being of an individual generated substance,[87] that is, its activity of being that runs along, for some duration, with the single flowing 'now' that pertains to the rotation of the heaven. The rotation of the heaven creates the days and nights which appear on earth and which are necessary for the being of any sublunary substance to have a duration and, as a result, a past and a future. An event ordered in the A series, say, a stage of life, variously has the properties of being future, present and past because it is variously related to a present activity of being. Therefore, the being in becoming, which characterizes the sublunary substances, is the result of two components: (i) time as a "perfecting element" or an inborn principle, which articulates the earlier and later within a durative activity of being; and (ii) the rotation of the heaven which makes an activity of being actual, that is, which makes it happen in the present time (or in *a* present time), a time that is flowing:

> […] the only possible way to resolve Aristotle's aporia [namely that what exists of time, i.e. the 'now', is not time, whereas what is time (i.e. the past and the future) does not exist][88] is to assume that the temporal measure is the present time. Insofar as this measure subsists, it is present; insofar as it is destroyed, it is past; as it recurs without interruption, it is future. There are therefore two times around the present time, because the present time is constantly other. At all events, **in the imperishable generation** [i.e. the becoming of the heaven] **all time is contracted into the present time.** It is in accordance with this everlastingly present time that we can also see how time measures motion or, in general, generation. For that [part] of generation that is each time present, that is measured in its totality [not by the 'now' but] by time. Therefore, as a totality, a thing does not become in the now, but *is* then, because it is then whatever it is in its totality simultaneously. Just like the generated time is the 'now' that is constantly other, so generation is the being that is constantly other; therefore, generation is an essence that is constantly other, and time is a now that is constantly other.[89]

---

86 On this expression of Damascius, see Chapter 3, n. 59.
87 Cf. *Parm.*, 152e 1–2: "Whenever it is, it is always now." ("Εστι γὰρ ἀεὶ νῦν ὅτανπερ ᾖ.)
88 Cf. Damascius, *In Parm.*, III, 172.13–14, referring to Aristotle, *Phys.*, IV 10, 218a 3–8. On Aristotle's aporiae about time, see below, 3.1.
89 Damascius, *In Parm.*, III, 185.9–24: "Ἤδη δὲ καὶ πρὸς τὸ δυοδέκατον λέγομεν ὡς οὕτω μόνως ἐπιλύεσθαι δυνατὸν τὴν Ἀριστοτέλους ἀπορίαν, εἶναι χρόνον ἐνεστῶτα ὑποθεμένοις τὸ χρονικὸν τοιόνδε μέτρον· ὅπερ ὡς μὲν παρὸν ἐνεστώς ἐστιν, ὡς δὲ φθειρόμενον παρεληλυθώς, ὡς δὲ ἐπιγιγνόμενον ἀδιαλείπτως μέλλων. Εἰσὶν ἄρα καὶ οἱ δύο περὶ τὸν ἐνεστῶτα χρόνον, ἄλλος γὰρ ἀεὶ καὶ

Thus, Damascius seems to have been the first philosopher to make a case for presentism, with respect, however, only to the activity that proceeds from the essence of the heaven. We can see in this activity the term outside the time-series, which McTaggart sought but did not find.[90] Had Damascius known McTaggart's analysis of time, he would have pointed out to him that his fault lied in his assessment of the A series. Such a series indeed does not exist in actuality. But this does not imply that time does not exist either. Time for Damascius is the unchanging order—the C series—of the leaps of generation, which are variously present because each one generated being has its *own* present that is actualized by the *unique* flowing present of the rotation of the heaven. The properties of being past and future emerge only secondarily, insofar the activity of being of a generated substance has a duration.

We shall now see that the flowing present, which runs along with the rotation of the heaven, proceeds from a further time, a time that is not flowing.

ἄλλος ὁ ἐνεστώς· ἕν γέ τοι τῇ ἀφθάρτῳ γενέσει ἐν τῷ ἐνεστῶτι συνέπτυκται πᾶς ὁ χρόνος. Κατὰ δὴ τὸν ἀεὶ ἐνεστῶτα τοῦτον δυνάμεθα καὶ ὅπως μετρεῖ τὴν κίνησιν ὁ χρόνος ἰδεῖν, ἢ καὶ ὅλως τὴν γένεσιν· ὃ γὰρ αὐτῆς ἀεὶ πάρεστιν, τοῦτο μετρεῖ ὅλον ὁ χρόνος. Διόπερ ὡς ὅλον ἕν γε τῷ νῦν οὐδὲ γίγνεται, ἀλλ' ἔστιν τότε, ἅτε ὅλον ὁμοῦ ὅ ποτέ ἐστιν ὂν τότε· ὡς δὲ ἄλλο καὶ ἄλλο τοιοῦτον νῦν ὁ γιγνόμενος, οὕτως ἄλλο καὶ ἄλλο τοιόνδε ὂν ἡ γένεσις, ὡς τήν τε γένεσιν ἄλλην ἀεὶ καὶ ἄλλην εἶναι οὐσίαν, καὶ τὸν χρόνον ἄλλο καὶ ἄλλο νῦν.

90 See McTaggart (1908: 468) and *supra*, n. 82.

3 Time all at once

> But those things that he says do not disturb me so much, but rather those things that he often said to me when he was alive, without convincing me, namely that the whole of time exists simultaneously in reality.[1]

We saw in the previous chapter that Damascius distinguishes between the activities that proceed from an essence and the very activity of being. He takes the flowing time, which is commonly taken to correspond to the image of eternity of Plato's *Timaeus*, to be the 'measure' of the activity that proceeds *from* the essence of the heaven, namely its rotation. This seems to leave the activity *of* the heaven's being without a measure of its own. Damascius thus conceived of a time in-between eternity and flowing time, a time which pertains to the heaven's activity of being. Since the being of the heaven does not properly come to be, as the extended being of any sublunary substance does, Damascius calls this time "the whole of time" (ὁ σύμπας χρόνος): the activity of the heaven's being does not go through earlier and later stages and, therefore, has no past or future. On the contrary, it creates through its external activity, i.e. its rotation, a past and a future for the sublunary substances. This 'whole of time' is closely related to what Damascius calls, in a fragment of his *On Place*, "the non-flowing now" (τὸ ἄρρευστον νῦν), which pertains to the integral presence of the enmattered form. Given that eternity is the cause of permanence in being, then time as the true and first image of eternity must be the cause of permanence in becoming.[2] All sublunary substances have their being in becom-

---

[1] Simplicius, *In Phys.*, 775.31–34: Ἀλλὰ ταῦτα μὲν οὐ τοσοῦτον ἐμὲ θράττει λεγόμενα παρ' αὐτοῦ, ἐκεῖνα δὲ μᾶλλον, ἅπερ καὶ ζῶν ἔτι πολλάκις πρὸς ἐμὲ λέγων οὐκ ἔπειθε, τὸ εἶναι ἅμα τὸν ὅλον χρόνον ἐν ὑποστάσει.

[2] Cf. Damascius, *apud Simplicium, In Phys.*, 775.12–16 (quoted in Chapter 2, n. 63): "Just as eternity is the cause, to that which undergoes the intelligible differentiation from the proper One-which-is, of its abiding in its own One-which-is in respect with its being, so time is the cause, to what descended from there into perception, of its dancing around the one intelligible radiance of the form (χορεύειν περὶ τὸ νοητὸν ἓν τοῦ εἴδους ἀπαύγασμα) and of its having the continuity of this dance (χορείαν) in order." In speaking about χορεύειν and χορεία, Damascius appeals to the common (par)etymology of the word χρόνος; cf. Proclus, *In Timaeum*, III, 9.15–18: "Indeed, people commonly think that the name 'eternity' is derived from the expression 'that which always is' (ὁ αἰών > τὸ ἀεὶ ὄν), just like they think that the name 'time' is derived from the word 'dance' (χρόνος > χορεία), which is a motion and has its existence in generation." (Καὶ γὰρ ἡ κοινὴ ἔννοια παρὰ τὸ ἀεὶ εἶναι τὸν αἰῶνα λέγεσθαι οἴεται, καθάπερ τὸν χρόνον παρὰ τὴν χορείαν κίνησιν οὖσαν καὶ ἐν γενέσει τὴν ὕπαρξιν ἔχουσαν.) Iamblichus, who is followed by Damascius, was probably the first to

ing, that is, they *evolve* around an irradiating intelligible form because of the first generated substance, i.e. the heaven, in which being and becoming coincide because of an integral time. Their evolving necessitates earlier and later stages and as they go through them in an orderly way, they acquire a past and a future.

Much of Damascius' novel thinking on time comes out as a reflexion on what is permanent in becoming. In order to understand this we have to go back to the formative theories of Damascius' philosophy of time: Aristotle's concept of 'the now' (τὸ νῦν) and its relation to time as "a number of motion according to the anterior and posterior",[3] expounded in *Physics* IV and VI; Plato's conception of 'the now' as the present time,[4] in which 'the one' partakes as it becomes and is older than itself (and also younger than itself and at the same age as itself), discussed within the second hypothesis of the *Parmenides*; and Iamblichus' interpretation of pseudo-Archytas' account of time, defined as "a universal extension of the nature of all"[5] and described as partless and non-existent.[6]

---

put on track the "natural", in accordance with Plato's *Cratylus*, account of the namegivers; cf. Iamblichus, *apud Simplicium, In Phys.*, 786.30–33: "Some [of the earlier thinkers] defined time, as the name makes clear, as some kind of dance around the intelligence." (Οἱ μὲν γάρ, ὥσπερ καὶ τοὔνομα δηλοῖ, χορείᾳ τινὶ τοῦ νοῦ [...] τὸν χρόνον ἀφωρίσαντο.) Proclus himself thought that the original word was χορόνοος, a word capturing both the imparticipable still time (νοῦς) and the participated circularly moving time (χορός); cf. *In Timaeum*, III, 27.32–28.6: "It seems to me that those who properly cognized time's nature thusly named it 'chronos', since they wished to say that it is a certain 'choronoos', that is, a dancing intellect. Perhaps they shortened the name to 'chronos' as a disguise. Or perhaps it was because it is simultaneously still and dancing, remaining still by means of one aspect of itself, but dancing by means of another aspect, as if it has a half that is intellect and a half that is dedicated to dancing." (Καί μοι δοκοῦσιν (οἱ) τὴν φύσιν αὐτοῦ ταύτην κατανενοηκότες οὕτως αὐτὸν ὀνομάσαι χρόνον, χορόνοόν τινα ἐθελήσαντες εἰπεῖν καὶ οἷον χορεύοντα νοῦν, συντεμόντες δὲ τάχα μὲν δι᾽ ἐπίκρυψιν χρόνον ὠνόμασαν, τάχα δὲ καὶ διότι μένων τε ἅμα καὶ χορεύων καὶ τῷ μὲν ἑαυτοῦ μένων, τῷ δὲ χορεύων, ὥσπερ ἐφ᾽ ἡμισείας ἐστὶ νοῦς καὶ χορευτικός. Translation by Baltzly, slightly modified.)

3 Aristotle, *Phys.*, IV 11, 219b 1–2: Τοῦτο γάρ ἐστιν ὁ χρόνος, ἀριθμὸς κινήσεως κατὰ τὸ πρότερον καὶ ὕστερον.
4 Cf. Plato, *Parm.*, 152b 3–4: κατὰ τὸν νῦν χρόνον [...] τὸν μεταξὺ τοῦ ἦν τε καὶ ἔσται.
5 Cf. Simplicius, *In Phys.*, 786.11–13: "But the divine Iamblichus, in the first book of his commentary on the *Categories*, says that Archytas defines time as being 'a number of a certain motion or a universal extension of the nature of the universe'." (Ὁ μέντοι θεῖος Ἰάμβλιχος ἐν τῷ πρώτῳ τῶν εἰς τὰς Κατηγορίας ὑπομνημάτων τὸν Ἀρχύταν ὁρίζεσθαί φησι τὸν χρόνον ὡς ἐστι "κινάσιός τι(νο)ς ἀριθμὸς ἢ καὶ καθόλω διάσταμα τᾶς τῶ παντὸς φύσιος".)
6 (Pseudo-)Archytas *apud Simplicium, In Phys.*, 785.16–17: "In general, time has the property of being partless and non-existent." ([...] ὁ χρόνος καθόλου μὲν ἴδιον ἔχει τὸ ἀμερές καὶ ἀνυπόστατον.)

3.1 The indivisible 'now' and the present time

According to the first two of Aristotle's notorious aporiae in *Physics* IV 10, the divisibility of time—time is commonly divided in past, present, and future—leads to a serious difficulty. For any divisible thing to exist, Aristotle says, either all of it or some part of it has to exist. Your divisible body, for instance, now exists in its entirety, as also does your reading of this part of the chapter (it seems that a substance exists in its entirety, whereas an activity exists part by part). However, no part of time exists: the past no longer is and the future is not yet.[7] The 'now', i.e. the present moment, seems to exist but the moment, Aristotle retorts, is not a part of time.[8] Time is not constituted by moments or instants,[9] as a line is not constituted by points. The 'now' is a non-part of time that separates the parts of time.[10]

Aristotle goes on to explain how the 'now' creates further problems. (a) It can either always be the same, that is, there should be only one and the same instant, or (b) it can always be destroyed, so that a new instant is generated each time.[11] Both alternatives turn out to be problematic. An instant is a limit (it separates the future from the past, or the past from the future) and there is no limitable thing (say a line, a plane or a body) which can have only one limit; moreover, if there is only one instant, all events will collapse into one simultaneous event,

---

7 Cf. Aristotle, *Phys.*, IV 10, 217b 33–34: "One part of time has been and is not, while the other is going to be and is not yet." (Τὸ μὲν γὰρ αὐτοῦ [sc. τοῦ χρόνου] γέγονε καὶ οὐκ ἔστιν, τὸ δὲ μέλλει καὶ οὔπω ἔστιν.)
8 Cf. Aristotle, *Phys.*, IV 10, 218a 3–6: "Further, if a divisible thing is to exist, it is necessary that, when it exists, all or some of its parts must exist. But of time some parts have been, while others have to be, and no part of it is though it is divisible; the now is not a part of time." (Πρὸς δὲ τούτοις παντὸς μεριστοῦ, ἄνπερ ᾖ, ἀνάγκη, ὅτε ἔστιν, ἤτοι πάντα τὰ μέρη εἶναι ἢ ἔνια· τοῦ δὲ χρόνου τὰ μὲν γέγονε τὰ δὲ μέλλει, ἔστι δ' οὐδέν, ὄντος μεριστοῦ· τὸ δὲ νῦν οὐ μέρος. Translation by Hardie, slightly modified.)
9 Cf. Aristotle, *Phys.*, IV 10, 218a 6–8: "For the part is measured and the whole must be made up of its parts; time, however, is not held to be made up of 'nows'." (Μετρεῖται γὰρ τὸ μέρος, καὶ συγκεῖσθαι δεῖ τὸ ὅλον ἐκ τῶν μερῶν· ὁ δὲ χρόνος οὐ δοκεῖ συγκεῖσθαι ἐκ τῶν νῦν.) The 'now' is instantaneous and cannot be *measured* as any part of time can. On this reading (μετρεῖται, against μετρεῖ τε, which is followed by other editors and translators of the *Physics*) see Pellegrin (2000: 246 n. 4).
10 Cf. Aristotle, *Phys.*, IV 10, 218a 8–9: "Moreover, the 'now' which obviously draws the boundary between the past and the future [...]." (Ἔτι δὲ τὸ νῦν, ὃ φαίνεται διορίζειν τὸ παρελθὸν καὶ τὸ μέλλον [...].)
11 Cf. Aristotle, *Phys.*, IV 10, 218a 9–10: "Does the 'now' always remain one and the same or is it [always] other and other? It is hard to say.". ([...] πότερον ἓν καὶ ταὐτὸν ἀεὶ διαμένει ἢ ἄλλο καὶ ἄλλο, οὐ ῥᾴδιον ἰδεῖν.)

which is absurd.[12] If, on the other hand, the instant is always destroyed and regenerated, and thus the directionality and irreversibility of time is assured, it is destroyed either in itself or in some other instant. Nonetheless, it is impossible for an instant to be destroyed in itself, because each instant subsists only when it is (such destruction would require a non-instant in the instant, which is contradictory). But it is also impossible for an instant to be destroyed in another instant because there are no successive instants, as there are no successive points in a line. Thus, an instant would then have to be destroyed in a non-successive instant, which yields the absurd consequence that before its destruction an instant exists simultaneously in itself and in all infinite instants that separate it from the non-successive instant, in which it will eventually be destroyed.[13] These difficulties clearly defied the very existence of the present. And a non-existing present would actually eliminate the whole of time; for it is a common assumption, from which the first of Aristotle's aporiae arises,[14] that the past and the future are non-existent parts of time.

---

[12] This would happen because no past event could be separated from another past event, and no future event could be separated from another future event, as there would be only one and the same instant that would separate the past from the future. McTaggart's B series—the earlier and later that are immune to change—would be destroyed and some sort of extreme presentism would arise.

[13] Cf. Aristotle, *Phys.*, IV 10, 218a 16–30: "The 'now' cannot have been destroyed in itself because it then existed; yet it cannot have been destroyed in another 'now'. For we may lay it down that one 'now' cannot be next to another, any more than point to point. If then it has not been destroyed in the successive 'now' but in another, it would exist simultaneously with the infinite 'nows' between the two, which is impossible. But, of course, neither is it possible for the 'now' to remain always the same. No limited divisible thing has a single limit, whether it is continuously extended in one or in more than one dimension; but the 'now' is a limit, and it is possible to take a limited time [i.e. through two 'nows']. Further, if existing simultaneously in time (i.e. being neither anterior nor posterior) means to be in one and the same 'now', then, if both what is anterior and what is posterior are in this same 'now', things which happened ten thousand years ago would be simultaneous with what has happened today, and nothing would be anterior or posterior than anything else." (Ἐν αὐτῷ μὲν οὖν ἐφθάρθαι οὐχ οἷόν τε διὰ τὸ εἶναι τότε, ἐν ἄλλῳ δὲ νῦν ἐφθάρθαι τὸ πρότερον νῦν οὐκ ἐνδέχεται. ἔστω γὰρ ἀδύνατον ἐχόμενα εἶναι ἀλλήλων τὰ νῦν, ὥσπερ στιγμὴν στιγμῆς. εἴπερ οὖν ἐν τῷ ἐφεξῆς οὐκ ἔφθαρται ἀλλ' ἐν ἄλλῳ, ἐν τοῖς μεταξὺ [τοῖς] νῦν ἀπείροις οὖσιν ἅμα ἂν εἴη· τοῦτο δὲ ἀδύνατον. ἀλλὰ μὴν οὐδ' αἰεὶ τὸ αὐτὸ διαμένειν δυνατόν· οὐδενὸς γὰρ διαιρετοῦ πεπερασμένου ἓν πέρας ἔστιν, οὔτε ἂν ἐφ' ἓν ᾗ συνεχὲς οὔτε ἂν ἐπὶ πλείω· τὸ δὲ νῦν πέρας ἐστίν, καὶ χρόνον ἔστι λαβεῖν πεπερασμένον. ἔτι εἰ τὸ ἅμα εἶναι κατὰ χρόνον καὶ μήτε πρότερον μήτε ὕστερον τὸ ἐν τῷ αὐτῷ εἶναι καὶ ἑνὶ [τῷ] νῦν ἐστιν, εἰ τά τε πρότερον καὶ τὰ ὕστερον ἐν τῷ νῦν τῳδί ἐστιν, ἅμα ἂν εἴη τὰ ἔτος γενόμενα μυριοστῷ τοῖς γενομένοις τήμερον, καὶ οὔτε πρότερον οὔτε ὕστερον οὐδὲν ἄλλο ἄλλου. Translation by Hardie, modified.)

[14] Time is made out of items that do not exist, namely the past and the future, and therefore cannot itself exist; cf. Aristotle, *Phys.*, IV 10, 217b 33–218a 3.

Aristotle actually solved these difficulties. He said that the instant, which separates the future from the past and the past from the future, is in some way always the same and in some other way always different, thus uniting the two branches of the dilemma.[15] The instant is always the same with respect to its ground of being (ὅ ποτε ὄν). An instant, for Aristotle, is not separately existing but is, we would say, a second-order property pertaining to the motion of a substance; its ground of being, that is, is always a moving substance (τὸ φερόμενον) which, as such, is in anterior and posterior states of being a moving substance in terms of spatial location.[16] On the other hand, an instant is always different with respect to what it itself is, namely an anterior and posterior for a percipient mind.[17] In virtue of the very nature of the perception of time as duration determined by two instants, one anterior and one posterior,[18] no instant, as individuated by a percipient mind, can be the same as another instant.[19] This instant of your reading, for instance, which is now projected by your mind as posterior to the instant from which your reading has begun, is anterior to a posterior instant, say, the instant at which your reading will have ended (please note the perfect aspect of the verbs used). This distinction

---

15 Cf. Aristotle, *Phys.*, IV 11, 219b 31–33: "Thus, the 'now' in one sense is always the same, in another it is not the same; for [this is true] also of the thing that is moving." (Ἔστι μὲν οὖν ὡς τὸ αὐτὸ τὸ νῦν αἰεί, ἔστι δ' ὡς οὐ τὸ αὐτό· καὶ γὰρ τὸ φερόμενον.)
16 See further Roark (2011: 80–99).
17 Cf. Aristotle, *Phys.*, IV 11, 219b 10–15: "The 'now' is the same as to its ground of being, but its being is different. It is the 'now' that delimits the time, insofar as it is anterior and posterior. [Thus,] the 'now' in one sense is the same, in another it is not the same; insofar as it is in other and other [i.e. state of being a moving substance], it is different (which is just what it is for it to be 'now'), but insofar as it has a ground of being, it is the same." (Τὸ γὰρ νῦν τὸ αὐτὸ ὅ ποτ' ἦν—τὸ δ' εἶναι αὐτῷ ἕτερον—τὸ δὲ νῦν τὸν χρόνον ὁρίζει, ᾗ πρότερον καὶ ὕστερον. τὸ δὲ νῦν ἔστι μὲν ὡς τὸ αὐτό, ἔστι δ' ὡς οὐ τὸ αὐτό· ᾗ μὲν γὰρ ἐν ἄλλῳ καὶ ἄλλῳ, ἕτερον (τοῦτο δ' ἦν αὐτῷ τὸ νῦν ⟨εἶναι⟩), ᾗ δέ ποτε ὄν ἐστι τὸ νῦν, τὸ αὐτό.)
18 Cf. Aristotle, *Phys.*, IV 11, 219a 30–219b 2: "When, therefore, we perceive the 'now' as one, and neither as before and after in a motion nor as the same but of an anterior and a posterior [motion], no time is thought to have elapsed, because there has been no motion either. On the other hand, when we do perceive the anterior and posterior, then we say that there is time. For time is just this: a number of motion in respect of the anterior and posterior." (Ὅταν μὲν οὖν ὡς ἓν τὸ νῦν αἰσθανώμεθα, καὶ μὴ ἤτοι ὡς πρότερον καὶ ὕστερον ἐν τῇ κινήσει ἢ ὡς τὸ αὐτὸ μὲν προτέρου δὲ καὶ ὑστέρου τινός, οὐ δοκεῖ χρόνος γεγονέναι οὐδείς, ὅτι οὐδὲ κίνησις. ὅταν δὲ τὸ πρότερον καὶ ὕστερον [sc. αἰσθανώμεθα], τότε λέγομεν χρόνον· τοῦτο γάρ ἐστιν ὁ χρόνος, ἀριθμὸς κινήσεως κατὰ τὸ πρότερον καὶ ὕστερον. Translation by Hardie, modified.)
19 Cf. Aristotle, *Phys.*, IV 11, 218b 27–28: "If the 'now' were not different but one and the same, there would not have been time." (Εἰ μὴ ἦν ἕτερον τὸ νῦν ἀλλὰ ταὐτὸ καὶ ἕν, οὐκ ἂν ἦν χρόνος. Translation by Hardie.) Note that I do not follow the Basel edition of Aristotle (1539), from which the standard division in chapters derives. A new chapter (11) should start, in my view, not at 218b 21 but at 219a 1.

between an anterior and posterior instant is necessary for your activity of reading to have a number, a "number of motion", as Aristotle says, which will be its duration. Moreover, in virtue of its separating the future from the past, one and the same instant is both posterior and anterior: it is posterior to all instants which divide a past time, and is anterior to all instants which divide a future time. Indeed, in virtue of its having simultaneously contradictory properties, namely its belonging simultaneously to an anterior and a posterior motion,[20] its being both a start (of the future time) and an end (of the past time),[21] the instant does not exist in reality, that is, outside the human soul. It is nonetheless through these contradictory properties that the human soul comes to know what the physical reality really is like, namely continuous. In a non-continuous space (like the atomic one), a point could not be *both* the start and the end of two parts of a divided line.[22] Aristotle would be happy to admit that the relevant aporiae had already correctly put the matter. Time is divisible in parts according to the instant *and* no part of time subsists. Once, however, one has understood the true nature of time, these difficulties cease to be real. For time, which is a concomitant of motion, which in its turn is a concomitant of space, is continuous; therefore, it has no parts, that is, it has no *actual* parts. Time is never actually divided by itself.[23] It is the human soul, the mind of the soul, that actually does the dividing by individuating instants as anterior and posterior cuts in some thing's motion. As we saw in the previous chapter, time, according to Aristotle, measures (μετρεῖ) the being of motions—thus creating their duration—and numbers (ἀριθμεῖ) the motions—thus creating a number of motion: a day, a month, a season, a years, a four-year cycle or 'Olympiad'—by dint of the human soul.[24] Time and instant, we can say today, were for Aristotle mind-depend-

---

20 Cf. Aristotle, *Phys.*, IV 11, 219a 32 (quoted n. 18): τὸ αὐτὸ μὲν προτέρου δὲ καὶ ὑστέρου τινός.
21 Cf. Aristotle, *Phys.*, IV 13, 222a 10–12: "The 'now' is the continuity of time, as has been said; for it connects the past and future time, and it is a limit of time; for it is the beginning of the future time and the end of the past time." (Τὸ δὲ νῦν ἐστιν συνέχεια χρόνου, ὥσπερ ἐλέχθη· συνέχει γὰρ τὸν χρόνον τὸν παρεληλυθότα καὶ ἐσόμενον, καὶ πέρας χρόνου ἐστίν· ἔστι γὰρ τοῦ μὲν ἀρχή, τοῦ δὲ τελευτή.)
22 Cf. Aristotle, *Phys.*, IV 11, 220a 10–11: "For also the point both connects and draws a boundary in a length; it is the beginning of one [segment] and the end of another." (Καὶ γὰρ ἡ στιγμὴ καὶ συνέχει τὸ μῆκος καὶ ⟨δι⟩ορίζει [scripsi : ὁρίζει codd.]· ἔστι γὰρ τοῦ μὲν ἀρχὴ τοῦ δὲ τελευτή.)
23 Cf. also Damascius *apud Simplicium, In Phys.*, 798.8 (quoted Chapter 2, n. 83): "[...] in itself time is one and continuous".
24 Cf. Aristotle, *Phys.*, IV 12, 220b 23–24: "We measure the motion by the time, and the time by the motion." (Τῷ μὲν γὰρ χρόνῳ τὴν κίνησιν, τῇ δὲ κινήσει τὸν χρόνον μετροῦμεν.) Say, by one year we measure a complete revolution of the sun along the ecliptic; by a complete revolution of the sun along the ecliptic we measure the time that has elapsed, namely one year. Despite the reluctance of several scholars, Aristotle states with no hesitancy that time would not exist without the human

ent entities.²⁵ And as the first of Aristotle's notorious aporiae implies,²⁶ time, unlike the continuum of space and motion, is not a basic ingredient of the universe. Time emerges from items—the past, the future, and the present moment that separates them—that do not exist except in the human soul. It is not obvious at all that Aristotle believed that other living beings, say, the planet Saturn or an ant, had their own past and their own future.

Thus, Aristotle brought forth the difficulties concerning the existence of time and the 'now' and provided solutions to these difficulties. But his solutions were not perceived as such by the Platonists of Late antiquity. Rather, these philosophers believed that Aristotle's aporiae and their solutions were meant to stimulate further reflection on the true nature of time, which was intrinsically related to a correct understanding of the 'now'. The true 'now', which exists outside the human soul, should not be understood as an extensionless limit. Time, as any follower of the *Timaeus* knows, is a "movable image of eternity", or "an eternal image, moving according to number, of the eternity that abides in unity", or "an imitation of eternity, which circles round according to number".²⁷ Thus, time for Plato was not just a moving entity, which accomplishes days, months and years that come and go, but it was also the image of a model. And despite the fact that the image is ontologically dependent on the model, the two items taken together, as they should be, are relatives. This means that the one does not exist without the other. If eternity exists—that is, if the unextended activity of being of the Living-Being-itself, through which the intelligible forms contemplated by the Demiurge are "activities by their essence",²⁸ exists—then time—that is, the durative activity of being of the cosmos, through which the generated substances depart from their essence—must also exist. By presenting time as ontologically dependent on motion, Aristotle's definition of time as a "number of motion according to the anterior and posterior" could not concern the true nature of time but only the way in which time is at first cog-

---

soul; cf. *Phys.*, IV 14, 223a 25–28: "But if nothing but soul, or in soul intelligence, is by nature qualified to count, there would not be time unless there were soul, but only the time's ground of being, if motion, for instance, can exist without soul. The anterior and posterior is in motion, and time is these insofar as they are numerable." (Εἰ δὲ μηδὲν ἄλλο πέφυκεν ἀριθμεῖν ἢ ψυχὴ καὶ ψυχῆς νοῦς, ἀδύνατον εἶναι χρόνον ψυχῆς μὴ οὔσης, ἀλλ' ἢ τοῦτο ὅ ποτε ὄν ἔστιν ὁ χρόνος, οἷον εἰ ἐνδέχεται κίνησιν εἶναι ἄνευ ψυχῆς. τὸ δὲ πρότερον καὶ ὕστερον ἐν κινήσει ἐστίν· χρόνος δὲ ταῦτ' ἐστὶν ᾗ ἀριθμητά ἐστιν.) This is meant, however, as a thought experiment: (a) the human soul will always exist; (b) motion, which is the matter of time, would not exist, if there were no soul in the universe.
25 This, of course, does not mean that time and instant are illusions. They have a real ground of being, namely the moving substance.
26 See n. 14.
27 Cf. Plato, *Timaeus*, 37c 6–38a 8. See Chapter 2, n. 1 and 2.
28 Cf. Simplicius, *In Phys.*, 773.34–774.5.

nized in the human soul. The true recognition of time, Damascius contends, requires us to distinguish the indivisible or partless 'now' (τὸ ἀδιαίρετον νῦν, τὸ ἀμερὲς νῦν), which is a limit of time (πέρας χρόνου), from the present time (ὁ ἐνεστὼς χρόνος), which is continuous and, as any continuous entity in this world, is infinitely divisible in thought. In reality, however, it is undivided. It is this time, Damascius says,[29] which is called "now" (νῦν) by Plato in the *Parmenides*; and this 'now' is different from the 'now', of which Aristotle speaks in his account of time in *Physics* IV and VI.

For concordist Platonists such as Damascius and his pupil Simplicius, Aristotle appeared to claim that time does not exist outside the human soul only to superficial readers, who were unable to see that the 'now', which is "the anterior and posterior", in Aristotle's definition of time, is not the only 'now' that exists. In his treatise *On Time*, Damascius criticizes those Peripatetics who did not read book *Delta* of the *Physics* in the light of book *Zeta* in the same treatise, a book in which Aristotle purposefully shows, to the detriment of Zeno's paradoxes, that nothing moves or changes in the indivisible 'now'; as a result, there can be no instantaneous motion. It would be contradictory for a divisible thing, such as motion, to be realized or even to exist within something indivisible, such as an instant. And yet time, this "movable image", is inseparable from motion. Damascius says, in a Platonic vein, that time "coexists" (συνών) and "runs along with" (συμπαραθέων) motion:

> I am astonished at how those who say that only the indivisible 'now' exists solve Zeno's argument by claiming that motion is not accomplished according to something indivisible, but rather progresses in a whole stride at once (ἀθρούστερον), and that it does not always [cover] the half before the whole, but sometimes, as it were, leaps over (οἶον ὑπεραλλομένης) whole and part, but did not realize the same thing happening in the case of time: for time always coexists with motion and, as it were, runs along with it,[30] so that it strides along together with [motion] in a whole continuous jump and does not infinitely traverse a [series of] now[s]. And [they do not realize] this, while on the one hand motion is evident in things and

---

29 Cf. Damascius, *In Parm.*, III, 192.4–5: "And it is called 'now' not in the sense of being a limit of time but in the sense of being a time that is creatively undivided." (Καὶ νῦν καλεῖσθαι οὐχ ὡς πέρας χρόνου ἀλλ᾽ ὡς χρόνον ἀμέριστον δημιουργικῶς.) We will see in Section 2 of this Chapter that the creatively undivided (or partless) 'now' is the non-flowing 'now', which structures the generation of a sublunary substance.

30 οἶον συμπαραθέοντος: this word comes from Plotinus, *Enneads*, III 7, 8.53–56: "If someone says that time is the extent of motion, [he means] not the extent of the motion itself but the extent in virtue of which the motion itself has its duration, as if the motion run along with it." (Εἰ δὲ τὸ διάστημα τῆς κινήσεως λέγοι τις χρόνον, οὐ τὸ αὐτῆς τῆς κινήσεως, ἀλλὰ παρ᾽ ὃ αὐτὴ ἡ κίνησις τὴν παράτασιν ἔχοι οἶον συμπαραθέουσα ἐκείνῳ [...].) But Damascius sees the relation between these two magnitudes inversely.

on the other hand Aristotle has clearly shown that nothing moves or changes at the now but only has moved or has changed at it,³¹ whereas, no doubt, things are changing and are moving in time. At any rate, the leap of motion, being a part of motion which occurs in the course of moving,³² will not be moving at the now, nor will that which is present occur in a time that is not present. So that in which the present motion occurs, this is the present time (χρόνος οὗτός ἐστιν ὁ ἐνεστώς), and it is infinitely divisible, just as motion; for each is continuous. And everything continuous is infinitely divisible [i.e. in thought].³³

Language can here help us to understand what Damascius thought Aristotle's point was. The difference between the progressive and the perfect aspect of the verb captures what really is the case with motion and its relation to the 'now' that is actualized by the human soul. It is with a view to this relation that Aristotle affirms in book *Zeta* of the *Physics* that a thing "cannot *be changing* at the now; it is necessary that at every 'now' it *has changed*".³⁴ At the indivisible 'now' a thing has moved (κεκίνηται) or *has* changed (μεταβέβληται)—that is, it has accomplished a part of its motion, as this part is actually individuated in a percipient mind— while it is moving and is changing in time. To the detriment of Zeno's paradoxes, a motion should be compared to a leap (ἅλμα): it covers, as it were, "at once" (ἀθρούστερον), that is, at one go, a continuous spatial distance. Surely, jumping, unlike the tortoise's walking and Achilles' running, can hardly be conceived as divided,³⁵ that is, as progressing successively step by step. But Damascius takes a further

---

31 Cf. Aristotle, *Phys.*, VI 6, 237a 14–15: Ἐν δὲ τῷ νῦν οὐκ ἔστιν μεταβάλλειν, ἀνάγκη μεταβεβληκέναι καθ' ἕκαστον τῶν νῦν.
32 ἐν τῷ κινεῖσθαι: Damascius has here in mind Aristotle's distinction between (accomplished) motion, which is numbered, and the being of motion, which is measured; cf. Aristotle, *Phys.* IV 12, 220b 33–221a 1: Ἐπεὶ δ' ἐστὶν ὁ χρόνος μέτρον κινήσεως καὶ τοῦ κινεῖσθαι...
33 Damascius *apud Simplicium, In Phys.*, 796.32–797.13: Θαυμάζω δὲ ἔγωγε πῶς τὸν μὲν Ζήνωνος ἐπιλύονται λόγον, ὡς οὐ κατά τι ἀδιαίρετον τῆς κινήσεως ἐπιτελουμένης, ἀλλὰ καθ' ὅλον βῆμα προκοπτούσης ἀθρούστερον, καὶ οὐκ ἀεὶ τὸ ἥμισυ πρὸ τοῦ ὅλου, ἀλλὰ ποτὲ καὶ ὅλον καὶ μέρος οἷον ὑπεραλλομένης, οὐ συνενόησαν δὲ οἱ τὸ ἀδιαίρετον μόνον νῦν εἶναι λέγοντες τὸ αὐτὸ καὶ ἐπὶ τοῦ χρόνου συμβαῖνον ἅτε συνόντος ἀεὶ τῇ κινήσει καὶ οἷον συμπαραθέοντος, ὥστε καὶ συμβηματίζοντος ὅλῳ πηδήματι συνεχεῖ καὶ οὐ κατὰ ⟨τὸ⟩ νῦν διεξιόντος ἐπ' ἄπειρον, καὶ ταῦτα κινήσεως μὲν οὔσης ἐναργοῦς ἐν τοῖς πράγμασι, τοῦ δ' Ἀριστοτέλους οὕτω δεικνύντος λαμπρῶς, ὅτι οὐδὲν ἐν τῷ νῦν κινεῖται οὐδὲ μεταβάλλεται, ἀλλ' ἐν τούτῳ μὲν κεκίνηται καὶ μεταβέβληται, μεταβάλλεται δὲ καὶ κινεῖται πάντως ἐν χρόνῳ. τὸ γοῦν ἅλμα τῆς κινήσεως μέρος ὂν κινήσεως τὸ ἐν τῷ κινεῖσθαι, οὐκ ἐν τῷ νῦν ἔσται κινούμενον, οὐδὲ ἐν μὴ ἐνεστῶτι χρόνῳ τό γε ἐνεστώς. ὥστε ἐν ᾧ κίνησις ἡ ἐνεστῶσα, χρόνος οὗτός ἐστιν ὁ ἐνεστὼς ἄπειρος ὢν τῇ διαιρέσει ἀπείρου οὔσης· ἑκάτερον γὰρ συνεχές. πᾶν δὲ συνεχὲς ἐπ' ἄπειρον διαιρετόν.
34 See n. 31.
35 Cf. Damascius, *In Parm.*, III, 192.18–20: "How, then, that which marches lets one leap go and seizes another, since it does not cut each one leap into other leaps?" (Πῶς οὖν τοῦ μὲν ἀφίεται,

step; he says that, in addition, so is time.³⁶ He says that a leap, which does not take place at the 'now' but in time, is present when it takes place in the present time. This, the ἐνεστὼς χρόνος, is the time that, unlike Aristotle's indivisible 'now', exists outside the human soul in the world of nature. This is the real 'now', whose flowing creates duration.

According to Damascius, when something moves, it does not move successively part by part, thus covering the half before the whole, but covers with its motion both whole and part; in other words, it covers a whole that is not actually divided in parts but, once it is covered, becomes itself a part of the continuum—a part, however, which, unlike a part of space, does not remain in the case of time and motion.³⁷ This is what the word ἀθρούστερον refers to. Covering both whole and part is for Damascius a central concept for understanding the true nature of time. Time, he invites us to think, is a measure composed by a ceaseless plurality of measures that come and go, each one of which is an undivided divisible; time, therefore—we can say,³⁸ like a quantum—is both continuous and discrete (συνεχής καὶ διωρισμένος):

> We must therefore take care not to believe that time is made of indivisibles. What then? Is time not continuous and discrete, as [Parmenides] demonstrates?³⁹ By all means, I answer. However, it is not made of indivisible parts but of extended [parts] that are discrete. For it is composed, as Strato [of Lampsacus] says, "of parts that do not remain", hence of discrete parts. But each part is a continuum, so [time] is, so to speak, a measure composed of a plurality of measures. Indeed, we have shown also in our Commentary on the *Timaeus* that time does not progress according to instants, because it could then not even progress, since instants are always infinite in number.⁴⁰ But, just as motion progresses by intervals and not by points, but, so to speak, by leaps, as Aristotle also said, so it is necessary that time also advance by

---

τοῦ δὲ ἐπιλαμβάνεται τῶν ἁλμάτων τὸ πορευόμενον, οὐ τέμνει τὸ ἅλμα ἕκαστον εἰς ἄλλα ἅλματα;) For the vocabulary here used by Damascius, see n. 46.

36 See also Sorabji (1983: 53–56). Sorabji thinks, however, that Damascius calls 'leap' the period of (still) time, which intervenes between two transitions, which he wrongly takes to be instantaneous. He is probably influenced by Shmuel Sambursky who writes: "The flux of our time [...] resembles a film consisting of many pictures, of which each presents a position of rest and is separated from that of its neighbour by a small yet finite jump" (Sambursky 1968: 164). But the leaps *are* the transitions (μεταβάσεις), which Damascius also calls "measures", and these measures are separated by a limit that is in no time. Galperine (1980: 337) rightly notes: "Ces bonds sont des diastèmes temporels ou encore des mesures (μέτρα). Et ce n'est pas briser la mélodie du devenir que la diviser ainsi en mesures, C'est l'articuler. Il n'y a pas de discontinu temporel. Mais il y a un rythme du temps". See also n. 78.

37 See Chapter 2.2.

38 Cf. Sambursky (1968: 155, 163–164).

39 Cf. Plato, *Parm.*, 152b 5-c 6.

40 Cf. Aristotle, *Phys.*, IV 10, 218a 19–20: ἐν τοῖς μεταξὺ [τοῖς] νῦν ἀπείροις οὖσιν ἅμα ἂν εἴη.

whole measures, which become suitable for measuring the leaps of movement. It is therefore in this sense that time [is composed] of measures, but of measures that are discrete and separated by limits. This is also why Parmenides introduced time after the continuous magnitude and the discrete plurality,[41] because time too, as it is composed of both [whole] measures and parts, is both continuous and discrete.[42]

According to his own avowal, Damascius detected the conception of 'leap' in Aristotle's account of motion and its relation to time in *Physics* VI. His intuition, however, we shall now see, comes from the Platonic dialogue that he is here commenting on, namely the *Parmenides*.

3.2 The present time and the non-flowing 'now'

Within the conclusions reached in the second hypothesis of the *Parmenides*, which posits 'the one' (as distinct from 'the many') as participating in being or essence,[43] the namesake Platonic persona makes, according to Damascius, a crucial distinction: he shows that his interlocutor must accept that the one, while "moving forward in time" (προέρχεται κατὰ χρόνον),[44] does not only *become* older than itself but also *is* older than itself:

---

[41] Damascius refers here to Parmenides' preceding discussion of the properties that characterize (according to his interpretation) the sphere of the fixed stars and the spheres of the seven planets, namely continuous magnitude (*Parm.*, 149d 8–151b 7) and discrete plurality (*Parm.*, 151b 7-e 2) respectively. To be both continuous and discrete (*Parm.*, 151e 2–155e 3) is then the property of time, which characterizes the sublunary realm.
[42] Damascius, *In Parm.*, III, 182.17–183.12: Εὐλαβητέον ἄρα τὸ ἐξ ἀμερῶν εἶναι τὸν χρόνον. Τί οὖν; οὐδὲ συνεχής ἐστι καὶ διωρισμένος, ὡς ἀποδείκνυσιν; Πάνυ γε φήσω, ἀλλ' οὐκ ἐκ μερῶν ἀμερῶν, ἀλλ' ἐκ διαστατῶν διωρισμένων συγκείμενος. Ἔστιν γὰρ σύνθετος, ὥς φησι Στράτων, "ἐκ μερῶν μὴ μενόντων", ταύτῃ οὖν ἐκ διωρισμένων· ἕκαστον δὲ μέρος συνεχές ἐστι· καὶ οἷον μέτρον ἐστὶν ἐκ πολλῶν μέτρων. Ἐδείκνυμεν γὰρ καὶ ἐν τοῖς εἰς Τίμαιον ὅτι οὐ κατὰ τὰ νῦν προκόπτει ὁ χρόνος· οὐδὲ γὰρ ἂν προέκοψεν, ἀπείρων ὄντων ἀεὶ τῶν νῦν. Ἀλλ' ὥσπερ ἡ κίνησις προκόπτει διαστηματικῶς, ἀλλ' οὐ κατὰ σημεῖον, ἀλλ' οἷον κατὰ ἄλματα, ὡς ἔλεγεν καὶ Ἀριστοτέλης, οὕτως ἀνάγκη καὶ τὸν χρόνον κατὰ μέτρα ὅλα προβαίνειν ἃ μετρητικὰ τῶν ἁλμάτων γίγνεται τῆς κινήσεως. Οὕτως ἄρα ἐκ μέτρων ὁ χρόνος· ἀλλὰ μέτρων πέρασι διειλημμένων καὶ διωρισμένων. Διὸ καὶ ὁ Παρμενίδης τὸν χρόνον παρήγαγεν μετὰ τὸ συνεχὲς πηλίκον καὶ τὸ διωρισμένον πλῆθος, ὅτι καὶ αὐτὸς ὡς ἐκ μέτρων τε καὶ μερῶν συνεχής τέ ἐστι καὶ διωρισμένος.
[43] Cf. Plato, *Parm.*, 142b 3 and 142b 5: ἓν εἰ ἔστιν ("if it *is* one"). In the first hypothesis, the hypothetical clause is enunciated differently; 137c 4: εἰ ἕν ἐστιν ("*one* if there is").
[44] Cf. Plato, *Parm.*, 152a 4–5: Ἀεὶ ἄρα πρεσβύτερον γίγνεται ἑαυτοῦ, εἴπερ προέρχεται κατὰ χρόνον.

— And it is older (is it not?) when, in becoming, it gets to the point of time between 'was' and 'will be', which is 'now';[45] for surely in marching (πορευόμενον) from its being once (ποτέ) to its being thereafter (ἔπειτα) it cannot skip the 'now' (νῦν)? – No. – And when it arrives at the 'now' it ceases (ἐπίσχει) to become older, and no longer *becomes*, but *is* already older, for if it went on (προϊόν) it would never be reached by the 'now', for it is the nature of that which goes on, to touch both the 'now' and the 'thereafter', letting go the 'now' and seizing the 'thereafter', while it comes to be between the two, [that is, between] the 'thereafter' and the 'now'. – True. – But if that which is becoming cannot pass the 'now', when it reaches the 'now', *it ceases to become and is then whatever it may happen to be becoming.* – Clearly. – And so the one, when in becoming older it reaches the 'now', ceases to become and is then older. – Certainly.[46]

We now arrive at a conception of 'now' substantially different from Aristotle's. Plato thinks that, as a thing becomes, it does not merely move from the past (the "was") to the future (the "will be") but is constantly between a 'now' and a 'thereafter'. The rationale behind this apparently strange contention is simple: if the thing is only in the 'thereafter', it does not become but *will be*; if the thing is only in the 'now', it does not become but *is*. The conception of an extended 'now'—what the Stoics will later call διάστημα,[47] i.e. interval—thus emerges. Whatever becomes is not between a 'now' and a 'thereafter' in the way in which the 'now' itself is between the 'once' and the 'thereafter', but is 'between' insofar as "it touches", as Plato says, "both the 'now' and the 'thereafter'". The 'now', then, has a part in which the thing that becomes is (for if it were in the whole of the 'now', it would be only in the 'now' and therefore would not *become* but *be*) and which it lets go (and thus this part of 'now' turns into a 'once') in order to "seize" the 'thereafter', which it was previously "touching" by moving towards

---

45 Literally: "When it is becoming according to the time now, which is between 'was and will be'".
46 Plato, *Parm.*, 152b 2-d 4: Ἔστι δὲ πρεσβύτερον ἆρ' οὐχ ὅταν κατὰ τὸν νῦν χρόνον ᾖ γιγνόμενον τὸν μεταξὺ τοῦ ἦν τε καὶ ἔσται; οὐ γάρ που πορευόμενόν γε ἐκ τοῦ ποτὲ εἰς τὸ ἔπειτα ὑπερβήσεται τὸ νῦν. – Οὐ γάρ. – Ἆρ' οὖν οὐκ ἐπίσχει τότε τοῦ γίγνεσθαι πρεσβύτερον, ἐπειδὰν τῷ νῦν ἐντύχῃ, καὶ οὐ γίγνεται, ἀλλ' ἔστι τότ' ἤδη πρεσβύτερον; προϊὸν γὰρ οὐκ ἄν ποτε ληφθείη ὑπὸ τοῦ νῦν. τὸ γὰρ προϊὸν οὕτως ἔχει ὡς ἀμφοτέρων ἐφάπτεσθαι, τοῦ τε νῦν καὶ τοῦ ἔπειτα, τοῦ μὲν νῦν ἀφιέμενον, τοῦ δ' ἔπειτα ἐπιλαμβανόμενον, μεταξὺ ἀμφοτέρων γιγνόμενον, τοῦ τε ἔπειτα καὶ τοῦ νῦν. – Ἀληθῆ. – Εἰ δέ γε ἀνάγκη μὴ παρελθεῖν τὸ νῦν πᾶν τὸ γιγνόμενον, ἐπειδὰν κατὰ τοῦτο ᾖ, ἐπίσχει ἀεὶ τοῦ γίγνεσθαι καὶ ἔστι τότε τοῦτο ὅτι ἂν τύχῃ γιγνόμενον. – Φαίνεται. – Καὶ τὸ ἓν ἄρα, ὅταν πρεσβύτερον γιγνόμενον ἐντύχῃ τῷ νῦν, ἐπέσχεν τοῦ γίγνεσθαι καὶ ἔστι τότε πρεσβύτερον. – Πάνυ μὲν οὖν. Translation by Jowett, modified.
47 Cf. *SVF*, II 510: "Of the Stoics Zeno said that time is an interval of every simple motion, whereas Chrysippus said that it is the interval of the motion of the cosmos." (Τῶν δὲ Στωϊκῶν Ζήνων μὲν πάσης ἁπλῆς κινήσεως διάστημα τὸν χρόνον εἶπε, Χρύσιππος δὲ διάστημα τῆς τοῦ κόσμου κινήσεως.)

it,[48] and which, by being not merely touched but seized, turns into a renewed part of 'now'. But if the 'now' has a part, then it is extended.

This passage of the *Parmenides* is important in one more respect. Plato thinks that, as 'the one' "marches" from the past to the future and thus necessarily "arrives at the 'now', it [then] ceases to become older", that is, it "no longer *becomes* [older], but *is* already older". In other words, as the thing that becomes moves forward to the 'thereafter', the part of it which is in the 'now' does not move but stands still; otherwise it would not be *now* (insofar as the thing that becomes is moving, it "touches" the 'thereafter' and not the 'now'). This contention introduces the idea of the present time (ὁ ἐνεστὼς χρόνος) as 'pending', which is what ἐνεστὼς literally means ('pending', 'begun but not completed'—actually, time is never completed). As the thing that becomes moves forward in time and each time reaches the 'now', "it *is* [then] what it happens to be becoming", in other words it has accomplished a part (or a stage) of what it is becoming. We can trace in this analysis of the *Parmenides* the origin not only of Damascius' conception of time as being both continuous (insofar as it moves and *becomes*) and discrete (insofar as it stands still and *is*) but also of Iamblichus' conception of a thing having its being in becoming, which was taken over by Damascius (and Simplicius).[49]

Parmenides further insists that, since 'the one' must be and become in a time equal to itself, it also does not become older and younger than itself, and is not older and younger than itself, but has the same age as itself.[50] Damascius goes on to explain that this occurs whenever 'the one' is in the 'now':

---

48 Also this idea was later taken over, and expressed in clearer terms, by the Stoics; cf. *SVF*, II 165: "The Stoics define the present as durative present because it extends to the future; for he who says 'I am doing' manifests both that he did something and that he will do it." (Τὸν ἐνεστῶτα οἱ Στωϊκοὶ ἐνεστῶτα παρατατικὸν ὁρίζονται ὅτι παρατείνεται καὶ εἰς μέλλοντα· ὁ γὰρ λέγων "ποιῶ" καὶ ὅτι ἐποίησέ τι ἐμφαίνει καὶ ὅτι ποιήσει.)
49 See above, Chapter 2, n. 60.
50 Cf. Plato, *Parm.*, 152d 8-e 10: "– But the present is always present with the one during all its being; for whenever it is, it is always now. – Certainly. – Then the one always both is and becomes older and younger than itself? – Truly. – And is it or does it become a longer time than itself or an equal time with itself? – An equal time. – But if it becomes or is for an equal time with itself, it is of the same age with itself? – Of course. – And that which is of the same age, is neither older nor younger? – No. – The one, then, becoming and being the same time with itself, neither is nor becomes older or younger than itself? – I should say not." (– Τό γε μὴν νῦν ἀεὶ πάρεστι τῷ ἑνὶ διὰ παντὸς τοῦ εἶναι· ἔστι γὰρ ἀεὶ νῦν ὅτανπερ ᾖ. – Πῶς γὰρ οὔ; – Ἀεὶ ἄρα ἐστί τε καὶ γίγνεται πρεσβύτερον ἑαυτοῦ καὶ νεώτερον τὸ ἕν. – Ἔοικεν. – Πλείω δὲ χρόνον αὐτὸ ἑαυτοῦ ἐστιν ἢ γίγνεται, ἢ τὸν ἴσον; – Τὸν ἴσον. – Ἀλλὰ μὴν τόν γε ἴσον χρόνον ἢ γιγνόμενον ἢ ὂν τὴν αὐτὴν ἡλικίαν ἔχει. – Πῶς δ' οὔ; – Τὸ δὲ τὴν αὐτὴν ἡλικίαν ἔχον οὔτε πρεσβύτερον οὔτε νεώτερόν ἐστιν. – Οὐ γάρ. – Τὸ ἓν ἄρα τὸν ἴσον χρόνον αὐτὸ ἑαυτῷ καὶ γιγνόμενον καὶ ὂν οὔτε νεώτερον οὔτε πρεσβύτερον ἑαυτοῦ ἐστιν οὐδὲ γίγνεται. – Οὔ μοι δοκεῖ. Translation by Jowett.)

How, then, does Parmenides conceive of the predicates 'neither younger nor older' in the midst of that-which-becomes according to the 'now'? For, once [the one] encounters the 'now', it has ceased to become. The answer is that each interval of time is called "now" in the sense of the present time, and not in the sense of the limit of time; for there is a certain interval of time which has been present all at once, [and is] not distinct in virtue of two 'nows'.[51] And that Parmenides called this interval "now", this is what he made clear by naming it "time", for he said: *"Is it not older, when, in becoming, it gets to the point of time between 'was' and 'will be', which is 'now'?"*.[52] And that this 'now' has an extension, and that it is a whole and has parts, this is what he also showed very clearly, when he added: *"For it is the nature of that which goes on, to touch both the 'now' and the 'thereafter', letting go the 'now' and seizing the 'thereafter'."*[53] It is therefore possible for it both to touch and to let go the 'now'; it will therefore touch one part and will let go another. The 'now' is therefore divisible; it is therefore time, and not a limit of time. Moreover, that-which-becomes progresses in becoming (ἐν τῷ γίγνεσθαι) but stops (ἐπίσχει) and stands still in being (ἐν τῷ εἶναι). Like motion, stationariness for the things here [i. e. in the sensible realm] is in time; therefore, that-which-is is stationary in time, just as that-which-becomes is moving [in time]. Hence the 'now' too is an interval of time, and time is made out of such intervals. Therefore, through the succession (διαδοχῇ) and, as it were, the motion of such intervals, time becomes always other, while through the abiding of each interval in a way as a whole, **that-which-is is always in one time, just as that which becomes is [always] in a different time.**[54]

---

51 This remark refers to the Aristotelian concept of the indivisible 'now'; cf. Aristotle, *Phys.*, IV 11, 219a 26 – 29: "When we think of the extremes as different from the middle and the soul pronounces that the 'nows' are two, one anterior and one posterior, it is then that we say that there is time, and this that we say is time." (Ὅταν γὰρ ἕτερα τὰ ἄκρα τοῦ μέσου νοήσωμεν, καὶ δύο εἴπη ἡ ψυχὴ τὰ νῦν, τὸ μὲν πρότερον τὸ δ' ὕστερον, τότε καὶ τοῦτό φαμεν εἶναι χρόνον. Translation by Hardie, slightly modified.) Cf. also *Phys.*, VI 8, 239a 33 – 35: "If this is not so and [the moving thing is] only at a single 'now', then it will be [over against a particular thing] not for a (period of) time but only in accordance with the limit of time." (Εἰ γὰρ μὴ οὕτως ἀλλ' ἐν ἑνὶ μόνῳ τῶν νῦν, οὐκ ἔσται χρόνον οὐδένα κατά τι, ἀλλὰ κατὰ τὸ πέρας τοῦ χρόνου.)
52 *Parm.*, 152b 3 – 4.
53 *Parm.*, 152c 3 – 5.
54 Damascius, *In Parm.*, III, 184.10 – 185.8: Πῶς οὖν ὁ Παρμενίδης ἐν μέσῳ τοῦ γιγνομένου κατὰ τὸ νῦν θεωρεῖ τὸ μήτε νεώτερον μήτε πρεσβύτερον; Ἐπειδὰν γὰρ ἐντύχῃ τῷ νῦν, πέπαυται γιγνόμενον. Ἢ καὶ τὸ διάστημα ἕκαστον τοῦ χρόνου νῦν καλεῖται ὡς ἐνεστὼς χρόνος, ἀλλ' οὐχ ὡς τὸ τοῦ χρόνου πέρας· ἔστι γάρ τι διάστημα χρόνου ὃ ἐνέστηκεν ὅλον ὁμοῦ, οὐ παρὰ τὰ δύο νῦν. Καὶ ὅτι τοῦτο τὸ διάστημα κέκληκεν "νῦν" ὁ Παρμενίδης ἐδήλωσεν "χρόνον" αὐτὸ ὀνομάσας· λέγει γάρ· "ἆρα οὐχ ὅταν κατὰ τὸν νῦν χρόνον ᾖ γιγνόμενον τὸν μεταξὺ τοῦ ἦν τε καὶ ἔσται;" Καὶ ὅτι πλάτος ἔχει τοῦτο τὸ νῦν, καὶ ὅλον τί ἐστι καὶ μέρη ἔχει, σαφέστατα παρέστησεν ἐπαγαγών· "τὸ γὰρ προϊὸν οὕτως ἔχει, ὡς ἀμφοτέρων ἐφάπτεσθαι, τοῦ τε νῦν (καὶ τοῦ ἔπειτα, τοῦ μὲν νῦν) ἀφιέμενον, τοῦ δ' ἔπειτα λαμβανόμενον". Ἔστιν ἄρα ἅπτεσθαι ἅμα καὶ ἀφίεσθαι τοῦ νῦν· μέρους μὲν ἄρα ἅψεται, μέρους δὲ ἀφεθήσεται· μεριστὸν ἄρα τὸ νῦν· χρόνος ἄρα, καὶ οὐ πέρας χρόνου. Ἔτι δὲ πορεύεται μὲν ἐν τῷ γίγνεσθαι τὸ γιγνόμενον, ἐπίσχει δὲ καὶ ἵσταται ἐν τῷ εἶναι· ὡς δὲ ἡ κίνησις, οὕτω καὶ ἡ στάσις ἐν χρόνῳ τοῖς τῇδε πράγμασιν, καὶ ἕστηκεν ἄρα ἐν χρόνῳ τὸ ὄν, ὥσπερ κινεῖται τὸ γιγνόμενον·χρονικὸν ἄρα καὶ τὸ νῦν διάστημα, καὶ ἐκ τοιούτων σύγκειται ὁ χρόνος. Τῇ μὲν οὖν διαδοχῇ καὶ οἷον κινήσει τῶν τοιούτων διαστημάτων ἄλλος ἀεὶ καὶ

This, we may surmise, was Damascius' solution to Aristotle's dilemma with regard to the nature of the 'now': is it one or always regenerated?[55] In pertaining to that-which-becomes (τὸ γιγνόμενον), time measures a duration that is generated through a succession of intervals or extended 'nows'. The being, however, which is *in* becoming, i.e. that-which-is (τὸ ὄν), is at each interval halted and is thus measured by one and the same 'now':

> Does the now introduce stationariness into generation? Certainly, what is stationary is stationary in all time, for the infinity of time, not only in the now, but also in the time that is flowing. And how can stationariness, which does not flow, coexist with the flowing time? We answer that, in the material world, also stationariness is generation: it has its being in becoming and it is not already entirely what it is. Now, time measures generation, the time that marches the generation that marches. We must not therefore understand the halt in the now[56] as a stationariness that has duration and is opposed to motion; rather, we must understand it either as what is arrested between the march of time and the march of generation, a 'that-which-is' and a 'now' (ὄν τε καὶ νῦν), a partless [thing] within an extended [march]: on the one hand the now within time, on the other hand that-which-is within generation [...].[57]

This "partless now" is called "non-flowing" (νῦν τὸ ἄρρευστον) in an otherwise obscure fragment from Damascius' *On Place*:

> It has become clear to us that there are three measures of three partitions. There is no other type in generation except these three, and no other measure. For the indivisible is also threefold; there is the monad, the now and the point. The material division of the monad, or, to speak more accurately, of the one, creates plurality, which is delimited by a certain number, like the single thing, which is delimited by the monad, [that is,] what is undivided in number. The flow of the now creates duration;[58] I call 'now' that which does not flow in the now of the flowing time, like the accomplished motion as beginning of motion with regard to motion. It

---

ἄλλος ὁ χρόνος, τῇ δὲ καὶ ὁπωσοῦν ἀθρόᾳ μονῇ τοῦ διαστήματος ἑκάστου ἐν ⟨ἑνὶ⟩ χρόνῳ ἀεὶ τὸ [scripsi : τὸ ἀεὶ] ὄν ἐστιν, ὥσπερ ἐν ἄλλῳ ⟨καὶ ἄλλῳ⟩ [addidi] τὸ γιγνόμενον.

55 Cf. Aristotle, *Phys.*, IV 10, 218a 9–10 (quoted n. 11).
56 τὴν ἐν τῷ νῦν ἐπίσχεσιν; cf. Plato, *Parm.*, 152b 6-c 1: ἆρ' οὖν οὐκ ἐπίσχει τότε τοῦ γίγνεσθαι πρεσβύτερον, ἐπειδὰν τῷ νῦν ἐντύχῃ [...] (quoted n. 46).
57 Damascius, *In Parm.*, III, 191.1–12: Ἆρα οὖν τὸ νῦν τὴν στάσιν εἰσάγει τῇ γενέσει; Καὶ μὴν ἐν τῷ ὅλῳ χρόνῳ καὶ τὸ ἑστὸς ἕστηκε τὸν ἄπειρον χρόνον, οὐδὲ ἐν τῷ νῦν μόνον, ἀλλὰ καὶ ἐν τῷ ῥέοντι χρόνῳ. Καὶ πῶς ἡ μὴ ῥέουσα τῷ ῥέοντι συνυφέστηκεν; Ἢ ὅτι γένεσίς ἐστι καὶ ἡ στάσις ἐν τῇ ὕλῃ, καὶ ἐν τῷ γίγνεσθαι ἔχει τὸ εἶναι, ἀλλ' οὐχ ὅλη ἤδη ἐστὶν ὅ ἐστιν· ὁ δὲ χρόνος μετρεῖ τὴν γένεσιν, πορευόμενος πορευομένην· οὐκ ἄρα τὴν ἐν τῷ νῦν ἐπίσχεσιν τὴν ἐν παρατάσει ἀκουστέον στάσιν ἀντικειμένην τῇ κινήσει· ἀλλ' ἤτοι τὸ μεταξὺ τῆς πορείας τοῦ τε χρόνου καὶ τῆς γενέσεως ὄν τε καὶ νῦν ἀπολαμβανόμενον ἀμερὲς μεριστῆς, τοῦ μὲν χρόνου τὸ νῦν, τῆς δὲ γενέσεως τὸ ὄν [...].
58 Cf. Alexander of Aphrodisias, *On Time*, 94.35 (Sharples 1982: 63): "The instant [= the now], in its travel [= flux], creates time".

was allotted to the now of time to measure this [non-flowing now], and to time to measure its flowing, as it was allotted to number to measure plurality [...].[59]

Damascius presents in this fragment the three 'partitions' that occur in generation,[60] as well as the three uniting 'measures', i.e. number, time and place, which intervene in order to give unity to the partitions.[61] Number is the measure of the division of the indivisible unity, place is the measure of the extension of the indivisible point, and time is the measure of the duration of the flowing 'now'. But what exactly is the "non-flowing now", which is measured by "the now of time", i.e. Plato's 'now',[62] which, through its flowing, creates the duration measured by time? It is surely not Aristotle's indivisible 'now', which is only a limit brought about by the human soul. It cannot be but the "one time in which that-which-is *always* is", as it becomes. This may seem difficult to grasp,[63] but we may tackle it by

---

59 Damascius *apud Simplicium*, *In Phys.*, 644.26–34: Πέφηνεν ἄρα ἡμῖν τρία μέτρα ὄντα τριῶν μερισμῶν· οὔτε δὲ ἄλλος ἐστὶ μερισμὸς ἐν τῇ γενέσει παρὰ τοὺς τρεῖς οὔτε ἄλλο μέτρον. καὶ γὰρ τὸ ἀδιαίρετον τριττόν· μονὰς γὰρ καὶ τὸ νῦν καὶ σημεῖον. τῆς μὲν οὖν μονάδος ἡ κατὰ τὴν ὕλην διαίρεσις, ἢ ἀκριβέστερον φάναι τοῦ ἑνός, ποιεῖ τὸ πλῆθος, ὃ περιγράφει τις ἀριθμός, ὡς τὸ ἓν πρᾶγμα ἡ μονὰς τὸ ἀδιαίρετον τοῦ ἀριθμοῦ. τοῦ δὲ νῦν ἡ ῥύσις ποιεῖ παράτασιν· λέγω δὲ νῦν τὸ ἐν τῷ νῦν τοῦ ῥέοντος (χρόνου) ἄρρευστον, οἷον τὸ κίνημα πρὸς τὴν κίνησιν ὡς ἀρχὴ κινήσεως. τοῦτο δὴ οὖν μετρεῖν εἴληχε τὸ τοῦ χρόνου νῦν, καὶ τὴν ῥύσιν ὁ χρόνος, καθάπερ τὸ πλῆθος ὁ ἀριθμός.
60 ἐν τῇ γενέσει, as contradistinguished to the οὐσία, which, unlike generation, is by itself the cause of its own existence. The generation evolves around the (intelligible) essence.
61 Place is presented in the remainder of this passage; cf. Damascius *apud Simplicium*, *In Phys.*, 644.35–645.4: "The expansion of the point produced extension, with which place coexists as the measure that determines the total position of the whole, in so far as, being extended in three dimensions, that is, in all dimensions [cf. Aristotle, *On the Heavens*, I 1, 268a 6–10], it will ensure the right disposition of the whole with regard both to its own omni-dimensional position and to all the parts in it, and, further, with regard to the position of all the parts in the totality of place and to each position of each part. Consequently, if [the whole] were not a sphere and had a different middle and boundary, it would still be positioned in place where it would have the right disposition". (Τοῦ δὲ σημείου ἡ ἔκτασις ποιεῖ τὴν διάστασιν, ᾗ μέτρον σύνεστιν ὁ τόπος ἀφοριστικὸν τῆς τε τοῦ ὅλου θέσεως ἁπάσης, μέχρις ὅσου διαστᾶσα τριχῇ, ὅ ἐστι πανταχῇ, εὖ ποιήσει κεῖσθαι τὸ ὅλον κατὰ τὴν ἑαυτοῦ πρὸς ἑαυτὸ πανταχῇ θέσιν καὶ τὰ ἐν αὐτῷ μέρη πάντα, καὶ ἔτι τῆς πάντων τῶν μερῶν θέσεως ἐν τῷ παντὶ τόπῳ καὶ τῆς ἑκάστου ἑκάστης· ὥστε καὶ εἰ σφαῖρα εἴη ἢ ἄλλως ἔχοι τι μέσον ἢ πέρας ἄλλο καὶ τοῦ τόπου κεῖσθαι ὅπου κείμενον εὖ κείσεται.)
62 Cf. Plato, *Parm.*, 152b 3: κατὰ τὸν νῦν χρόνον.
63 Already Simplicius had expressed his perplexity at this teaching of his master; cf. Simplicius, *In Phys.*, 782.27–28: "Damascius seems to demand that this everlastingness, which is stationary and numerically the same, be also in things generated, which is very surprising." ([...] ἔοικε καὶ ἐν τοῖς γενητοῖς εἶναι τὸ ἀεὶ τοῦτο βουλόμενος τὸ ἑστὼς καὶ κατ' ἀριθμὸν τὸ αὐτό, ὅπερ ἄν τις θαυμάσειεν.)

taking as an example you, who are a (male) human being. In becoming, you go through the various stages of what it is to be a generated human being. As you become, you become a small child (παιδίον), then a child (παῖς), then a youth (μειράκιον), then a young man (νεανίσκος), then a man (ἀνήρ), then a senior (πρεσβύτης) and, finally, an old man (γέρων).[64] You move forward in your becoming by reaching *successively* all the stages of a generated human being. This is, of course, true but only partially. For you become *continuously* by evolving around the intelligible essence of humanity through "the leaps of generation" (τὰ ἅλματα τῆς γενέσεως).[65] Each single such leap is measured by the flowing now, which runs along with it, and the sum of these leaps is measured by the flowing time. If time progresses through leaps, so must generation. At each stage and at each leap, however, you are *always* a human; your humanity is integrally present at each leap because of the "non-flowing now".

The distinction between two sorts of 'now', one flowing and being extended, the other being extensionless and integral, can be traced back to Damascius' constant source of inspiration, namely Iamblichus:

> The numerical diversity in constant alteration is an indication of the differentiation of the participating things, while the permanence of their form indicates the stable identity of the partless now.[66]

Simplicius, who quotes this passage, was reluctant to posit such an integral now as really existing within nature,[67] and indeed it is not clear whether Iamblichus thought that such a now exists outside the intellective realm.[68] At any rate, we

---

[64] These are the seven stages of life (ἡλικίαι) divided into seven-year periods (ἑβδομάδες), as, for instance, by 'Hippocrates' in the *Hebdomads*. Cf. Aristotle, *Politics*, VII 17, 1336b 40–1337a 1: "Those who divide the stages of life into seven-years periods speak in general terms correctly; but we must follow the division presented by nature." (Οἱ γὰρ ταῖς ἑβδομάσι διαιροῦντες τὰς ἡλικίας ὡς ἐπὶ τὸ πολὺ λέγουσιν οὐ κακῶς, δεῖ δὲ τῇ διαιρέσει τῆς φύσεως ἐπακολουθεῖν.) I owe this reference to Singer (2022: 41).
[65] See n. 70.
[66] Iamblichus *apud Simplicium, In Cat.*, 354.24–27: Ἡ μὲν κατ' ἀριθμὸν ἑτερότης ἀεὶ ἀλλοιουμένη τῆς τῶν μετεχόντων ἐστὶν διαφορότητος δεῖγμα, τὸ δὲ εἶδος ταὐτὸ μένον τὴν τοῦ ἀμεροῦς νῦν ἐνδείκνυται ταὐτότητα. Translation by Gaskin, slighlty modified.
[67] Cf. Simplicius, *In Cat.*, 354.26–27: "And this is well said [by Iamblichus], if we are to be able to comprehend in reasoning what is stable in the flux of generation." (Καὶ λέγεταί γε ταῦτα καλῶς, εἰ τὸ ἑστὼς ἐν τῇ ῥοῇ τῆς γενέσεως δυνηθείημεν τῷ λογισμῷ συλλαβεῖν. Translation by Gaskin.)
[68] Cf. Iamblichus *apud Simplicium, In Cat.*, 355.4–14: "And so when [Archytas] says that the instant comes to be and is destroyed, one should understand here not the generation and destruction of the now itself, but that of the things participating or not participating in it. For rendering them continuous and joining them up is the function of nothing other than the partless [now], but its

will see shortly that in virtue of positing the enmattered form, which is unmixed with matter, as a separate principle and object of the fourth hypothesis of the *Parmenides*,[69] Damascius was able to clear this out.

Thus, Plato's *Parmenides* read against the background of Iamblichus' distinctions with regard to the 'now' were fundamental for Damascius' conception of time. Both philosophers teach that time has essentially a double nature: it is both flowing and stationary, both continuous and discrete, both becoming and being. Every one of us partakes in a present time, which is unceasingly flowing and therefore temporalizes extrinsically our duration, that is, the *extended* activity of our being (in other words, our temporality), which is ordered by the time that is immanent to our generated essence. Like the extension of our activity of being, our generation (our coming to be) occurs through leaps. But unlike the sum of these leaps, a single leap, a leap by itself, is ungenerated:

> Certainly, even the leaps of generation, being such [i.e. undivided], cannot be generated. For if they were generated, they would be infinitely divisible [i.e. in reality], and in this way generation could never progress to an end; this is why the leap of generation is not generated, that is, with regard to the very aggregation of progression. This is why it is also called "being" (ὄν), if compared to the generation composed of the leaps, just as the leap of time is called "now", if compared to time, which is composed of these leaps.[70]

---

coming to be always different and being destroyed and its sempiternal flowing most appropriately belongs to the now that is participated in generation. Now, how is it that the same thing [i.e. the now] both becomes always different and remains the same in form, is both divided and indivisible, is both altered and comprehends in one the limit [of the previous time] and the beginning [of the next time]? Well, because the now which is participated in nature, and which is inseparable from things coming to be, is different from the now which is separate and exists in itself: the latter stands fast in the same form in the same way, while the former is observed in continuous motion."
(Κἂν γίνεσθαι οὖν καὶ φθείρεσθαι λέγῃ τὸ νῦν, οὐκ αὐτοῦ τοῦ νῦν τὴν γένεσιν καὶ φθορὰν ἀκουστέον, ἀλλὰ τῶν μετεχόντων αὐτοῦ ἢ οὐ μετεχόντων· τὸ μὲν γὰρ συνέχειν καὶ συνάπτειν οὐκ ἄλλου τινός ἐστιν ἢ τοῦ ἀμεροῦς, τὸ δὲ ἄλλο καὶ ἄλλο γίνεσθαι καὶ φθείρεσθαι καὶ τὸ ἀεὶ ῥεῖν τῆς ἐν τῇ γενέσει μετουσίας τοῦ νῦν ἐστιν οἰκειότατον. πῶς οὖν τὸ αὐτὸ καὶ ἄλλο καὶ ἄλλο γίνεται καὶ μένει τὸ αὐτὸ κατ' εἶδος, καὶ διαιρεῖται καὶ ἔστιν ἀδιαίρετον, καὶ ἀλλοιοῦται καὶ ἐν ἑνὶ τὸ πέρας καὶ τὴν ἀρχὴν συνείληφεν; ἢ ὅτι ἄλλο μὲν ἦν τὸ ἐν τῇ φύσει μετεχόμενον νῦν καὶ ἀχώριστον ὂν τῶν γινομένων, ἄλλο δὲ τὸ χωριστὸν καὶ καθ' ἑαυτό, καὶ τὸ μὲν ἐν εἴδει τῷ αὐτῷ ἔστηκεν ὡσαύτως, τὸ δὲ ἐν φορᾷ συνεχεῖ θεωρεῖται. Translation by Gaskin, modified.)

69 Iamblichus recognized the enmattered form as the object of the sixth hypothesis of the *Parmenides*. See Dalsgaard Larsen 1972: 421–423.

70 Damascius, *In Parm.*, III, 192.8–15: Ἀμέλει καὶ τὰ ἄλματα τῆς γενέσεως τοιαῦτα (οὐκ) ἂν εἴη γενητά· εἰ γὰρ γενητά, ἐπ' ἄπειρον μεριστά, οὕτω δὲ οὐκ ἂν προέλθοι ποτὲ εἰς τέλος ἡ γένεσις· διὸ τὸ ἅλμα τῆς γενέσεως ἀγένητόν ἐστι, κατ' αὐτήν γε τὴν συναίρεσιν τῆς προκοπῆς. Διὸ καὶ ὂν λέγεται ὡς πρὸς τὴν σύνθετον ἐκ τῶν ἁλμάτων γένεσιν, ὥσπερ καὶ τὸ ἅλμα τοῦ χρόνου νῦν ὀνομάζεται ὡς πρὸς τὸν χρόνον, ὅς ἐστιν ἐκ τῶνδε τῶν ἁλμάτων σύνθετος.

One single leap does not convey generation and, to this extent, is ungenerated. The ungenerated leap of generation relates to generation as the non-flowing now relates to time (the temporality), i.e. the sum of the flowing 'nows' that compose it. A non-flowing 'now' pertains to each ungenerated leap. These 'nows', which are not flowing, structure the existence of every substance that has its being in becoming. They appear as 'once' and 'thereafter' and are indeed such within the temporalization that reigns over the sublunary world, but they are all together present in the enmattered form (τὸ ἔνυλον εἶδος), that is, in the participation (μέθεξις) itself, which makes a participating generated substance participate in an ungenerated intelligible form.[71] The enmattered form is *not* mixed with matter and has therefore to be distinguished from the common form (τὸ κοινὸν εἶδος), i.e. the form of the individual matter-form composites (τὰ σύνθετα).[72] While such com-

---

71 According to Damascius, the enmattered form is the same as "the form in itself" (τὸ εἶδος καθ' αὐτό, see also next note) and is a principle—*Parmenides* was considered by the Neoplatonists to be concerned only with principles—insofar as it is necessary for the orderly arrangement (διακόσμησις) of the sublunary word. This form is the object of the fourth hypothesis of the *Parmenides* both as a (not real) unity ('the one-that-is-becoming', τὸ γιγνόμενον ἕν) and as a (real) plurality ('the formal others', τὰ εἰδητικὰ ἄλλα, which are 'one' by participation in the one irradiating intelligible form). The matter and 'the material others' (τὰ ὑλικὰ ἄλλα) are the object of the fifth hypothesis. Cf. Damascius, *In Parm.*, IV, 53.10–14: "The aim of the [fourth] hypothesis is to examine this kind of form [i.e. the enmattered form]. This also belongs to the principles because it is a cause contributory to the sublunary orderly arrangement. For [Parmenides] will not discuss about the beings that exist now, which are individuals [i.e. the matter-form composites], but universally about this kind of nature." (Σκοπὸς ἄρα τῇδε τῇ ὑποθέσει περὶ τοῦ τοιούτου διελθεῖν εἴδους. οὐκ ἔξω δὲ οὐδὲ τοῦτο τῶν ἀρχῶν, ὅτι συναίτιον καὶ τοῦτο τῆς ὑποσελήνου διακοσμήσεως. οὐ γὰρ περὶ τῶν νῦν ὄντων διαλεχθήσεται, ἀτόμων ὄντων, ἀλλὰ καθόλου περὶ τῆς τοιᾶσδε φύσεως.) For the details of this doctrine see Golitsis (forthcoming).
72 According to Damascius' interpretation, Parmenides deals with the common form in the sixth hypothesis (in which he tackles it as the form of "the composite one", which is 'one' only seemingly) and in the eighth hypothesis (in which he tackles it as the form of "the composite others", to which each one of us belongs). Cf. Damascius, *In Parm.*, IV, 122.8–123.8: "So as [the one-that-is not] was, so will the others also be. But that was the composite one and the phenomenal one, and so the others will also be of the same kind, that is, composite and phenomenal. Parmenides expressly declares that they are phenomenal; that they are also composite, he says it clearly (when he asserts) that they have mass and that they are extended forms. Only the composite has a mass, for neither matter nor form in itself [i.e the enmattered form] has one. So, what things does Parmenides introduce through 'the others'? Surely, the composite parts of the composite one. And to remain within [Parmenides'] talking about the principles, we will say that 'the others' are the more particular elements, e. g. the elements in accordance with the nations and the states, from which the regionally different animals are composed and born, and not only the animals, but also the plants and the inanimate beings. Let me put it like this: let the wholes be the one-that-is-not and let the particular and the individuals—not [just] those that exist now, but those which always come to be and perish—be the others than the one-that-is-not. For both the individuals *qua* indi-

pounds *come to be* progressively, their temporality is wholly present "with respect to the very aggregation of progression", that is, in the *being* of the enmattered form.[73] This explains the fact that the order of the life stages and, more precisely, of the "leaps of generation" of any generated substance is always the same for any living being belonging to the same species. Time, therefore, emerges as an active power of ordering on two levels: (a) as a measure that inheres in the compound, and it is then the flowing time that is made out of the flowing now; (b) as a measure that inheres in the enmattered form, and it is then not properly time but a non-flowing now.

Damascius also drew from Plato's *Parmenides* the conception that the flowing time is not absolutely continuous (as Aristotle had thought on the basis of the single and continuous rotation of the outermost celestial sphere carrying the fixed stars, to which all numbers of time are ultimately reducible) but rather successive in the way of a recurring 'leap' that runs along with the 'leap' of motion and generation. Damascius adduces a well-known passage from the *Phaedrus* in order to show that in motion and, thus,[74] also in time some sort of rest or stationariness (στάσις) inheres:

> That time is composed of discrete measures, and not of indivisible 'nows',[75] is shown by the example of the soul that [Proclus] adduces.[76] Let us assume, indeed, that the cognition (νόη-

---

viduals are an ultimate principle—of me, for instance, and of you and of each individual—as also is the form that common is to the individuals." (Οἷον ἄρα ἐκεῖνο [sc. τὸ ἓν μὴ ὄν], τοιαῦτα καὶ τὰ ἄλλα αὐτοῦ· ἐκεῖνο δὲ τὸ σύνθετον ἓν καὶ τὸ φαινόμενον ἕν, τοιαῦτα ἄρα καὶ τὰ ἄλλα, σύνθετα καὶ φαινόμενα. ὅτι μὲν γὰρ φαινόμενα, διαρρήδην ὁ Παρμενίδης ἀποφαίνεται, ὅτι δὲ καὶ σύνθετα, σαφῶς λέγει (ἐνδεικνύμενος) ὄγκον αὐτὰ ἔχειν καὶ εἴδη εἶναι διαστατά. μόνον δὲ ὤγκωται τὸ σύνθετον· οὔτε γὰρ ἡ ὕλη οὔτε τὸ εἶδος αὐτὸ καθ' αὑτό. ποῖα οὖν εἰσήγηται διὰ τῶν ἄλλων; ἢ τὰ σύνθετα μέρη τοῦ συνθέτου ἑνός. καὶ ἵνα μὴ ἀποστῶμεν τοῦ περὶ ἀρχῶν λέγειν, τὰ μερικώτερα στοιχεῖα φήσομεν εἶναι τὰ ἄλλα, οἷον τὰ κατὰ ἔθνη ἢ πόλεις, ἐξ ὧν τὰ ἐθνικὰ καὶ διάφορα ζῷα συντίθεται καὶ γεννᾶται, καὶ οὐ ζῷα μόνον, ἀλλὰ καὶ ὅσα φυτὰ καὶ ὅσα ἄψυχα. εἰ δὲ βούλει, τὰ μὲν ὅλα ἔστω ἓν μὴ ὄν, τὰ δὲ καθ' ἕκαστα καὶ ἄτομα, οὐ τὰ νῦν ὄντα, ἀλλὰ τὰ ἀεὶ τοιαῦτα γιγνόμενα καὶ φθειρόμενα, ἔστω τὰ ἄλλα τοῦ ἑνὸς μὴ ὄντος. καὶ τὰ ἄτομα γάρ, ᾗ ἄτομα ἁπλῶς, ἀρχή τις ἐσχάτη ἐμοῦ, εἰ τύχοι, καὶ σοῦ, καὶ ἑκάστου τῶν κατὰ μέρος, καὶ αὐτὸ τὸ κοινὸν τῶν ἀτόμων εἶδος.) Cf. also Simplicius, *In Phys.*, 777.12: [...] τὸ κοινὸν εἶδος μέν[ει] τῷ πάλιν καὶ πάλιν. ("[...] the common form remains because it recurs").

73 Cf. Damascius, *In Parm.*, III, 185.19–21 (quoted Chapter 2, n. 87): "Therefore, as a totality, a thing does not become in the now, but *is* then, because it is then whatever it is in its totality simultaneously."

74 Note that, in quite an un-Aristotelian way, there is here equivalence: a Platonist can also straightforwardly say "in time and, thus, also in motion".

75 Cf. Aristotle, *Phys.*, VI 9, 239b 5–9: Ζήνων δὲ παραλογίζεται· [...] οὐ γὰρ σύγκειται ὁ χρόνος ἐκ τῶν νῦν τῶν ἀδιαιρέτων. (Zeno's reasoning is fallacious; [...] for time is not composed of indivisible 'nows'.)

σις) of the soul is continuous, but let us divide it by its transitions [from one form to another], when it contemplates justice, then temperance, then knowledge.⁷⁷ Does it abide in each one form only at the [indivisible] 'now', or does it stop in each form for a whole time? For, if the latter is true, its accomplished cognitions (νοήματα) will look like leaps, and in this way the intervals of the transitions will also appear to be in time and not at the 'now'; indeed, to have cognized (νενοηκέναι) occurs at the 'now', but to cognize (νοεῖν) occurs in time. The discreteness [of the psychic cognition] is composed of the parts which correspond to the [separate] acts of cognizing and contemplating, otherwise [the psychic cognition] would abide in any intelligible [form] at no time; but it is absurd that [the soul] is only moving and that there is no stationariness in its intellections.⁷⁸

We find anew in this passage the notion of 'leap'. Psychic cognition or intellection occurs continuously but discursively, and its discursive intellectual contents are measured by temporal intervals that run along with it continuously—or, rather, successively, since some sort of stationariness separates them; otherwise they would not be intervals.⁷⁹ What we get from this example anew is the idea that time, like motion, actually 'jumps'; "the march of time" (ὁ πορευόμενος χρόνος),

---

76 In the relevant part (now lost) of his commentary on the *Parmenides*.
77 This alludes to Plato, *Phaedrus*, 247d 1-e 2: "Now the divine intellect, since it is nurtured on intelligence and pure knowledge, and [the intellect] of every soul which is capable of receiving that which befits it, rejoices in seeing the Being for a period of time and by gazing upon truth is nourished and made happy until the revolution brings it again to the same place. In the revolution it contemplates absolute justice, temperance, and knowledge, not such knowledge as has a generation, nor the varying knowledge that is associated with one or another of the things we call beings, but the real knowledge which abides in the real Being." (Ἅτ' οὖν θεοῦ διάνοια νῷ τε καὶ ἐπιστήμῃ ἀκηράτῳ τρεφομένη, καὶ ἁπάσης ψυχῆς ὅση ἂν μέλῃ τὸ προσῆκον δέξασθαι, ἰδοῦσα διὰ χρόνου τὸ ὂν ἀγαπᾷ τε καὶ θεωροῦσα τἀληθῆ τρέφεται καὶ εὐπαθεῖ, ἕως ἂν κύκλῳ ἡ περιφορὰ εἰς ταὐτὸν περιενέγκῃ. ἐν δὲ τῇ περιόδῳ καθορᾷ μὲν αὐτὴν δικαιοσύνην, καθορᾷ δὲ σωφροσύνην, καθορᾷ δὲ ἐπιστήμην, οὐχ ᾗ γένεσις πρόσεστιν, οὐδ' ἥ ἐστίν που ἑτέρα ἐν ἑτέρῳ οὖσα ὧν ἡμεῖς νῦν ὄντων καλοῦμεν, ἀλλὰ τὴν ἐν τῷ ὅ ἐστιν ὂν ὄντως ἐπιστήμην οὖσαν. Translation by Fowler, modified.)
78 Damascius, *In Parm.*, III, 183.19 – 184.9: Ὅτι δὲ ἐκ μέτρων διωρισμένων σύγκειται ὁ χρόνος, ἀλλ' οὐκ ἐκ τῶν ἀμερῶν νῦν, δηλοῖ αὐτοῦ τὸ ἐπὶ ψυχῆς παράδειγμα. Ἔστω μὲν γὰρ συνεχὴς ἡ ψυχικὴ νόησις, διοριζέσθω δὲ ταῖς μεταβάσεσι, καθορώσης μὲν δικαιοσύνην, καθορώσης δὲ σωφροσύνην, καθορώσης δὲ ἐπιστήμην. Ἆρα οὖν καθ' ἕκαστον εἶδος ἐν (τῷ) [scripsi : ἐν cod.] νῦν διατρίβει μόνον, ἢ χρόνον ὅλον ἔστηκεν ἐν ἑκάστῳ; Εἰ μὲν γὰρ τοῦτο, ἅλμασιν ἐοικότα ἔσται τὰ νοήματα· οὕτω δὲ καὶ τὰ διαστήματα τῶν μεταβάσεων ἐν χρόνῳ φανεῖται, ἀλλ' οὐκ ἐν τῷ νῦν· τὸ μὲν γὰρ νενοηκέναι ἐν τῷ νῦν, τὸ δὲ νοεῖν ἐν τῷ χρόνῳ. Ὁ δὲ διορισμὸς ἐκ τῶν μερῶν σύγκειται τῶν κατὰ τὸ νοεῖν τε καὶ καθορᾶν, ἢ οὐκ ἂν ἐνέμεινεν τινι νοητῷ χρόνον οὐδένα· τοῦτο δὲ ἄτοπον, κινεῖσθαι μόνον, [οὐ] στάσιν δὲ μηδεμίαν ἐνεῖναι ταῖς νοήσεσιν.
79 The term 'interval' (διάστημα, in the sense of non-spatial extension) comes from the Stoics; see n. 47. Damascius, however, probably considered the term as eminently Pythagorean, since he believed that it was for the first time used by Archytas, whose doctrine Plato would then exploit.

in which Parmenides' 'one' partakes, as it becomes and is older than itself (and, consequently, also younger than itself),[80] is in reality a succession of leaps, which *qua* leaps are both continuous and discrete.

According to Damascius' interpretation of the second hypothesis of the *Parmenides*, the 'one' revealed by the conclusions of becoming and being older than itself and of becoming and being younger than itself (and of not becoming and being older than itself and younger than itself) through a succession of leaps is the divine Henad of the sublunary world—to put it simply, the sublunary world as a unity. We can say that Damascius extended the Stoic definition of time as "the interval concomitant to the motion of the cosmos",[81] i.e. the pace with which the outermost celestial sphere is moving and which is necessary for any generation to occur,[82] from the supralunary natural time to the sublunary natural time but also, as the passage quoted above shows, to the (superior) psychic time. Such a multitude of times, of course, is far remote from the Stoic doctrine. It actually stems from Iamblichus, who was eager to trace it back to an ancient Pythagorean philosopher, namely Archytas of Tarentum.

---

[80] Since everything that is older is older than something younger, and "the one" is older than itself, it is also younger than itself; and since it is younger than itself, then it also becomes younger (for also when it is older by reaching the 'now', it becomes older by letting it go); cf. Plato, *Parm.*, 152d 4–8: "– And it is older than that than which it was becoming older, and it was becoming older than itself. – Yes. – And that which is older is older than that which is younger? – True. – Then the one is younger than itself, when in becoming older it reaches the present? – Certainly." (– Οὐκοῦν οὗπερ ἐγίγνετο πρεσβύτερον, τούτου καὶ ἔστιν· ἐγίγνετο δὲ αὐτοῦ; – Ναί. – Ἔστι δὲ τὸ πρεσβύτερον νεωτέρου πρεσβύτερον; – Ἔστιν. – Καὶ νεώτερον ἄρα τότε αὐτοῦ ἐστι τὸ ἕν, ὅταν πρεσβύτερον γιγνόμενον ἐντύχῃ τῷ νῦν. – Ἀνάγκη. Translation by Jowett.)

[81] *SVF* II, 509, 3–4. See also n. 47.

[82] There are, of course, further such 'paces', namely those with which the rest of the heavenly bodies move; cf. Damascius, *In Parm.*, III, 191.15–19: "There are different measures for different leaps; the leaps of the star which moves more slowly are smaller, those of the star that moves more swiftly are greater; this is why the latter completes the same circle more quickly. Now, since the motions are different, it is necessary that the times be so also." (Ἄλλου δὲ ἄλλο μέτρον τῶν ἁλμάτων· τοῦ μὲν βράδιον κινουμένου ἀστέρος ἐλάττω, τοῦ δὲ τάχιον μείζω, διὸ θᾶττον διανύει τὸν αὐτὸν κύκλον· ἀνάγκη δὲ ἄλλων καὶ ἄλλων οὐσῶν τῶν κινήσεων, ἄλλους εἶναι καὶ ἄλλους τοὺς χρόνους.)

3.3 The flowing time and the still essence of the higher times

Iamblichus reported in his commentary on Aristotle's *Categories* that Archytas, in his treatise *On the Universe*,[83] defined time as "a number of a certain motion or a universal extension of the nature of the universe".[84] For us, this definition brings artificially together the Aristotelian and the Stoic definition of time but, for the late Platonists, it was considered to be the source of both Aristotle and Chrysippus, who transposed Archytas' definition, so Iamblichus contended, to manifestations of time that were different than those intended by the (purportedly) ancient Pythagorean philosopher. Aristotle conceived of time as a number adventitious to a natural motion, whereas Archytas, according to Iamblichus' interpretation, meant the essential number that causally precedes and orders the first motion of all motions,[85] namely the projection of the essential reasons of the particular souls in the transcendent soul, a projection that is precisely 'measured' by this first psychic time.[86] The extension, on the other hand, Iamblichus contended, was meant by

---

[83] Περὶ τῶ παντός (in the Dorian dialect used by the pseudo-Pythagoreans), as quoted by Simplicius (*In Phys.*, 785.15–16), whose source was Iamblichus. On this pseudepigraphous treatise, also known as Περὶ τῶ καθόλου λόγω ("On the universal reason"), see Szlezák (1972).
[84] Iamblichus *apud Simplicium, In Phys.*, 786.11–13 (quoted n. 5).
[85] This Iamblichean concept was later taken over by Proclus, who calls this essential number "Number-itself" (αὐτοαριθμός); cf Proclus, *In Timaeum*, III, 32.25–27: "Accordingly, this is what time is in reality: the number itself which [counts] each of the numbers of all of the periods [of time found within the cosmos]. (Ἐκεῖνο τοίνυν ἐστὶν ὁ τῷ ὄντι χρόνος, ὅς ἐστιν αὐτοαριθμὸς πασῶν τῶν περιόδων ἑκάστην ἀριθμῶν. Translation by Baltzly.)
[86] Cf. Iamblichus *apud Simplicium, In Phys.*, 786.13–22: "[Iamblichus] explains the definition: '"A certain motion" refers not to one [motion] out of many (for the other motions will be [thus] excluded from time), nor to the community of the many [motions] (for this is not one), but to that which is truly single and pre-exists all others as the monad of motions, which is rightly primary and cause of all other motions; it is the first change of the soul, which is born as the soul projects to itself the formal principles [of all generated things]. The number of this motion does not supervene or come from outside, as Aristotle thinks, but is set above motion in a rank of cause and advances it according to fitting measures, being an essence advancing an essential activity and, as it were, bringing to birth the self-moving projections of the essential formal principles of the soul'." (Ἐξηγεῖται δὲ τὸν ὁρισμὸν αὐτός, ὡς "κινήσεως μὲν εἴρηταί τινος οὐχὶ μιᾶς τῶν πολλῶν (αἱ γὰρ ἄλλαι χρόνου λελείψονται) οὐδὲ τῆς τῶν πολλῶν κοινότητος (αὕτη γὰρ οὐ μία), ἀλλὰ τῆς τῷ ὄντι μιᾶς καὶ πασῶν τῶν ἄλλων προϋπαρχούσης οἷον μονάδος τῶν κινήσεων, ἣ ἐστι πρώτη δικαίως καὶ αἰτία πασῶν, ἡ ψυχικὴ κατὰ τὴν προβολὴν τῶν λόγων ἐκφυομένη πρώτη μεταβολή. ταύτης δὴ ἀριθμὸς οὐκ ἐπιγινόμενος οὐδὲ ἔξωθεν, ὡς Ἀριστοτέλης οἴεται, ἀλλὰ προτεταγμένος αὐτῆς ἐν αἰτίας τάξει καὶ προποδίζων αὐτὴν κατὰ μέτρα τὰ πρόσφορα, οὐσία ὤν, οὐσιώδη οὖσαν ἐνέργειαν, οἷον ἐκμαιευομένη τῶν ψυχῆς οὐσιωδῶν λόγων τὰς αὐτοκινήτους προβολάς".) The "essential activity", in this context, is the activity of being. Simplicius considers this time to be an aspect of the transcendent soul,

Archytas in the sense of the duration of time that pertains to nature and maintains in a continuum all natural reasons.[87]

Moreover, Iamblichus thought that the attributes used by Archytas, namely 'partless' (ἀμερές) and 'inexistent' (ἀνυπόστατον),[88] are not applied to the same time, which, according to some Aristotelianizing interpreters, was the flowing time,[89] but to two different times: 'partless' is the time that pertains to the stationary formal reasons (i.e. the intellective time), whereas 'inexistent' is the time that pertains to the motions (viz. the activities of being) that proceed in generation

---

which is, as he says, 'self-timed' or 'time-itself' (αὐτόχρονος); cf. Simplicius, *In Phys.*, 785.2–3: "The soul is not in time but is time-itself, except that it is soul as to its life-giving [property] but time as to its measuring the duration of being." (Οὔτε ἡ ψυχὴ ἔγχρονος ἀλλ' αὐτόχρονος, πλὴν ὅτι ψυχὴ μὲν κατὰ τὸ ζωοποιόν ἐστι, χρόνος δὲ κατὰ τὸ μετρητικὸν τῆς τοῦ εἶναι παρατάσεως). His doctrine, therefore, is slightly different from both Iamblichus' and Proclus'.

87 Cf. Iamblichus *apud Simplicium, In Phys.*, 786.22–29: "'One must understand', [Iamblichus] says, 'that by "universal extension of the nature of the universe" the Ancients meant what we observe as continuous in the formal principles and which extends itself by being divided. For what this [extension] displays in the world of generation—the extension between this now and the preceding now, and between this motion and the preceding motion—this is observed as pre-existing much prior and more principally in the essence as pre-existing the universal natural principles; and the extension of time, which is the eldest of all [things] and holds together the principles of nature, completes this [extension in the world of generation]'." ("Τὸ δὲ καθόλου διάστημα τῆς τοῦ παντὸς φύσεως ὑποληπτέον", φησί, "τοὺς ἀρχαίους λέγειν τὸ ἐν τοῖς λόγοις θεωρούμενον συνεχὲς αὐτῶν καὶ εἰς μερισμὸν διιστάμενον. ὃ γὰρ ἐπὶ τῶν ἐν γενέσει μεταβολῶν ἐπιδείκνυσι τούτου τοῦ νῦν παρὰ τὸ πρόσθεν νῦν καὶ ταύτης τῆς κινήσεως παρὰ τὴν πρόσθεν κίνησιν, τοῦτο δὴ πολὺ πρότερον καὶ ἀρχηγικώτερον ἐπὶ τῆς οὐσίας τῶν ὅλων φυσικῶν λόγων προϋπάρχον θεωρεῖται, καὶ κυρίως συμπληροῖ τὸ διάστημα τοῦ πρεσβυτάτου πάντων χρόνου τοῦ συνεχίζοντος τοὺς τῆς φύσεως λόγους".) Cf. also Iamblichus *apud Simplicium, In Cat.*, 352.2–6: "The universal extension of the nature of the universe embraces all the natures of the universe universally, and permeates them wholly and completely; and it determines time as originating from the first [natural] reasons above and permeating as far as whatever [reason], and as determining its extension universally in terms of the transition and movement of the reasons as a whole." (Τὸ γὰρ καθόλου διάστημα τῆς τοῦ παντὸς φύσεως πάσας τὰς φύσεις τοῦ παντὸς καθόλου περιείληφεν καὶ δι' ὅλων αὐτῶν διήκει παντελῶς, τόν τε χρόνον ἄνωθεν ἀρχόμενον ἀπὸ τῶν πρώτων λόγων μέχρι τινὸς διήκοντα ἀφωρίσατο, ὡς κατὰ τὴν μετάβασιν καὶ κίνησιν τῶν ὅλων λόγων καθόλου τὸ διάστημα ἀφορίζοντα. Translation by Gaskin, modified.)

88 See above, n. 6.

89 Cf. Iamblichus *apud Simplicium, In Cat.*, 353.16–19: "[...] some consider the partlessness of time in connection with the 'now' of time, which is [for them] both a limit and a beginning of time, and [they consider] the inexistence of time in connection with the 'now' of time, to the extent that the past has been destroyed, while the 'now' is no sooner thought of and mentioned that it has become past." (Ἐν δὴ τούτοις οἱ μὲν ἄλλοι τὸ μὲν ἀμερὲς κατὰ τὸ νῦν τοῦ χρόνου θεωροῦσιν, ὅπερ καὶ πέρας ἐστὶν καὶ ἀρχὴ χρόνου, τὸ δὲ ἀνυπόστατον, καθ' ὅσον τὸ μὲν παρεληλυθὸς ἔφθαρται, τὸ δὲ νῦν ἅμα νοούμενον καὶ λεγόμενον παρελήλυθεν. Translation by Gaskin, slightly modified.)

3.3 The flowing time and the still essence of the higher times —— 75

from those reasons.[90] Thus, time for Iamblichus is primarily still; motion comes about not with time but with the generated things that participate in time:

> "And where", [Iamblichus] says, "must we conceive the flux and the extension of time? We shall answer that it is in things that participate in time. For these things that ever become cannot receive without motion the still essence of time but at different times with different parts of themselves they make contact with it and what happens to them is falsely attributed to the essence of time".[91]

Now, Damascius disagreed with Iamblichus' interpretation of Archytas but was clearly inspired by his concepts. He thought that the ancient Pythagorean philosopher referred not only to psychic but also to natural motion and that by 'extension' he wished to convey the idea that time in nature measures not only the extended and generated being of motion but also the extended and generated being of rest.[92]

---

90 Cf. Iamblichus *apud Simplicium, In Phys.*, 787.10–17: "Iamblichus demands that 'partless' and 'inexistent' should be taken as applying to two different times, assigning [to time] partlessness in accordance with the formal principles, which remain motionless in themselves, and inexistence in accordance with the motions that proceed from them, since these do not preserve the partless and unmoved essence [of the formal principles], and [also] partlessness in accordance with the activity and perfection that remains in the essences, and inexistence in accordance with the inclination away from being towards generation, since [this time] has not preserved the purity of the first essence." (Τὸ δὲ 'ἀμερές' καὶ 'ἀνυπόστατον' ὁ Ἰάμβλιχος ἐπ' ἄλλου καὶ ἄλλου χρόνου ἀκούειν ἀξιοῖ κατὰ μὲν τὰ εἴδη τῶν λόγων τὰ ἑστῶτα ἐν ἑαυτοῖς τὸ ἀμερὲς ἀφοριζόμενος, κατὰ δὲ τὰς προϊούσας ἀπ' αὐτῶν κινήσεις, ἐπειδὴ αὗται οὐ διασῴζουσι τὴν ἀμέριστον καὶ ἀκίνητον οὐσίαν, τὸ ἀνυπόστατον, καὶ κατὰ μὲν τὴν μένουσαν ἐν οὐσίαις ἐνέργειαν καὶ τελειότητα τὸ ἀμερές, κατὰ δὲ τὴν ἐξιοῦσαν εἰς γένεσιν ῥοπὴν ἀπὸ τοῦ ὄντος τὸ ἀνυπόστατον, ὅτι τὸ τῆς πρώτης οὐσίας καθαρὸν οὐ διέσωσε.)
91 Iamblichus *apud Simplicium, In Phys.*, 787.17–21: "Καὶ ποῦ", φησί, "δεῖ νοεῖν τὴν τοῦ χρόνου ῥοήν τε καὶ ἔκστασιν; ἐν τοῖς μετέχουσιν αὐτοῦ φήσομεν. γινόμενα γὰρ ταῦτα ἀεὶ οὐ δύναται τὴν ἐκείνου σταθερὰν οὐσίαν ἀκινήτως δέξασθαι, ἄλλοτε δὲ ἄλλοις μέρεσι τοῖς ἑαυτῶν ἐκείνης ἐφαπτόμενα τὸ ἑαυτῶν πάθημα ἐκείνης καταψεύδεται.
92 Cf. Simplicius, *In Phys.*, 787.29–788.4: "Damascius, I think, if nearer the ground, yet more suitably to the text of Archytas, understands the number of a certain motion as being not of a motion as form and as unmoved, but of a changing motion; so that it is not of the psychic alone, but equally of all change; and very likely Archytas says 'a certain' because change always belongs to individuals and is individual (for the universal is unchangeable). [He says that] it is the universal extension of the nature of the universe because it measures not only motion but also rest, which Aristotle well understood by saying that for motion 'this is what being in time means, that its being is measured; it is clear that this is to be in time for other things too, namely that their being is measured by time'. So in the case of rest, also, the extension of being is measured by time. So that, even if time is said to belong to motion, it is [actually] said to belong to the duration of being that occurs in generation." (Ὁ δὲ Δαμάσκιος, οἶμαι κἂν χθαμαλώτερον ἀλλ' οἰκειότερόν γε πρὸς τὴν Ἀρχύτου λέξιν, ἀριθμὸν μέν τινος κινήσεως ἀκούει οὐ τῆς ὡς εἴδους καὶ ἀκινήτου, ἀλλὰ

Nonetheless, Damascius is conceptually indebted to Iamblichus in two important respects.

First, he took over from Iamblichus the idea of a generated thing participating in an essence by "making contact" with it with different parts of itself, in other words, of having its being *in* becoming. But whereas Iamblichus ascribes such being in becoming to the things that move forward in time, whereas time itself stands still, Damascius ascribes it also to motion and time.[93] By 'measuring' whatever has its being in becoming—that is, the generated substances, whose activity of being, unlike the activity of being of the intelligible and the intellective forms, is in continuous flux—time itself, according to Damascius, on some level, must be in continuous flux by coming to be at different parts of its own essence. This transposition was of crucial importance for Damascius' conception of the flowing time as distinct from the flowing now. The former is durative and is, strictly speaking, the sublunary time, i.e. the time made out of the days and nights;[94] the latter is a recurring interval of time and is, strictly speaking, the supralunary time, which, as we shall see in the following section, does not properly come to be (in the sense of having a properly durative activity of being) but has its being actually coinciding with its becoming.

Secondly, Damascius espoused Iamblichus' idea of time being still. In his view, however, such a time should not be identified solely with the intellective (that is, the essence of) time. Still is not only the primary time that is manifested in the intellective intellect, i.e. the Demiurge,[95] but still are also the reasons (*logoi*, i.e.

τῆς μεταβολικῆς, ὥστε οὐ τῆς ψυχικῆς μόνης, ἀλλὰ πάσης ὁμοίως μεταβολῆς, ἴσως δὲ καὶ ὅτι ἀτόμων ἀεὶ καὶ ἄτομος ἡ μεταβολή, διὰ τοῦτο 'τινός' (τὸ γὰρ καθόλου ἀμετάβλητον)· καθόλου δὲ διάστημα τῆς τοῦ παντὸς φύσεως, ὅτι οὐ μόνης κινήσεως ἀλλὰ καὶ ἡρεμίας, ὅπερ καὶ Ἀριστοτέλης καλῶς νοήσας εἶπεν [*Phys.* IV 12, 221a 6–9] ὅτι "τοῦτό ἐστι" τῇ κινήσει "τὸ ἐν χρόνῳ εἶναι, τὸ μετρεῖσθαι αὐτῆς τὸ εἶναι· δῆλον ὅτι καὶ τοῖς ἄλλοις τοῦτό ἐστι τὸ ἐν χρόνῳ εἶναι τὸ μετρεῖσθαι αὐτῶν τὸ εἶναι ὑπὸ τοῦ χρόνου"· ὥστε καὶ τῆς ἠρεμίας ἡ τοῦ εἶναι διάστασις ὑπὸ τοῦ χρόνου μετρεῖται. ὥστε [scripsi : ὥσπερ codd. Diels] καὶ εἰ τῆς κινήσεως ὁ χρόνος λέγεται, τῆς παρατάσεως λέγεται ταύτης τῆς τοῦ εἶναι τῆς ἐν γενέσει.)

93 Damascius *apud Simplicium, In Phys.*, 775.9–10 (quoted Chapter 2, n. 61): "Although motion and time are in continuous flux, they are not unreal, but have their being in becoming. But becoming is not simply non-being, but is to exist at different times in different part of being".

94 Cf. Damascius, *In Parm.*, III, 175.13–17: "Fourth, we must understand that the time that we [i.e. the human beings] acknowledge is composed of nights and days; and this kind of time exists in the sublunary world. This is why Timaeus too made of the Earth the guardian of night and day [cf. *Timaeus*, 40b 8-c 2]." (Τέταρτον ἐννοητέον ὅτι ὁ μὲν συνεγνωσμένος οὗτός ἐστιν ὁ ἐκ νυκτῶν καὶ ἡμερῶν συγκείμενος, ὁ δὲ τοιοῦτος ὑπὸ σελήνην ἐστί· διὸ καὶ ὁ Τίμαιος τὴν γῆν ἐποίει φύλακα νυκτὸς καὶ ἡμέρας.)

95 The time *in* the Demiurge is the (primal) image of the eternity that pertains to the Living-Being-itself, an eternity that is distinct from Eternity-itself). Cf. Damascius, *In Parm.*, III, 181.13–182.9: "I

3.3 The flowing time and the still essence of the higher times — 77

the immaterial principles) that stem from the essential time: first, the time that preexists in the unchanging essence of the soul and, then, the time that coexists with the essence of nature:

> Asking what it is that creates everlastingly the 'some time' which becomes again and again [i.e. the recurring interval of time] and never abandons the again and again, Damascius adds: "Assuredly, since this [i.e. the recurring interval of time] is natural, nature will create it, and before nature soul; for all change begins from soul. And how can nature, which is the creator of sempiternal bodies and pours from herself the ever-flowing time, not be [herself] sempiternal and full of sempiternal *logoi*? Therefore, the sempiternal *logos* of time which pertains to the essence of nature, this should be the time which is everlastingly totally present (παρών) and whole. Similarly, the form of time that pre-exists in the soul will everlastingly be numerically the same time. And if in the unchanging soul and the nature of this sort

---

guess [that the fontal time is in the Demiurge] because time does not have a life-giving property but a property that is demiurgic and measures the forms. And, if it also measures the movement of the soul, nothing is against my contention; for the fontal judgment judges the soul by being in the Demiurge, and the fontal perception is linked to "Nature suspended on the back of the Goddess" [cf. *Chaldean Oracles*, fr. 54] by being in him. Moreover, the Demiurge, who brings the soul into being, needs the vivifying crater, whereas he conceives time within himself, as Timaeus says [cf. *Timaeus*, 38c 3–4], because he has the fontal time in himself. Moreover, and thirdly, the paradigm of time is not the first eternity, but [the eternity] that coexists with the Living-Being-itself, as we have indicated many times; and, consequently, time will manifest itself in the third of the intellectives, and not in the intellective life which is analogous to the first eternity, whereas the Demiurge is, so to speak, the Living-Being-itself in the intellective [gods]. Moreover, although the time once revealed to the Theurgists is a god linked to the zones, nevertheless its symbols manifest rather its kinship with the demiurge, thus its character of being younger and older, that of being a cause of generation for the things that come to be, its misogynistic character, which implies that it is of a particular nature that is neither vivifying nor feminine. Let this be and be said in the way that pleases the god [Time]!" (Στοχάζομαι δὲ ὅτι οὐκ ἔστι ζωογονικῆς ἰδιότητος ὁ χρόνος, ἀλλὰ δημιουργικῆς καὶ μετρητικῆς τῶν εἰδῶν. Εἰ δὲ μετρεῖ καὶ τὴν ψυχῆς κίνησιν, οὐδὲν παρὰ τοῦτο· καὶ γὰρ ἡ πηγαία κρίσις ἐν τῷ δημιουργῷ οὖσα κρίνει τὴν ψυχήν, καὶ ἡ πηγαία αἴσθησις ἐν αὐτῷ οὖσα συνέζευκται τῇ φύσει ἀπαιωρουμένῃ τῶν τῆς θεοῦ νώτων. Ἔτι δὲ ὁ δημιουργὸς τὴν μὲν ψυχὴν ὑφιστῶν ἐπιδεῖται τοῦ ζωογονικοῦ κρατῆρος, τὸν δὲ χρόνον αὐτὸς ἐπινοεῖ καθ' ἑαυτόν, ὥς φησιν ὁ Τίμαιος, ἅτε ἔχων ἐν ἑαυτῷ τὸν πηγαῖον χρόνον. Ἔτι δὲ ἐκ τρίτων τὸ τοῦ χρόνου παράδειγμα οὐκ ἔστιν ὁ πρῶτος αἰών, ἀλλ' ὁ συνὼν τῷ αὐτοζώῳ, ὡς πολλάκις ἐδείξαμεν· καὶ ὁ χρόνος ἄρα ἐν τῷ τρίτῳ τῶν νοερῶν ἐκφανήσεται, ἀλλ' οὐκ ἐν τῇ νοερᾷ ζωῇ, ἥτις ἀναλογεῖ τῷ πρώτῳ αἰῶνι, ὁ δὲ δημιουργὸς οἷον αὐτοζῷόν ἐστιν ἐν τοῖς νοεροῖς. Καὶ δὴ ἐπὶ τούτοις, εἰ καὶ ζωναῖός ἐστιν οἷος ὁ θεουργοῖς ἐκφανείς ποτε χρόνος, ἀλλὰ τὰ συνθήματα αὐτοῦ δημιουργικὴν ἐμφαίνει μᾶλλον συγγένειαν, οἷον τὸ νεώτερον καὶ πρεσβύτερον, τὸ αἴτιον γενέσεως τοῖς γιγνομένοις, τὸ μισογύναιον, ὡς ἂν οὐ ζωογονικῆς οὐδὲ θηλυπρεποῦς ὄντος ἰδιοτροπίας· τοῦτο μὲν οὖν ὅπη ἂν τῷ θεῷ δοκῇ, ταύτῃ ἐχέτω τε καὶ λεγέσθω.) Note that this image of eternity, i.e. the fontal time (or Time as god), is prior to the "first image", i.e. the "whole of time" that pertains to the activity of being of the heaven, which is mentioned by Damascius *apud Simplicium, In Phys.*, 781.11–13 (quoted Chapter 1, n. 2), and which will be discussed in the next section.

[i.e. the unchanging essence of nature] time is assembled into the total form of time, then this [time] is also the whole of time, which everlastingly stays in the everlastingness and is in no way flowing; it has in one the earlier and the later and that 'now' which we call the present (ἐνεστώς) time. From this stationary (ἑστώς), indivisible [time] the flowing time will be divided into three in a certain way".[96]

Damascius explains a little further in his *On Time* that the flowing time manifests itself in three domains:

(1) In the changing activities that pertain to the unchanging 'natures' (i.e. the essences of soul and nature), and it is then (i) the psychic time that measures the ordered projection of the essential reasons of the generated ensouled things, and (ii) the natural time, i.e. the flowing now, which measures primarily the ordered rotation of the heaven.[97] This latter time is 'the everlastingness' (τὸ ἀεί) that pertains not to the heaven's activity of being, but to the activity that proceeds from the essence of the heaven; in other words it is the undivided interval of time (named, in this context, τὸ ποτέ, 'the some time'), which recurs everlastingly.

(2) In the unceasingly changing natures, i.e. the forms of the matter-form compounds, which are everlasting formally through their participating in the intelligible forms. This is the properly durative time which measures the extension of the activity of being of the generated substances (whereas the participation itself is measured by the non-flowing now).

(3) In the recurring day and night, and it is then the sublunary time, as well as in the activities that proceed from the generated substances.[98]

---

[96] Damascius *apud Simplicium, In Phys.*, 780.1–12: Ζητήσας γὰρ τί τὸ ἀεὶ ποιοῦν ἔσται τὸ ποτὲ πάλιν καὶ πάλιν γινόμενον οὐδέποτε παυόμενον τοῦ πάλιν καὶ πάλιν, ἐπάγει· Ἡ φυσικόν γε ὂν ἡ φύσις ποιήσει καὶ ψυχὴ πρὸ τῆς φύσεως· αὕτη γὰρ πάσης ἐξάρχει μεταβολῆς. καὶ πῶς ἡ φύσις ἀιδίων σωμάτων οὖσα δημιουργὸς καὶ τὸν ἀεὶ ῥέοντα χρόνον ἀφ' ἑαυτῆς ἐκχέουσα, πῶς οὐκ ἀίδιος καὶ λόγων πλήρης ἀιδίων; οὐκοῦν καὶ ὁ τοῦ χρόνου λόγος ἀίδιος ἐνουσιωμένος αὐτῇ οὗτος ἂν εἴη χρόνος ὁ ἀεὶ παρὼν ὅλος καὶ σύμπας. ὁμοίως δὲ καὶ ὁ ἐν τῇ ψυχῇ λόγος τοῦ χρόνου προϋπάρχων ἀεὶ κατ' ἀριθμὸν ὁ αὐτός ἔσται χρόνος. εἰ δὲ ἐν τῇ ἀμεταβλήτῳ ψυχῇ καὶ φύσει τῇ τοιαύτῃ χρόνος ἔσται συνηγμένος εἰς ὅλον τὸ χρόνου εἶδος, καὶ σύμπας χρόνος οὗτός ἐστιν ἀεὶ μένων ἐν τῷ ἀεὶ καὶ οὐδαμῇ ῥέων, ἔχων ἐν ἑνὶ τὸ πρότερον καὶ ὕστερον καὶ τὸ νῦν αὐτὸ ὃ λέγομεν ἐνεστῶτα χρόνον. ἀπὸ γοῦν τοῦ ἑστῶτος ἀδιαιρέτου ὁ ῥέων τριχῇ διαιρεῖται ὅπως ἂν διαιροῖτο.
[97] Damascius seems to join, in this context, nature and heaven, as Aristotle does in *Metaphysics*, XII 7, 1072b 13–14: "The heaven and the nature, therefore, depend on such a first principle." (Ἐκ τοιαύτης ἄρα ἀρχῆς ἤρτηται ὁ οὐρανὸς καὶ ἡ φύσις.)
[98] Cf. Simplicius, *In Phys.*, 780.12–19: "One part [of the flowing time] is in the changing activities of the unchanging natures, whether psychic or corporeal, activities that preserve the everlastingness only in form. Another part [of the flowing time] is seen in the unendingly changing natures, whereby the everlastingness is formally preserved in their totalities. A third part [of the flowing time] is

The whole of time as such, however, "the everlastingness itself",[99] as Damascius also calls it, pertains to the activity of being of the heaven.

3.4 The whole of time in the heaven

Given that the heaven is generated,[100] its being cannot be true being but being in becoming. In other words, the activity of being of the heaven does not subsist all at once but is extended. Its extension, however, need not surpass the tiniest temporal extension, namely the undivided divisible which is the 'leap' of the flowing present. As every generated activity of being, the activity of being of the heaven coexists with motion.[101] But the being of the heaven does not properly come to be. It does not go through earlier and later stages and, therefore, it requires no past or future. Unlike, for instance, each one of us, who receive our humanity "in flux",[102] the heaven does not receive its form in this way. The being of the heaven cannot but coincide with its becoming and this is so in virtue of the integral time that pertains not only to its essence but also to its activity of being. The activity of being the heaven is wholly present at each single leap of time.

As we have seen in the previous sections, an integral time pertains to each enmattered form or *essence*, which explains that the individuals belonging to the same species come to be through the same "leaps of generation". The *activity of being* of the enmattered form, however, which is manifested in the composite form (εἶδος κατὰ τὸ σύνθετον) that is mixed with matter, is ordered by the flowing time. The heaven is

---

in the things that come to be and cease to come to be, and this [occurs] either in circle, like the revolution of the generated universe [i.e. the day and night] or, if you prefer, a single rotation of the sun from and to the same place, or else rectilinearly, as is seen in the individual perishable things." (Τὸ μέν ἐστιν ἐν ταῖς ἐνεργείαις τῶν ἀμεταβλήτων φύσεων ταῖς μεταβαλλομέναις εἴτε ψυχαίων εἴτε σωματοειδῶν σῳζούσαις τὸ ἀεὶ κατὰ εἶδος μόνον, τὸ δὲ ἐν ταῖς μεταβαλλομέναις ἐπ' ἄπειρον οὐσίαις ὁρᾶται ⟨τοῦ⟩ ἀεὶ σῳζομένου κατὰ εἶδος ἐν ταῖς ὁλότησιν αὐτῶν, τὸ δὲ ἐν τοῖς γινομένοις καὶ ἀπογινομένοις πεπερασμένον (καὶ) τοῦτο ἢ κατὰ κύκλον, ὡς ἡ τοῦ ὅλου γεννητοῦ περίοδος ἢ τοῦ ἡλίου εἰ τύχοι ἀπὸ τοῦ αὐτοῦ ἐπὶ τὸ αὐτὸ μία περιφορά, ἢ κατ' εὐθυπορίαν ὡς ἐπὶ τῶν ἀτόμων καὶ φθαρτῶν θεωρεῖται.)

99 Cf. Damascius *apud Simplicium, In Phys.*, 779.26: "It is impossible for the everlastingness itself not to exist everlastingly." (Ἀδύνατον τὸ ἀεὶ πρᾶγμα μὴ εἶναι ἀεί.)

100 As we have already seen in Chapter 1 (see n. 2), 'generated', in a Platonic context, does not necessarily mean created in time but being not self-constituted; the intelligible realm, which Plato designates in the *Timaeus* as "that which is always and has no generation" (27d 6), is self-constituted.

101 See Chapter 2, n. 39.

102 Cf. Simplicius, *In Phys.*, 798.18 (speaking of a river in the sensible realm): τὸ εἶδος ἐν ῥοῇ δεχόμενος.

also mixed with matter, but this matter is divine and does not properly extend the activity of being of the heaven. Time is indeed "a *movable* image of eternity", as Plato says in the *Timaeus*, but this is so only because the essence of the heaven is moved accidentally through its activity. In clarifying the time dealt with within the second hypothesis of the *Parmenides*, Damascius contradistinguishes this sublunary time, which alters the essences of the sublunary things, to the "essential time" in the heaven:

> [...] if Parmenides' demonstrations take essences as their object, and if it is from essences that he draws his demonstrations, it is also clear that he cannot take time [as acting] in [the category of] actions, but in essence itself, since "younger and older" are properties of the essences themselves, and it is clearly seen, I think, that, the essence is altered according to the ages in the sublunary things. For there is an essential time in the heaven but [this time] is unchangeable and always identical, whereas the time that changes according to the ages is the time here below.[103]

Unlike the generation of the sublunary substances, the generation of the heaven is imperishable. Unlike any sublunary substance, which *is* in the 'now' but *becomes* in time, the heaven both *is* and *becomes* in the 'now'. In it, Damascius says, all time is contracted.[104] Thus, the heaven exists for ever in the present. We can say, of course, that the heaven accomplished a rotation yesterday and will accomplish a new one tomorrow, but this is so only from our own perspective. Past and future are necessary parts of our own (durative) activity of being and not of heaven's. As the activity of being of the heaven is wholly present at each single leap of time, so is also the activity that proceeds from its essence. The motion of the heaven, we have to assume, is regenerated with each leap of time.

Damascius says in his *On Time* that the measure of the everlasting rotation of the heaven, that is, the measure of the activity that proceeds from the essence of the heaven, is the ποτέ, that is, a point of time that "comes into being again and again and always recurs". Like the item that it measures, this flowing time is itself an activity. As the rotation is the external activity of the heaven, so the flowing time is the external activity of "the whole of time", which inheres in the essence

---

103 Damascius, *In Parm.*, III, 175.4–12: Τρίτον δὲ εἰ οὐσίας ἀποδείκνυσι καὶ ἀπὸ οὐσιῶν λαμβάνει τὰς ἀποδείξεις, φανερὸν ὅτι καὶ τὸν χρόνον οὐκ ἂν ἐν ταῖς ἐνεργείαις λαμβάνοι, ἀλλὰ κατ' αὐτὴν τὴν οὐσίαν, ἐπεὶ καὶ τὸ νεώτερον καὶ πρεσβύτερον [καὶ] πάθη αὐτῶν ἐστιν τῶν οὐσιῶν, καί που λαμπρῶς ἡ οὐσία ὁρᾶται ἀλλοιουμένη κατὰ τὰς ἡλικίας ἐν τοῖς ὑπὸ σελήνην πράγμασιν. Ἔστι μὲν γὰρ ἐν οὐρανῷ χρόνος οὐσιώδης, ἀλλ' οἷον ἀμετάβλητος καὶ ὁ αὐτὸς ἀεί, κατὰ δὲ τὰς ἡλικίας μεταβαλλόμενος ⟨ὁ⟩ [addidi] ἐνθάδε ἐστὶν διαρρήδην.
104 Cf. Damascius, *In Parm.*, III, 185.15–16: ἐν γέ τοι τῇ ἀφθάρτῳ γενέσει ἐν τῷ ἐνεστῶτι συνέπυκται πᾶς ὁ χρόνος (quoted Chapter 2, n. 87).

of the heaven. Unlike the ποτέ, whose everlasting recurring creates the flowing time, the whole of time is identical to the 'always' (ἀεί) that is the same not formally but numerically. Damascius calls this "the always itself", "the everlastingness itself". It is this, and not the flowing time, which was born together with the heaven, as Plato has it in the *Timaeus*. The whole of time, in which the essence of "the first of the things that become" partakes and thus always exists, is, according to Damascius, the first image of eternity;[105] the flowing time is just the second:

> Therefore, that which creates [the point of time which becomes again and again] is sempiternal and is in the time that is everlasting [i.e. in the whole of time]; and it creates through its being [i.e. its essence] the first of the generated things.[106] For if it creates through its activities, still more does it through its being; for the essence is creative before the activities, and the sempiternal is before that which is not such. Therefore, it will fix the time that exists everlastingly and never flows in the sempiternal among the things that become according to their essence, or rather it will bind those things to the sempiternal through this time. **For the essence of the heaven participated in the everlastingness itself and became** sempiternal **in accordance with this everlastingness, that is, it became a substance for the whole of time.** So the time that is connatural and cogenerated with what is total and sempiternal [i.e. the heavens], whether it originates from the soul or from its own nature, (this is what creates everlastingly the point of time which becomes again and again). For this, which neither flows to the later nor coexists with what is flowing, truly is the whole of time, from which the flowing time winds off part by part. And it is because of this time that the time which is each time present never ceases to become, although it is each time ceased, [that is,] because this time [i.e. the whole of time] stands still and is everlastingly the same in number and activates the time which is everlasting in form. For as the activity of the heaven is an inexhaustible circular motion [that becomes] again and again, so the time of the circular motion is the activity of the time that is there assembled into one.[107]

---

105 Cf. Damascius *apud Simplicium, In Phys.*, 781.11–13 (quoted Chapter 1, n. 2).
106 That is, the heaven and the heavenly bodies.
107 Damascius *apud Simplicium, In Phys.*, 780.20 – 781.1: Εἰ δ' οὖν, τὸ ποιοῦν ἀίδιον καὶ ἐν χρόνῳ τῷ ἀεί, ποιεῖ δὲ τῷ εἶναι τὰ πρῶτα τῶν γινομένων. εἰ γὰρ ταῖς ἐνεργείαις ποιεῖ, πολλῷ μᾶλλον τῷ εἶναι· δημιουργικὴ γὰρ ἡ οὐσία πρὸ τῶν ἐνεργειῶν καὶ τὸ ἀίδιον πρὸ τοῦ μὴ τοιούτου. ὥστε καὶ ἐν τοῖς ἀιδίοις τῶν γινομένων ἐνστηρίξει κατ' οὐσίαν τὸν ἀεὶ ὄντα καὶ μηδέποτε ῥέοντα χρόνον, μᾶλλον δὲ ταῦτα ἐκείνῳ συνδήσει πρὸς τὸ ἀίδιον. τοῦ γὰρ ἀεὶ μετασχοῦσα ἡ τοῦ οὐρανοῦ οὐσία γέγονεν ἀίδιος κατ' αὐτὸ τὸ ἀεί, ταὐτὸν δὲ εἰπεῖν τὸν σύμπαντα χρόνον οὐσιωθεῖσα. ὁ ἄρα τῷ ὅλῳ καὶ ἀιδίῳ χρόνῳ ὁμοφυής καὶ ὁμόγονος, εἴτε ἀπὸ ψυχῆς ἀρχόμενος εἴτε ἀπὸ τῆς ἑαυτοῦ φύσεως, (τὸ ἀεὶ ποιοῦν ἐστι τὸ ποτὲ πάλιν καὶ πάλιν γινόμενον). τοῦτο μὲν γὰρ εἰς ὕστερον οὐ ῥέον οὐδὲ ῥέοντι συνὸν ὁ σύμπας τῷ ὄντι χρόνος ἐστίν, ἀφ' οὗ ὁ ῥέων κατὰ μέρος ἐκμηρύεται· καὶ διὰ τοῦτον οὐ παύεται γινόμενος καίτοι ἑκάστοτε παυόμενος ὁ ἑκάστοτε ἐνιστάμενος, ὅτι ἐκεῖνος ἀεὶ κατ' ἀριθμὸν ὁ αὐτὸς ἔστηκεν ἐνεργῶν τὸν ἀεὶ κατ' εἶδος. ὡς γὰρ τοῦ οὐρανοῦ ἡ ἐνέργεια κυκλοφορία πάλιν καὶ πάλιν ἀνέκλειπτος, οὕτω καὶ χρόνου ἐκεῖ τοῦ εἰς ἓν συνηγμένου ὁ τῆς κυκλοφορίας χρόνος ἐνέργεια.

The Platonist philosopher takes pains to refute an objection that a Peripatetic philosopher would raise, namely that this image, that is, "the whole of time", is ultimately not different from the model of which it is supposed to be the image:

> And how, someone may ask, does the time, which, as we say, is assembled into one, differ from eternity? Aristotle, for sure, would say that "that which contains each time that each time becomes" is eternity. And it is likely that Alexander [of Aphrodisias] probably follows Aristotle more in saying this. But one might retort to Alexander that it should be considered whether Aristotle would treat as identical the being and the everlastingness of the essence of the fifth body and [the being and the everlastingness] of the essence of the unmoved object of desire.[108] For if the latter is the cause and the former from the cause, as he himself agrees,[109] and if he demands that 'generation' be not predicated of corporeal sempiternity (for he says that this very name should de rejected), if, then, they differ, he would admit that the everlastingness is of two kinds, one being the cause, the other from the cause. But we [i.e. Platonists] who agree that whatever receives its existence from something else is generated and becoming[110] would reasonably not call this eternity, but time, positing this as the first image of eternity[111].[112]

Damascius' point is that the Peripatetics lack the Platonic (and more sophisticated) notion of 'generation' as a predicate of something that is not self-constituted but receives its existence integrally at each point of time (which implies that it is not created in time). They were thus constrained to name 'eternity' not only the everlastingness as a cause, which pertains to the Unmoved Mover, but also the everlastingness as an effect, which pertains to the entire heaven. The latter, however, Damascius points out, should more properly be called 'time' because it is, as the Peripatetics would concede, "from a cause", that is, in the Platonic jargon, an image, actually the first image of eternity. By qualifying this first time as eternity,

---

108 That is, the unmoved mover of the heavens.
109 That is, Alexander of Aphrodisias, who would agree in that with Aristotle, *Metaphysics*, XII 7, 1072b 13–14: ἐκ τοιαύτης ἄρα ἀρχῆς ἤρτηται ὁ οὐρανός.
110 Cf. Plato, *Timaeus*, 28a 4–6.
111 Cf. Plato, *Timaeus*, 37d 5.
112 Damascius *apud Simplicium*, 781.1–13: Καὶ τί διοίσει, φαίη τις ἄν, τοῦ αἰῶνος ὁ συνηγμένος εἰς ἓν ὡς λέγομεν χρόνος; ὁ γοῦν Ἀριστοτέλης αἰῶνα τοῦτον ἂν λέγοι εἶναι ἐν ᾧ περιέχεσθαι τὸν ἑκάστοτε γινόμενον ἕκαστον χρόνον. καὶ τάχα ἂν κατακολουθοίη μᾶλλον Ἀριστοτέλει τοῦτο λέγων Ἀλέξανδρος. ἢ πρὸς μὲν Ἀλέξανδρον εἴποι τις ἄν, ὡς εἴη σκεπτέον, εἰ ταὐτὸν Ἀριστοτέλης θήσεται τὸ εἶναι καὶ τὸ ἀεὶ τῆς τε τοῦ πέμπτου σώματος οὐσίας καὶ τῆς τοῦ ἀκινήτου ὀρεκτοῦ. εἰ γὰρ αὕτη μὲν αἰτία, ἐκείνη δὲ ἀπ' αἰτίας, ὡς αὐτὸς ὁμολογεῖ, καὶ εἰ μὴ γένεσιν ἀξιοῖ κατηγορεῖν τῆς σωματικῆς ἀϊδιότητος (τοῦτο γὰρ μόνον τὸ ὄνομα παραιτεῖσθαί φησιν), εἰ δ' οὖν διαφέροι, συγχωρήσειεν ἂν καὶ τὸ ἀεὶ διττὸν εἶναι, τὸ μὲν αἰτίαν, τὸ δ' ἀπ' αἰτίας. ἡμεῖς δὲ οἱ τὸ ὑπὸ ἑτέρου ὑφιστάμενον γενητὸν εἶναι καὶ γινόμενον ὁμολογοῦντες εἰκότως ἂν οὐκ αἰῶνα καλοῖμεν αὐτὸν ἀλλὰ χρόνον, αἰῶνος εἰκόνα πρώτην τιθέμενοι ταύτην.

the Peripatetics were erroneously led to exempt the things whose received existence is not contained in a given period of time—that is, the heaven and the heavenly bodies—from being in time:

> This also is strange, that that which is for ever numerically the same [i.e. the heavenly substance] is not in time because its essence does not flow and is by its nature outside flux; for [Aristotle] says that it is only eternal, like the incommensurability of the diagonal with regard to the side.[113] But if the multitemporal [i.e. the longest lasting substance] is in time, why not also the totitemporal, to coin a term? [114]

For Damascius, eternity does not contain any given period of time whatsoever but transcends time. It is the model of (in the Peripatetic jargon: it causes) not a period of time but the whole of time, which pertains to the "totitemporal" existence,[115] firstly to the activity of being of the heaven and, secondly, to the activity that proceeds from its essence. The whole of time in nature and heaven is, therefore, twofold. It is, of course, what the Peripatetics philosophers misleadingly call 'eternal', namely that outside which there is no time, and such is the time that pertains to the everlasting rotation of the heaven. But the 'leap' of time that equals a leap of this rotation, this leap that always recurs and never ceases to exist, cannot exist if it does not proceed from an essence. Thus, everlastingness-itself was generated together with the essence of the heaven and was bound to its activity of being:

> What is the whole of time? It is that outside which we can take no time. But outside everlastingness what manifestation of time could we tell? (Surely, to Aristotle the everlastingness seemed to transcend time and to be akin to eternity; for he declares clearly in his discussion of time that it is possible to take a time outside every time.[116]) Therefore, the everlastingness is the greatest time. So, is the everlastingness which is ever and ever becoming, i.e. the flowing time, is this the greatest time? But this time never arrives at being a whole nor becomes all at once, and the everlastingness does not exist everlastingly; rather, it does not exist even in a point of time. For it is hard even to imagine how the everlastingness could exist in a point of time; for in that case a point of time and everlastingness will be the same and simultaneous. But nor can the everlastingness exist in the everlastingness—for we say that the everlastingness does not exist at once but flows part by part. [...] However, if 'the everlastingness'

---

113 Cf. Aristotle, *Phys.*, IV 12, 221b 3–7 (quoted Chapter 2, n. 68) and 222a 4–6: "[...] such as the incommensurability of the diagonal [with regard to the side]: this is so always and will not be in time." ([...] οἷον τὸ ἀσύμμετρον εἶναι τὴν διάμετρον ἀεὶ ἔστι, καὶ οὐκ ἔσται τοῦτ' ἐν χρόνῳ.)
114 Damascius *apud Simplicium*, 776.20–24: Ἄτοπον δὲ καὶ ἐκεῖνο, τὸ ἀεὶ ταὐτὸν κατ' ἀριθμὸν μὴ εἶναι ἐν χρόνῳ, διότι μὴ ῥεῖ ἡ οὐσία μηδὲ πέφυκε ῥεῖν· ἀεὶ δὲ εἶναι μόνον, ὡς τὸ ἀσύμμετρον, φησί, τῆς διαμέτρου πρὸς τὴν πλευράν. καίτοι εἰ τὸ πολυχρονιώτατον ἐν χρόνῳ, διὰ τί μὴ καὶ τὸ παγχρόνιον, εἴ τις ὀνομάζοι καὶ τοῦτο;
115 I here follow Urmson's rendering of πολυχρονιώτατον and παγχρόνιον.
116 Cf. Aristotle, *Phys.*, IV 12, 221a 27.

refers to something and is not an empty name, it is impossible for the everlasting thing not to exist everlastingly; in fact, it denotes the sempiternal. And sempiternal is [the thing] which cannot sometimes or always be non-existent, and for which it is not possible to be non-existent, and which exists necessarily. Therefore, if the everlastingness does not exist, or exists but not everlastingly, then none of the things generated will be sempiternal. Consequently, neither the heaven nor the universe will be numerically the same, but everything will flow, if the everlastingness is in flux; it will of course neither be nor become; for it will be a point of time that each time will come to be and not the everlastingness.[117]

Damascius claims that the whole of time is not only the time that pertains to the everlasting rotation of the heaven but also, and firstly, the time that pertains to its activity of being. Time is expandable and there is always more time not in virtue of eternity proper but in virtue of a time that exists all at once in the essence of the heaven. In saying that time was generated together with the heaven as an image of eternity, Plato meant to say that time guarantees not the timeless but the everlasting existence of the heaven. The last Platonic successor explains that this existence does not consist in being coextensive with the whole of past and future, but in having an activity of being integrally present.

---

117 Damascius *apud Simplicium, In Phys.*, 779.14–32: Τίς δὲ ὁ σύμπας χρόνος; ἢ οὗ μὴ ἔστιν ἔξω τινὰ λαβεῖν. τοῦ δὲ ἀεὶ τί ἂν ἐκτὸς εἴποιμεν δήλωμα χρόνου; (τῷ γοῦν Ἀριστοτέλει καὶ ὑπὲρ χρόνον ἔδοξε τοῦτο καὶ τῷ αἰῶνι προσήκειν· παντὸς γὰρ εἶναι χρόνου λαβεῖν τι ἔξω σαφῶς ἀποφαίνεται ἐν τοῖς περὶ χρόνου λόγοις.) τὸ ἀεὶ ἄρα ἐστὶν ὁ μέγιστος χρόνος. πότερον οὖν τὸ ἀειγενὲς ἀεὶ καὶ ὁ ῥέων χρόνος οὗτος ὁ μέγιστος; ἀλλ' οὗτος οὐδέποτε πάρεισιν εἰς τὸ εἶναι σύμπας οὐδὲ γίνεται ὅλος ἄθρους, οὐδὲ ἔστιν ἀεὶ τὸ ἀεί, μᾶλλον δὲ οὐδὲ ποτέ· ἐν μὲν γὰρ τῷ ποτὲ πῶς ἂν εἴη τὸ ἀεί, χαλεπὸν καὶ πλάσαι· ταὐτὸν γὰρ ἔσται καὶ ἅμα τὸ ποτὲ καὶ τὸ ἀεί. ἀλλὰ μὴν οὐδὲ ἐν τῷ ἀεί· αὐτὸ γὰρ τοῦτο λέγομεν οὐκ εἶναι ἅμα τὸ ἀεί, ῥεῖν δὲ κατὰ μέρος. ἄτοπον οὖν τὸν μέν τινα καὶ ἐλάχιστον ὑφίστασθαι χρόνον, τὸν δὲ σύμπαντα μηδέποτε. καίτοι εἰ σημαίνει τι τὸ ἀεὶ καὶ μὴ ἔστιν ὄνομα κενόν, ἀδύνατον τὸ ἀεὶ πρᾶγμα μὴ εἶναι ἀεί· δηλοῖ γὰρ τὸ ἀίδιον. ἀίδιον δέ ἐστιν ὃ ἀδύνατον ποτὲ μὴ εἶναι ἢ μηδέποτε εἶναι, καὶ ὅπερ οὐκ ἐνδέχεται μὴ εἶναι, καὶ ἀναγκαῖον εἶναι. ἐπεὶ καὶ εἰ τὸ ἀεὶ μὴ ἔστιν ἢ ἔστι μὴ ἀεί, οὐδὲν ἔσται τῶν γενητῶν ἀίδιον· ὥστε οὔτε οὐρανὸς ἀεὶ οὔτε κόσμος κατ' ἀριθμὸν ὁ αὐτός, ἀλλὰ ῥευσεῖται πάντα τοῦ ἀεὶ ἐν ῥοῇ ὄντος, οὔτε δὴ ὄντος οὔτε γινομένου· τὸ γὰρ ποτὲ ἑκάστοτε γενήσεται καὶ οὐ τὸ ἀεί.

4 Epilogue: stillness and circularity as pertinent features of the Hellenic philosophy of time

> And it was not once, nor will it be, since it is now, together, whole, one, continuous.[1]

Parmenides of Elea was probably the first philosopher to conceive of a being (for him *the* being) which transcends past and future and, moreover, stands still.[2] In the verses quoted above, the old philosopher denies the "was" and "will be" as attributes of this one being. Plato was to do the same in the first hypothesis of the *Parmenides* and in the *Timaeus* with regard to 'the one' and the Living-being-itself respectively.[3] This idea led Plato to a conception of beings, namely the intelligible forms, whose existence denies any temporal succession. The concept of a timeless and extensionless present thus emerged.[4] Unlike the present that exists in time, this present, which was called eternity, does not become past by moving forward

---

[1] Parmenides, 28 B 8 DK (lin. 5–6): οὐδέ ποτ' ἦν οὐδ' ἔσται, ἐπεὶ νῦν ἔστιν ὁμοῦ πᾶν, / ἕν, συνεχές.

[2] Cf. Parmenides, 28 B 8 DK (lin. 26–30): "Moreover, it is immovable in the bonds of mighty chains / without beginning and without end; since coming into being and passing away / have been driven afar, and true belief has cast them away. / It is the same, and it rests in the self-same place, abiding in itself, and thus it remains constant in its place." (Αὐτὰρ ἀκίνητον μεγάλων ἐν πείρασι δεσμῶν / ἔστιν ἄναρχον ἄπαυστον, ἐπεὶ γένεσις καὶ ὄλεθρος / τῆλε μάλ' ἐπλάχθησαν, ἀπῶσε δὲ πίστις ἀληθής. / ταὐτόν τ' ἐν ταὐτῶι τε μένον καθ' ἑαυτό τε κεῖται / χοὔτως ἔμπεδον αὖθι μένει. Translation by Jowett.) Note, however, that late Platonist interpreters of Parmenides considered that the philosopher from Elea was pointing in his poem to the One-which-is, that is, to put it roughly, to the intelligence which appears as the second principial hypostasis in Plotinus' metaphysics. See Golitsis 2008: 100–108.

[3] Cf. Plato, *Parm.*, 141d 6-e 6; *Timaeus*, 38a 1–8: "[...] 'was' and 'will be' are terms properly applicable to the becoming which proceeds in time, since both of these are motions; but it belongs not to that which is ever changeless in its uniformity to become either older or younger through time, nor ever to have become so, nor to be so now, nor to be about to be so hereafter, nor in general to be subject to any of the conditions which becoming has attached to the things which move in the world of sense, these being generated forms of time, which imitates eternity and circles round according to number." ([...] τὸ δὲ ἦν τό τ' ἔσται περὶ τὴν ἐν χρόνῳ γένεσιν ἰοῦσαν πρέπει λέγεσθαι—κινήσεις γάρ ἐστον, τὸ δὲ ἀεὶ κατὰ ταὐτὰ ἔχον ἀκινήτως οὔτε πρεσβύτερον οὔτε νεώτερον προσήκει γίγνεσθαι διὰ χρόνου οὐδὲ γενέσθαι ποτὲ οὐδὲ γεγονέναι νῦν οὐδ' εἰς αὖθις ἔσεσθαι, τὸ παράπαν τε οὐδὲν ὅσα γένεσις τοῖς ἐν αἰσθήσει φερομένοις προσῆψεν, ἀλλὰ χρόνου ταῦτα αἰῶνα μιμουμένου καὶ κατ' ἀριθμὸν κυκλουμένου γέγονεν εἴδη. Translation by Lamb.) On Plato's conception of time in these two dialogues see Mesch (2003) and Karfík (2022).

[4] See Owen (1966).

to the future but stands still. It could therefore be the eternal model that explained the circular sempiternity of time.[5]

The Platonists of Late Antiquity espoused, of course, wholeheartedly the image-model relation of time to eternity, of circularity to stillness. But as they operated within the sacred Chaldean theology revealed by the Theurgists, a theology that posited Time as a God lower than Eternity but still a separate god, they ascribed stillness not only to eternity, which is for the intelligible forms the cause of their abiding in unity, but also to time-itself. For late Platonists, such as Iamblichus and Proclus and, especially, Damascius, who brought the Hellenic philosophy of time into a completion, time existed on different levels. We can recapitulate Damascius' doctrine roughly by saying that time manifests itself firstly (that is, ontologically) as a god and intellective time in the intellection of the Demiurge, who contemplates the eternal intelligible living being and causes the presence of time in the lower levels. In virtue of the intellective time, a psychic time pre-exists in the soul that transcends and animates the particular souls, which produce motion in the generated universe. No ordering of any transition whatsoever could occur, had it not been for this second still time. It next exists in nature and heaven as a further integral time that pertains to the heaven's activity of being and, finally, as the flowing time that coexists with the heaven's rotation and any bodily motion. No ordering of the "leaps of generation" as earlier and later and, derivatively, as future, present and past could occur in the sublunary world, had it not been for this lower mundane time. It is the flowing time that actualizes the biological time of every sublunary substance and also creates the historical time of the sublunary realm. But for this flowing time to recur everlastingly, it had to be bound to an essence whose motion was not constitutive of its being. The activity of being of the heaven is not brought into completion through motion but is moved accidentally; had it not been so, past, present, and future states of the heaven's being would have existed. But past, present and future only belong to substances that come to be and perish. "In the imperishable generation", however, i.e. in the activity of being of the heaven, "all time is contracted into the present time".[6] "For as the activity of the heaven is an inexhaustible circular motion [that becomes] again

---

5 Cf. Plato, *Timaeus*, 38c 1–3: "Whereas the pattern is existent through all eternity, the copy, on the other hand, is through all time, continually having existed, existing, and being about to exist." (Τὸ μὲν γὰρ δὴ παράδειγμα πάντα αἰῶνά ἐστιν ὄν, ὁ δ' αὖ διὰ τέλους τὸν ἅπαντα χρόνον γεγονώς τε καὶ ὢν καὶ ἐσόμενος. Translation by Lamb.)
6 Cf. Damascius, *In Parm.*, III, 185.15–16: ἕν γέ τοι τῇ ἀφθάρτῳ γενέσει ἐν τῷ ἐνεστῶτι συνέπυκται πᾶς ὁ χρόνος (quoted Chapter 2, n. 87).

and again, so the time of the circular motion is the activity of the time that is there assembled into one".[7]

The last Platonic successor teaches that a definite amount of flowing time, which, taken by itself, is the infinite sum of the flowing 'nows', is the measure of—that is, equals—the durative activity of one's being. But he further teaches that there is also a "non-flowing now", which measures a durative activity of being in a contracted form. This non-flowing now is parallel to the integral or contracted time that pertains to the activity of being of the heaven. An adventitious event, however, such as sudden death, mutilation, wound or illness, can stop or alter the activity of being of a sublunary substance and thus destroy the temporality that inheres in any enmattered form. Nonetheless, no adventitious events can occur to the heaven. The heaven will never stop to have all of its activity of being at once, within the extension of a single leap of time. It will therefore never stop to "circle round according to number",[8] so as to participate everlastingly in the intellective intelligence that contemplates the intelligible living being. It will thus keep alive and going the rest of the perceptible cosmos.

Everlastingness is intimately connected to circularity and stillness. We saw that the modern philosopher J. M. E. McTaggart postulated that the fundamental series in which events must be situated so as to be thought in time is the so-called A series, according to which an event has, in a way that turns out to be logically incoherent and illusory, the properties of being future, present and past. It is this thinking of time as giving shape to the A series that emerges also from the first of Aristotle's aporiae, which defies the very existence of time.[9] For the ancient philosophers, however, past, present and future only belong to the perishable substances, which necessitate earlier and later stages of being in order to exist. To put in McTaggart's terms, the Hellenic philosophy of time posits as fundamental not the A series but the B series. The earlier and later stages of being are variously future, present and past in the various individual substances, but are invariably the same for any given individual substance within the same species and for the sublunary world as a whole. The events that are intrinsic to the durative activity of being of a sublunary substance (in other words, the temporality or biological time that inheres in an enmattered form) are normally repeated in every matter-form compound: our cycle of life is regenerated through the cycle of life of our offspring. Cataclysm and regeneration also occur to the sublunary world periodically and everlastingly.

---

7 Cf. Damascius, *apud Simplicium, In Phys.*, 780.33–781.1.
8 Plato, *Timaeus*, 38a 7–8.
9 Cf. Aristotle, *Phys.*, IV 10, 217b 33–218a 3.

Several late Platonists derived the Greek word for time, χρόνος, from the expression χορεία τοῦ νοῦ, "dance around the intelligence"—the intelligence being the Demiurge's eternally actual and integral cognizing of the intelligible forms in the Living-Being-itself. As a generated sublunary substance comes to be and thus goes through the various stages of being, for instance, a human being, it evolves around an irradiating intelligible form that it is eternally contemplated by the Demiurge. The generated activities of being acquire a future and a past as the sublunary substances presently 'dance', in an unchangeably ordered way, through the earlier and later stages that pertain integrally to their enmattered form. Surely, a dance is not arbitrary but ordered and, moreover, is cyclical: the steps and the moves are repeated. For the Hellenes, generation and becoming are cyclical, and so is time. The unreality of time, which McTaggart brought forth with his analysis, is ultimately derived from a linear conception of time, which is in its turn dictated both by modern science—as the universe expands, it leaves its past expansion behind it—and the creationist religion that Christianity is.

Of course, the Hellenes knew that any cycle of life encloses events that move in a straight line, that is, extrinsic events that are not repeated, such as "the things that are and that shall be and that were before" known by "the best of bird-diviners", i.e. Calchas son of Thestor.[10] Any such event, which is extrinsic to a generated activity of being in the sublunary world, is temporalized in accordance with a flowing now, which is the same not numerically but only in form. Since the flowing 'nows' are not identical, extrinsic events cannot be repeated. This is the historical time of the sublunary world, which, although it is governed by the cyclical temporality, receives a linear temporalization. This double nature of sublunary time, which is intrinsically cyclical and extrinsically linear, was also revealed to the late Platonists by the Theurgists:

> The Theurgists [...] celebrate the god [Time] as 'older' and 'younger' and 'unrolled in a spiral' [...]. [This god] draws round all the things that are moved and brings them back to the beginning of their regular cycles, whether they be swift or slow. In addition to this, they celebrate him as 'limitless' on account of its power (for that which comes round again and again has an infinite power). Together with these [epithets], they also celebrate him as 'having a spiral

---

10 Cf. Homer, *Iliad*, A, lin. 69–70: Κάλχας Θεστορίδης οἰωνοπόλων ὄχ' ἄριστος / ὃς ᾔδη τά τ' ἐόντα τά τ' ἐσσόμενα πρό τ' ἐόντα. Cf. also Hesiod, *Theogony*, lin. 36–38: "Come you, let us begin with the Muses who gladden the great spirit of their father Zeus in Olympus with their songs, telling of things that are and that shall be and that were before with consenting voice." (Τύνη, Μουσάων ἀρχώμεθα, ταὶ Διὶ πατρὶ / ὑμνεῦσαι τέρπουσι μέγαν νόον ἐντὸς Ὀλύμπου / εἰρεῦσαι τά τ' ἐόντα τά τ' ἐσσόμενα πρό τ' ἐόντα / φωνῇ ὁμηρεῦσαι [...]. Translation by Evelyn-White, slightly modified.)

form',¹¹ since he is such as to measure things that undergo rectilinear motion as well as those that are moved in a circle, and since the helix includes in a unified manner both what is straight and what is moved in a circle.¹²

This, however, was Chaldean wisdom, which surpassed philosophy. The properly Hellenic thinking about time brought about an idea that seems quite contrary to our common day experience of time as flowing like a river which never rests: the idea of time's being still. It is because time is ultimately still that the universe and its inhabitants, so most of the Hellenes firmly believed, are everlasting either numerically or in species. To say it with Damascius' words:

> In itself time is rather a cause of changelessness for things which, to the extent that they depart from themselves, they depart from what they are, so that time rather belongs to rest than to motion.¹³

---

11 Cf. *Chaldean Oracles*, fr. 199.
12 Proclus, *In Timaeum*, III, 20.25–21.5: [...] καὶ ὑμνοῦσι πρεσβύτερον καὶ νεώτερον καὶ κυκλοέλικτον (τοῦτον) τὸν θεὸν [...] πάντα τὰ κινούμενα περιάγει καὶ ἀποκαθίστησι περιόδοις θάττοσιν ἢ βραδυτέραις, καὶ πρὸς τούτοις ἀπέραντον διὰ τὴν δύναμιν (τὸ γὰρ πάλιν καὶ πάλιν ἀνακυκλεῖν ἀπειροδυναμίας ἐστί), καὶ ἑλικοειδῆ φασι μετὰ τούτων, ὡς καὶ τῶν κατ' εὐθεῖαν κινουμένων καὶ τῶν κύκλῳ μετρητικὸν κατὰ μίαν δύναμιν, ὡς ἡ ἕλιξ ἑνοειδῶς περιέχει τὸ εὐθὺ καὶ περιφερές. Translation by Baltzly, slightly modified. Cf. also *In Timaeum*, III, 40.21–24.
13 Damascius *apud Simplicium*, *In Phys.*, 775.24–26: καθ' ἑαυτὸν ἀμεταβλησίας αἴτιος ἂν εἴη τοῖς ὅσον ἀφ' ἑαυτῶν ἐξισταμένοις τοῦ εἶναι ὅπερ εἰσίν, ὥστε μᾶλλον ἠρεμίας ἤπερ κινήσεως ὁ χρόνος.

5 Appendix: Damascius, *On Time*

Damascius' *On Time* is unfortunately lost but some fragments of this treatise are preserved through quotations by Simplicius in his Commentary on Aristotle's *Physics* (in the so-called 'Corollary on time'). The following edition of the preserved fragments is based on a fresh collation of the independent textual witnesses of Simplicius' commentary on book IV of the *Physics*.[1] These witnesses date all from the early Palaeologan period: 1) codex *Marcianus gr.* 227 [**F**], copied by George of Cyprus (1241–1289), in all probability before George's ascension (as Gregory II) to the patriarchal throne of Constantinople in 1281; 2) codex *Marcianus gr.* 229 [**E**], copied by Ioannikios, an otherwise unknown scholar who collaborated with George of Cyprus in the production of other philosophical manuscripts; 3) codex *Mosquensis* GIM 3649 [**M**], copied by Theodora Raoulaina Palaiologina (*ca.* 1240–*ca.* 1300),[2] niece of the emperor Michael VIII Palaiologos (reigned 1259–1282) and an acquaintance of George of Cyprus; she probably copied the manuscript (or had it copied) after she became a nun in 1274, following her second husband's death and her opposition to Michael's unionist religious policy. It seems reasonable to admit that all three manuscripts, copied in Constantinople by scribes who were acquainted with each other, were produced in the 1270's. Nonetheless, George used a model different from the model used by Ioannikios and Theodora.

A full *apparatus fontium* and an *apparatus criticus* to the fragments here presented can be found in the critical edition of Simplicius' 'corollaries' on place and on time.[3] Here I quote in footnotes the sources quoted by Damascius, as well as the deviations [*scripsi* or *addidi*] from the manuscript tradition of the text [*codd.*]. A translation with notes and some intermediary comments faces the edition of the Greek text.

---

[1] On the manuscript tradition of Simplicius' Commentary on Aristotle's *Physics* see Harlfinger (1987); Golitsis/Hoffmann 2014.
[2] Zorzi (2019) disputes the attribution of the handwriting of the *Mosquensis* (or, alternatively, of the *Vaticanus gr.* 1899, a further manuscript which bears an epigram identifying the erudite princess as the scribe, or both) to Theodora. Fonkič (1974) was the first to draw attention to the manuscript kept in the Historical Museum of Moscow.
[3] Golitsis/Hoffmann (2023).

Δαμασκίου Περὶ χρόνου

A Fragmenta

[Fr. 1 = Simplicius, *In Phys.*, 774.35–775.21 Diels] Ἔστιν οὖν ὁ χρόνος μέτρον τῆς τοῦ εἶναι ῥοῆς, εἶναι δὲ λέγω οὐ τοῦ κατὰ τὴν οὐσίαν μόνον ἀλλὰ καὶ τοῦ κατὰ τὴν ἐνέργειαν. καὶ θαυμαστῶς ὁ Ἀριστοτέλης εἶδέ τε τοῦ χρόνου τὴν φύσιν καὶ ἐξέφηνεν, εἰπὼν ὅτι καὶ τῇ κινήσει «καὶ τοῖς ἄλλοις τοῦτό ἐστι τὸ ἐν χρόνῳ εἶναι τὸ μετρεῖσθαι αὐτῶν τὸ εἶναι ὑπὸ τοῦ χρόνου».[5] ὥσπερ δὲ ἡ κίνησις οὐ κατὰ τὰ ἀμερῆ γίνεται (οὐδὲ γὰρ σύγκειται ἐκ κινημάτων· οὐδὲ γὰρ ἡ γραμμὴ ἐκ στιγμῶν, ἀλλὰ τὰ μὲν πέρατα καὶ τῆς γραμμῆς καὶ τῆς κινήσεως ἀμερῆ ἐστι, τὰ δὲ μέρη αὐτῶν ἐξ ὧν σύγκειται συνεχῆ ὄντα οὐκ ἔστιν ἀμερῆ ἀλλὰ μεριστά), οὕτω δὲ καὶ τοῦ χρόνου τὰ μὲν ὡς πέρατα τὰ νῦν ἀμερῆ ἐστι, τὰ δὲ ὡς μέρη οὐκέτι· συνεχὴς γὰρ ὢν ὁ χρόνος διαιρούμενα ἔχει καὶ αὐτὸς τὰ μέρη εἰς ἀεὶ διαιρετά.[6] ὥστε κἂν ἐν συνεχεῖ ῥοῇ ᾖ ἥ τε κίνησις καὶ ὁ χρόνος, οὐκ ἔστιν ἀνυπόστατα ἀλλ᾽ ἐν τῷ γίνεσθαι τὸ εἶναι ἔχει· τὸ δὲ γίνεσθαι οὐ τὸ μὴ εἶναι ἁπλῶς ἐστιν, ἀλλὰ τὸ ἄλλοτε ἐν ἄλλῳ μέρει τοῦ εἶναι ὑφίστασθαι. ὥσπερ γὰρ ὁ αἰὼν αἴτιός ἐστι τοῦ κατὰ τὸ εἶναι μένειν ἐν τῷ ἑαυτοῦ ἑνὶ ὄντι τὸ τὴν νοητὴν διάκρισιν ὑπομεῖναν ἀπὸ τοῦ οἰκείου ἑνὸς ὄντος, οὕτως ὁ χρόνος αἴτιος τοῦ χορεύειν περὶ τὸ νοητὸν ἐν τοῦ εἴδους ἀπαύγασμα τὸ εἰς αἴσθησιν ἐκεῖθεν ὑπελθὸν καὶ τεταγμένην ἔχειν τὴν τῆς χορείας συνέχειαν. ὡς γὰρ διὰ τὸν τόπον οὐ σύγκειται τὰ μέρη τῶν διεστώτων, οὕτω διὰ τὸν χρόνον οὐ συγχεῖται τὸ εἶναι τῶν Τρωικῶν τῷ τῶν Πελοποννησιακῶν εἶναι, οὐδὲ ἐν ἑκάστῳ τὸ εἶναι τοῦ βρέφους τῷ εἶναι τοῦ νεανίσκου. καὶ δῆλον ὅτι πανταχοῦ κινήσει σύνεστιν ὁ χρόνος καὶ μεταβολῇ, συνέχων ἐν τῷ γίνεσθαι τὰ ἐν τούτῳ τὴν ὕπαρξιν ἔχοντα, ὅπερ ταὐτόν ἐστι τῷ χορεύειν ποιῶν περὶ τὸ ὂν τὸ γινόμενον. [Fr. 2 = Simplicius, *In Phys.*, 775.24–26 Diels] ⟨ἀλλὰ⟩[7] καθ᾽ ἑαυτὸν ἀμεταβλησίας αἴτιος ἂν εἴη τοῖς ὅσον ἀφ᾽ ἑαυτῶν[8] ἐξισταμένοις τοῦ εἶναι ὅπερ εἰσίν, ὥστε μᾶλλον ἠρεμίας ἤπερ κινήσεως ὁ χρόνος.[9]

---

5 Aristotle, *Phys.*, IV 12, 221a 8–9.
6 Cf. Aristotle, *Phys.*, VI 2, 232b 24–25: Λέγω δὲ συνεχὲς τὸ διαιρετὸν εἰς ἀεὶ διαιρετά. *On the Heavens*, I 1, 268a 6–7: Συνεχὲς μὲν οὖν ἐστι τὸ διαιρετὸν εἰς ἀεὶ διαιρετά, σῶμα δὲ τὸ πάντῃ διαιρετόν.
7 The next fragment is qualified as τὸ δὲ ἑξῆς by Simplicius (*In Phys.*, 775.23–24); this suggests that it comes right after the previously quoted passage.
8 scripsi : ἐφ᾽ ἑαυτοῖς codd. Cf. Damascius, *apud Simplicium, In Phys.*, 625.26–27: ταῖς ἐνεργείαις ἀφ᾽ ἑαυτῶν ἐκστάντα κινεῖσθαι λέγεται καὶ μεταβάλλειν.
9 Cf. Aristotle, *Phys.*, IV 11, 219a 8–10: ὥστε ἤτοι κίνησις ἢ τῆς κινήσεώς τί ἐστιν ὁ χρόνος. ἐπεὶ οὖν οὐ κίνησις, ἀνάγκη τῆς κινήσεώς τι εἶναι αὐτόν.

Damascius, *On Time*

A Fragments

[I. Flowing time and time and the whole of time.]

[**Fr. 1**] Time is the measure of the flow of being, and by being I mean not only the being according to essence but also the being according to activity. Aristotle admirably saw the nature of time and made it clear, saying that both for motion and "for other things this is to be in time, that their being is measured by time".[10] Just as motion does not take place according to indivisible parts (for it is not composed of accomplished motions; for neither the line is composed of points, but the limits of both the line and the motion are indivisible, whereas the parts of them of which they are composed, being continuous, are not indivisible but divisible), so in the same way the limits of time, the instants, are indivisible, whereas its parts are not. For, since time is continuous, it too has parts that are infinitely divisible. So that, even if motion and time are in continuous flux, they are not unreal, but have their being in becoming. But becoming is not simply non-being, but is to exist at different times in different part of being. For just as eternity is the cause, to that which undergoes the intelligible differentiation from the proper One-that-is, of its abiding in its own One-that-is with respect to its being, so time is the cause, to what descended from there into perception, of its dancing around the one intelligible radiance of the form and of its having the continuity of this dance in order. For just as because of place the parts of distended things do not merge together, so because of time the being of the Trojan war is not confounded with the being of the Peloponnesian war, nor in each person the being of the baby with the being of the adolescent. And it is clear that everywhere time coexists with motion and change, holding together in becoming those things that have their being therein, which is the same thing as to make that- which-becomes dance around that-which-is. [**Fr. 2**] ⟨However,⟩ in itself time is rather a cause of changelessness for things which, to the extent that they depart from themselves, they depart from what they are, so that it rather belongs to rest than to motion.[11]

---

10 Aristotle, *Phys.*, IV 12, 221a 8–9.
11 This is meant as a rectification of Aristotle's contention that "time necessarily is something that belongs to motion" (*Phys.*, IV 11, 219a 9–10). It seems that Simplicius omits thereafter a critical comment by Damascius on Aristotle's definition of time as "the number of motion according to the anterior and posterior" (219b 1–2). Given that, as **fr. 1** makes it clear, Damascius believed that Aristotle was aware of the true "nature" of time, the standard definition of time would concern the way in which time is first cognized in the human soul, that is, through the indivisible instant (which exists only in the human soul).

[Fr. 3 = Simplicius, *In Phys.*, 776.2–33 Diels] Θαυμάσειε δ' ἄν τις ἔτι μειζόνως τοῦ ἐν χρόνῳ ὄντος ἀκούσας τὸν ἀφορισμόν, ὅτι οὗ ἔστιν ἔξω χρόνον λαβεῖν (οὕτω γὰρ περιλαμβάνεσθαι ὑπὸ τοῦ χρόνου ὡς κατὰ τὴν περιοχήν), μετροῦντα καὶ ἀριθμοῦντα τὸ ⟨ἐ⟩ν χρόνῳ[12] ὅρων ἔξωθεν ὄντα τοῦ περιεχομένου ὡς τὸν τόπον. καὶ δὴ λέγει τοῦτο καὶ αὐτός.[13] ἀλλ' εἰ τοῦτο, πῶς πάθος τι τῆς κινήσεως ὁ χρόνος,[14] οἷον μέτρησις; ὁ γὰρ τόπος οὐ τοιοῦτος. καὶ εἰ μέτρησις, κἂν μηδὲν εἴη λαβεῖν ἔξω, μεμέτρηται καὶ ἐν χρόνῳ. παράλογον δὲ ἐπισυμβαίνει καὶ τοῦτο, μὴ εἶναι χρόνον τὸν σύμπαντα χρόνον, οὐ λέγω τὸ εἶδος οἷον τὴν μορφήν, ὡς αὐτὸς ἔφη πάντα ἅμα εἶναι τὸν χρόνον,[15] καθάπερ εἴ τις λέγοι πάντα ἅμα τὸν ἄνθρωπον εἶναι Σωκράτη, ἀλλὰ τὸν κοινὸν ἀεὶ ῥέοντα χρόνον, ὃν περιειλῆφθαι λέγει ὑπὸ τοῦ αἰῶνος.[16] καίτοι ἀεὶ ῥέοντα χρόνον ταὐτὸν ὁμολογοῦμεν ἐν ᾧ καὶ τὴν ἀεὶ τῶν εἰδῶν μεταβολὴν γίνεσθαι καὶ τῶν σωμάτων τὴν ἀεικινησίαν. ἀλλ' ὅμως οὐκ ἐν χρόνῳ αὗται κατὰ τὸ[ν][17] ἀφωρισμένον· τοῦ γὰρ ἀεὶ γινομένου χρόνου τί ἂν ἔξωθεν εἴη νοεῖν; παράδοξον δὲ καὶ τὸ μὴ τοῦ χρόνου ὅλου τὰ μόρια χρόνον ποιεῖν.[18] ἔδει γάρ, εἰ τὸ παρελθὸν καὶ ἐνεστηκὸς καὶ μέλλον χρόνου μέρη, ἢ τὸ πέρυσι καὶ τῆτες καὶ εἰς νέωτα εἰ μέρη χρόνου, καὶ τὸν ὅλον ἐξ αὐτῶν χρόνον ⟨χρόνον⟩[19] ποιεῖν, οὗ ὄνομα τὸ ἀεί. ἄτοπον δὲ καὶ ἐκεῖνο, τὸ ἀεὶ ταὐτὸν κατ' ἀριθμὸν μὴ εἶναι ἐν χρόνῳ, διότι μὴ ῥεῖ ἡ οὐσία μηδὲ πέφυκε ῥεῖν· ἀεὶ δὲ εἶναι μόνον, ὡς τὸ ἀσύμμετρον, φησί, τῆς διαμέτρου πρὸς τὴν πλευράν.[20] καίτοι εἰ τὸ πολυχρονιώτατον ἐν χρόνῳ, διὰ τί μὴ καὶ τὸ παγχρόνιον,

---

12 τὸ ⟨ἐ⟩ν χρόνῳ scripsi (cf. *Phys.* IV 12, 221a 27) : τὸν χρόνον codd.
13 Cf. Aristotle, *Phys.*, IV 12, 221a 26–30: Ἐπεὶ δέ ἐστιν ὡς ἐν ἀριθμῷ τὸ ἐν χρόνῳ, ληφθήσεταί τις πλείων χρόνος παντὸς τοῦ ἐν χρόνῳ ὄντος· διὸ ἀνάγκη πάντα τὰ ἐν χρόνῳ ὄντα περιέχεσθαι ὑπὸ χρόνου, ὥσπερ καὶ τἆλλα ὅσα ἔν τινί ἐστιν, οἷον τὰ ἐν τόπῳ ὑπὸ τοῦ τόπου.
14 Cf. Aristotle, *Phys.*, IV 11, 219a 8–10: Ὥστε ἤτοι κίνησις ἢ τῆς κινήσεώς τί ἐστιν ὁ χρόνος. ἐπεὶ οὖν οὐ κίνησις, ἀνάγκη τῆς κινήσεώς τι εἶναι αὐτόν.
15 Cf. Aristotle, *Phys.*, IV 11, 219b 10: Ὁ δ' ἅμα πᾶς χρόνος ὁ αὐτός.
16 Cf. Aristotle, *On the Heavens*, I 9, 279a 25–27: Τὸ τοῦ παντὸς οὐρανοῦ τέλος καὶ τὸ τὸν πάντα χρόνον καὶ τὴν ἀπειρίαν περιέχον τέλος αἰών ἐστιν.
17 scripsi (sc. τὸ ἐν χρόνῳ) : τὸν codd.
18 Cf. Aristotle, *Phys.*, IV 10, 217b 33–218a 3: Τὸ μὲν γὰρ αὐτοῦ γέγονε καὶ οὐκ ἔστιν, τὸ δὲ μέλλει καὶ οὔπω ἔστιν. ἐκ δὲ τούτων καὶ ὁ ἄπειρος καὶ ὁ ἀεὶ λαμβανόμενος χρόνος σύγκειται. τὸ δ' ἐκ μὴ ὄντων συγκείμενον ἀδύνατον ἂν εἶναι δόξειε μετέχειν οὐσίας.
19 addidi.
20 Cf. Aristotle, *Phys.*, IV 12, 221b 3–7 and 222a 4–6: Ὥστε φανερὸν ὅτι τὰ αἰεὶ ὄντα, ᾗ αἰεὶ ὄντα, οὐκ ἔστιν ἐν χρόνῳ· οὐ γὰρ περιέχεται ὑπὸ χρόνου, οὐδὲ μετρεῖται τὸ εἶναι αὐτῶν ὑπὸ τοῦ χρόνου· σημεῖον δὲ τούτου ὅτι οὐδὲ πάσχει οὐδὲν ὑπὸ τοῦ χρόνου ὡς οὐκ ὄντα ἐν χρόνῳ. [...] οἷον τὸ ἀσύμμετρον εἶναι τὴν διάμετρον ἀεί ἐστι, καὶ οὐκ ἔσται τοῦτ' ἐν χρόνῳ.

[**Fr. 3**][21] One might be more astonished on hearing [Aristotle's] definition of what is in time, namely [that in time is] that with regard to which it is possible to take a time exterior to it (for [he says that] it is enclosed by time in that it is contained), which measures and counts what is in time by being outside the limits of what it contains, like place. Assuredly, this is what Aristotle himself says.[22] But, if this is so, (1) how can time be a certain affection of motion, such as its measuring? For place is not such [i.e. an affection]. And (2) if [time is] measuring, even if it is not possible to take a time exterior to it, [the motion] has been measured and [therefore] is in time. Moreover, (3) there follows this absurdity: the whole of time will not be time;[23] [by 'the whole of time'] I do not mean the form in the sense of *morphê* [i.e. the form-in-itself],[24] as he himself said that time is all at once,[25] just as one may say that the human being Socrates is all at once, but the common ever-flowing time, which he says is contained by eternity.[26] Yet we agree that the ever-flowing time is the same as that in which the everlasting change of the forms[27] and the everlasting motion of the [heavenly] bodies occur. But according to the definition [of what is in time] these are not in time; for what could we conceive of external to the time that becomes for ever? It is also paradoxical (4) that the parts of the totality of time do not constitute time. For, if the past, the present and the future are parts of time, or if last year, this year and next year are parts of time, then the totality of time that is composed of them ought to be a time, whose name is 'the everlastingness'. This also is strange, (5) that that which is for ever numerically the same [i.e. the heavenly substance] is not in time because its essence does not flow and is by its nature outside flux; for he says that it is only eternal, like the incommensurability of the diagonal with regard to the side. [28] But if the multitemporal [i.e. the longest

---

21 Although one might be tempted to link this fragment with **fr. 11** (θαυμάζω δὲ ἔγωγε...), I think that the phrase θαυμάσειε δ' ἄν τις ἔτι μειζόνως, which introduces it, is to be understood along the line of criticism of Aristotle's 'definitions', which is discernible in **fr. 2**; of course, these criticisms of Damascius did not really concern Aristotle but the superficial interpreters of his definitions.
22 Cf. Aristotle, *Phys.*, IV 12, 221a 26–30.
23 Stevens (2021: 215 n. 1 and n. 3) thinks that this deduction is not valid; Damascius should say that the totality of time is not *in* time, which is not the same thing as to say that the totality of time itself is not time. Damascius, however, points to a contradiction. His argument is that the everlasting motion of the supralunary bodies and the everlasting generation and corruption of the sublunary bodies take place in something that cannot be time, since there is no time exterior to the everlastingness. And yet this everlastingness is the totality of time.
24 On this sense of μορφή see Golitsis (2017b).
25 Cf. Aristotle, *Phys.*, IV 11, 219b 10.
26 Cf. Aristotle, *On the Heavens*, I 9, 279a 25–27.
27 That is, the coming to be and passing away of the numerically different individuals.
28 Cf. Aristotle, *Phys.*, IV 12, 221b 3–7 and 222a 4–6.

εἴ τις ὀνομάζοι καὶ τοῦτο; διὰ τί δὲ τὸ μὲν πανταχοῦ, οἷον τὸ πᾶν ἢ εἰ βούλει τὸ ὑπουράνιον πᾶν, ἐν τόπῳ λέγομεν κατειληφός γε πάντα τὸν τόπον (ποῦ γὰρ ὅλον τὸ πανταχοῦ;), ἐπὶ δὲ τοῦ χρόνου μὴ οὕτω νοοῦμεν ἐν χρόνῳ εἶναι τῷ ὅλῳ τὸ ἀεὶ ὂν ταὐτὸν ἐν ταὐτῷ κατ' ἀριθμόν; ὃ γάρ ἐστι πρὸς τόπον τὸ πανταχοῦ, τοῦτο πρὸς χρόνον τὸ ἀεί. διὰ τί δὲ τόπος μέν ἐστιν ἀίδιος οἷον ἡ κοίλη τοῦ οὐρανοῦ περιφέρεια καὶ τὸ μέσον τοῦ κόσμου, κατὰ ταὐτὸν δὲ εἰπεῖν καὶ ἀριθμὸς ἀεὶ ὁ αὐτὸς οἷον ὁ τῶν ἀστέρων, χρόνος δὲ μόνος εἷς ὁ φθαρτὸς καὶ γενητὸς οὗ ἔξω πλείων ἀεί; καὶ γὰρ εἰ κατὰ τὸν ἀριθμόν, ἀλλ' οὐδὲ τοῦ ἀιδίου ἀριθμοῦ ἔξω τις ἀίδιος, πᾶς δὲ καὶ αὐτὸς ἀριθμός.

[**Fr. 4** = Simplicius, *In Phys.*, 779.14–32 Diels] Τίς δὲ ὁ σύμπας χρόνος; ἢ οὗ μὴ ἔστιν ἔξω τινὰ λαβεῖν. τοῦ δὲ ἀεὶ τί ἂν ἐκτὸς εἴποιμεν δήλωμα χρόνου; (τῷ γοῦν Ἀριστοτέλει καὶ ὑπὲρ χρόνον ἔδοξε τοῦτο καὶ τῷ αἰῶνι προσήκειν· παντὸς γὰρ εἶναι χρόνου λαβεῖν τι ἔξω σαφῶς ἀποφαίνεται ἐν τοῖς περὶ χρόνου λόγοις.[29]) τὸ ἀεὶ ἄρα ἐστὶν ὁ μέγιστος χρόνος. πότερον οὖν τὸ ἀειγενὲς ἀεὶ καὶ ὁ ῥέων χρόνος οὗτος ὁ μέγιστος; ἀλλ' οὗτος οὐδέποτε πάρεισιν εἰς τὸ εἶναι σύμπας οὐδὲ γίνεται ὅλος ἄθρους, οὐδὲ ἔστιν ἀεὶ τὸ ἀεί, μᾶλλον δὲ οὐδὲ ποτέ[30]· ἐν μὲν γὰρ τῷ ποτὲ πῶς ἂν εἴη τὸ ἀεί, χαλεπὸν καὶ πλάσαι· ταὐτὸν γὰρ ἔσται καὶ ἅμα τὸ ποτὲ καὶ τὸ ἀεί. ἀλλὰ μὴν οὐδὲ ἐν τῷ ἀεί· αὐτὸ γὰρ τοῦτο λέγομεν οὐκ εἶναι ἅμα τὸ ἀεί, ῥεῖν δὲ κατὰ μέρος. ἄτοπον οὖν τὸν μέν τινα καὶ ἐλάχιστον ὑφίστασθαι χρόνον, τὸν δὲ σύμπαντα μηδέποτε. καίτοι εἰ σημαίνει τι τὸ ἀεὶ καὶ μὴ ἔστιν ὄνομα κενόν, ἀδύνατον τὸ ἀεὶ πρᾶγμα μὴ εἶναι ἀεί· δηλοῖ γὰρ τὸ ἀίδιον. ἀίδιον δέ ἐστιν ὃ ἀδύνατον ποτὲ μὴ εἶναι ἢ μηδέποτε εἶναι, καὶ ὅπερ οὐκ ἐνδέχεται μὴ εἶναι, καὶ ἀναγκαῖον εἶναι. ἐπεὶ καὶ εἰ τὸ ἀεὶ μὴ ἔστιν ἢ ἔστι μὴ ἀεί, οὐδὲν ἔσται τῶν γενητῶν ἀίδιον· ὥστε οὔτε οὐρανὸς ἀεὶ οὔτε κόσμος κατ' ἀριθμὸν ὁ αὐτός, ἀλλὰ ῥευσεῖται πάντα τοῦ ἀεὶ ἐν ῥοῇ ὄντος, οὔτε δὴ ὄντος οὔτε γινομένου· τὸ γὰρ ποτὲ ἑκάστοτε γενήσεται καὶ οὐ τὸ ἀεί.

---

[29] Cf. Aristotle, *Phys.*, IV 12, 221a 27: Ληφθήσεταί τις πλείων χρόνος παντὸς τοῦ ἐν χρόνῳ ὄντος.
[30] scripsi : οὐδέποτε codd.

lasting] is in time, why not also the totitemporal, to coin a term? And why do we say that what is everywhere, such as the universe or, if you prefer, the sub-celestial universe, is in place by occupying the whole of place (for where is the everywhere as a whole?), but in the case of time do not conceive as being in the totality of time that which is everlastingly numerically the same and in the same state? For as the everywhere is to place, so is the everlasting to time. Why is place sempiternal, such as the hollow periphery of the heavens and the centre of the universe, and the same holds also for the number of the stars, which is always the same, but there is only one time, i.e. the time that comes to be and passes away, beyond which there is always a greater time? For if [this is true] with regard to number, nonetheless there is no sempiternal number outside the sempiternal number; this [i.e. the sempiternal number] is the whole and the same number.

[**Fr. 4**] What is the whole of time? It is that outside which we can take no time. But outside everlastingness what manifestation of time could we tell? (Surely, to Aristotle the everlastingness seemed to transcend time and to be akin to eternity; for he declares clearly in his discussion of time that it is possible to take a time outside every time.[31]) Therefore, the everlastingness is the greatest time. So, is the everlastingness which is ever and ever becoming, i.e. the flowing time, is this the greatest time? But this time never arrives at being a whole nor becomes all at once, and the everlastingness does not exist everlastingly; rather, it does not exist even in a point of time. For it is hard even to imagine how the everlastingness could exist in a point of time; for in that case a point of time and everlastingness will be the same and simultaneous. But nor can the everlastingness exist in the everlastingness—for we say that the everlastingness does not exist at once but flows part by part. Therefore,[32] it is paradoxical that some time, even the minutest time, should exist, but never the whole of time. However, if 'the everlastingness' refers to something and is not an empty name, it is impossible for the everlasting thing not to exist everlastingly; in fact, it denotes the sempiternal. And sempiternal is [the thing] which cannot sometimes or always be non-existent, and for which it is not possible to be non-existent, and which exists necessarily. Therefore, if the everlastingness does not exist, or exists but not everlastingly, then none of the things generated will be sempiternal. Consequently, neither the heaven nor the universe will be numerically the same, but everything will flow, if the everlastingness is in flux; it will of course neither be nor become; for it will be a point of time that each time will come to be and not the everlastingness.

---

31 Cf. Aristotle, *Phys.*, IV 12, 221a 27. See also in the previous fragment.
32 If the whole of time is the everlastingness, and the everlastingness exists neither in itself nor in some time, then the whole of time does not exist.

Ζητήσας γὰρ τί τὸ ἀεὶ ποιοῦν ἔσται τὸ ποτὲ πάλιν καὶ πάλιν γινόμενον οὐδέποτε παυόμενον τοῦ πάλιν καὶ πάλιν, ἐπάγει·[**fr. 5** = Simplicius, *In Phys.*, 780.1–12 Diels] Ἤ φυσικόν γε ὂν ἡ φύσις ποιήσει καὶ ψυχὴ πρὸ τῆς φύσεως· αὕτη γὰρ πάσης ἐξάρχει μεταβολῆς. καὶ πῶς ἡ φύσις ἀιδίων σωμάτων οὖσα δημιουργὸς καὶ τὸν ἀεὶ ῥέοντα χρόνον ἀφ' ἑαυτῆς ἐκχέουσα, πῶς οὐκ ἀίδιος καὶ λόγων πλήρης ἀιδίων; οὐκοῦν καὶ ὁ τοῦ χρόνου λόγος ἀίδιος ἐνουσιωμένος αὐτῇ οὗτος ἂν εἴη χρόνος ὁ ἀεὶ παρὼν ὅλος καὶ σύμπας. ὁμοίως δὲ καὶ ὁ ἐν τῇ ψυχῇ λόγος τοῦ χρόνου προϋπάρχων ἀεὶ κατ' ἀριθμὸν ὁ αὐτὸς ἔσται χρόνος. εἰ δὲ ἐν τῇ ἀμεταβλήτῳ ψυχῇ καὶ φύσει τῇ τοιαύτῃ χρόνος ἔσται συνηγμένος εἰς ὅλον τὸ χρόνου εἶδος, καὶ σύμπας χρόνος οὗτός ἐστιν ἀεὶ μένων ἐν τῷ ἀεὶ καὶ οὐδαμῇ ῥέων, ἔχων ἐν ἑνὶ τὸ πρότερον καὶ ὕστερον καὶ τὸ νῦν αὐτὸ ὃ λέγομεν ἐνεστῶτα χρόνον. ἀπὸ γοῦν τοῦ ἑστῶτος ἀδιαιρέτου ὁ ῥέων τριχῇ διαιρεῖται ὅπως ἂν διαιροῖτο· μήπω γὰρ περὶ τούτου ⟨λέγωμεν⟩. [**Fr. 6** = Simplicius, *In Phys.*,780.20–781.13 Diels][33] Εἰ δ' οὖν, τὸ ποιοῦν ἀίδιον καὶ ἐν χρόνῳ τῷ ἀεί, ποιεῖ δὲ τῷ εἶναι τὰ πρῶτα τῶν γινομένων. εἰ γὰρ ταῖς ἐνεργείαις ποιεῖ, πολλῷ μᾶλλον τῷ εἶναι· δημιουργικὴ γὰρ ἡ οὐσία πρὸ τῶν ἐνεργειῶν καὶ τὸ ἀίδιον πρὸ τοῦ μὴ τοιούτου. ὥστε καὶ ἐν τοῖς ἀιδίοις τῶν γινομένων ἐνστηρίξει κατ' οὐσίαν τὸν ἀεὶ ὄντα καὶ μηδέποτε ῥέοντα χρόνον, μᾶλλον δὲ ταῦτα ἐκείνῳ συνδήσει πρὸς τὸ ἀίδιον. τοῦ γὰρ ἀεὶ μετασχοῦσα ἡ τοῦ οὐρανοῦ οὐσία γέγονεν ἀίδιος κατ' αὐτὸ τὸ ἀεί, ταὐτὸν δὲ εἰπεῖν τὸν σύμπαντα χρόνον οὐσιωθεῖσα. ὁ ἄρα τῷ ὅλῳ καὶ ἀιδίῳ χρόνος ὁμοφυὴς καὶ ὁμόγονος, εἴτε ἀπὸ ψυχῆς ἀρχόμενος εἴτε ἀπὸ τῆς ἑαυτοῦ φύσεως, ⟨τὸ ἀεὶ ποιοῦν ἐστι τὸ ποτὲ πάλιν καὶ πάλιν γινόμενον⟩. τοῦτο μὲν γὰρ εἰς ὕστερον οὐ ῥέον οὐδὲ ῥέοντι συνὸν ὁ σύμπας τῷ ὄντι χρόνος ἐστίν, ἀφ' οὗ ὁ ῥέων κατὰ μέρος ἐκμηρύεται· καὶ διὰ τοῦτον οὐ παύεται γινόμενος καίτοι ἑκάστοτε παυόμενος ὁ ἑκάστοτε ἐνιστάμενος, ὅτι ἐκεῖνος ἀεὶ κατ' ἀριθμὸν ὁ αὐτὸς ἕστηκεν ἐνεργῶν τὸν ἀεὶ

---

[33] After quoting fr. 7, Simplicius introduces **fr. 6** with the words "he adds the following to those quoted before" (*In Phys.*, 780.20: τοῖς δὲ προειρημένοις συνῆψε ταῦτα), i.e. **fr. 5**.

Asking what it is that creates everlastingly the 'some time' which becomes again and again and never abandons the again and again, Damascius adds: [**fr. 5**] Assuredly, since this [i.e. the 'some time' which becomes again and again] is natural, nature will create it, and before nature soul; for all change begins from soul. And how can nature, which is the creator of sempiternal bodies and pours from herself the ever-flowing time, not be [herself] sempiternal and full of sempiternal forms (*logoi*)? Therefore, the sempiternal form (*logos*) of time which pertains to the essence of nature, this should be the time which is everlastingly totally present (*parôn*)[34] and whole. Similarly, the form of time that pre-exists in the soul will everlastingly be numerically the same time. And if in the unchanging soul and the nature of this sort [i.e. unchanging] time is assembled into the total form (*eidos*) of time, then this [time] is also the whole of time, which everlastingly stays in the everlastingness and is in no way flowing; it has in one the earlier and the later and that 'now' which we call the present (*enestôs*) time. From this stationary (*hestôs*), indivisible [time] the flowing time will be divided into three in a certain way; but let us not speak of it [i.e. this division] yet.[35] [**Fr. 6**] Therefore, that which creates [the point of time which becomes again and again] is sempiternal and is in the time that is everlasting [i.e. in the whole of time]; and it creates through its being [i.e. its essence] the first of the things that become.[36] For if it creates through its activities, still more does it through its being; for the essence is creative before the activities, and the sempiternal is before that which is not such. Therefore, it will fix the time that exists everlastingly and never flows in the sempiternal among the things that become according to their essence, or rather it will bind those things to the sempiternal through this time. For the essence of the heaven participated in the everlastingness itself and became sempiternal in accordance with this everlastingness, that is, it became a substance for the whole of time. So the time that is connatural and cogenerated with what is total and sempiternal [i.e. the heavens], whether it originates from the soul or from its own nature, ⟨this is what creates everlastingly the point of time which becomes again and again⟩. For this, which neither flows to the later nor coexists with what is flowing, truly is the whole of time, from which the flowing time winds off part by part. And it is because of this time that the time which is each time present never ceases to become, although it is each time ceased, [that is,] because this time [i.e. the whole of time] stands still and is everlastingly the same in number and activates the time which is everlasting in form. For as

---

34 παρών, in this context, has not the same sense as ἐνεστώς, i.e. the present time that is flowing. Stevens (2021: 223 n. 2) translates παρών as 'actuel'.
35 Damascius will explicate the tripartite division of the flowing time in **fr. 7**.
36 That is, the heavens and the heavenly bodies.

κατ' εἶδος. ὡς γὰρ τοῦ οὐρανοῦ ἡ ἐνέργεια κυκλοφορία πάλιν καὶ πάλιν ἀνέκλειπτος, οὕτω καὶ χρόνου ἐκεῖ τοῦ εἰς ἓν συνηγμένου ὁ τῆς κυκλοφορίας χρόνος ἐνέργεια. καὶ τί διοίσει, φαίη τις ἄν, τοῦ αἰῶνος ὁ συνηγμένος εἰς ἓν ὡς λέγομεν χρόνος; ὁ γοῦν Ἀριστοτέλης αἰῶνα τοῦτον ἂν λέγοι εἶναι ἐν ᾧ περιέχεσθαι τὸν ἑκάστοτε γινόμενον ἕκαστον χρόνον. καὶ τάχα ἂν κατακολουθοίη μᾶλλον Ἀριστοτέλει τοῦτο λέγων Ἀλέξανδρος. ἢ πρὸς μὲν Ἀλέξανδρον εἴποι τις ἄν, ὡς εἴη σκεπτέον, εἰ ταὐτὸν Ἀριστοτέλης θήσεται τὸ εἶναι καὶ τὸ ἀεὶ τῆς τε τοῦ πέμπτου σώματος οὐσίας καὶ τῆς τοῦ ἀκινήτου ὀρεκτοῦ. εἰ γὰρ αὕτη μὲν αἰτία, ἐκείνη δὲ ἀπ' αἰτίας, ὡς αὐτὸς ὁμολογεῖ, καὶ εἰ μὴ γένεσιν ἀξιοῖ κατηγορεῖν τῆς σωματικῆς ἀιδιότητος (τοῦτο γὰρ μόνον τὸ ὄνομα παραιτεῖσθαί φησιν), εἰ δ' οὖν διαφέροι, συγχωρήσειεν ἂν καὶ τὸ ἀεὶ διττὸν εἶναι, τὸ μὲν αἰτίαν, τὸ δ' ἀπ' αἰτίας. ἡμεῖς δὲ οἱ τὸ ὑπὸ ἑτέρου ὑφιστάμενον γενητὸν εἶναι καὶ γινόμενον ὁμολογοῦντες[37] εἰκότως ἂν οὐκ αἰῶνα καλοῖμεν αὐτὸν ἀλλὰ χρόνον, αἰῶνος εἰκόνα[38] πρώτην τιθέμενοι ταύτην.

[Fr. 7 = Simplicius, In Phys., 780.12–19 Diels] Τὸ μέν ἐστιν ἐν ταῖς ἐνεργείαις τῶν ἀμεταβλήτων φύσεων ταῖς μεταβαλλομέναις εἴτε ψυχαίων εἴτε σωματοειδῶν σῳζούσαις τὸ ἀεὶ κατὰ εἶδος μόνον, τὸ δὲ ἐν ταῖς μεταβαλλομέναις ἐπ' ἄπειρον οὐσίαις ὁρᾶται ⟨τοῦ⟩ ἀεὶ σῳζομένου[39] κατὰ εἶδος ἐν ταῖς ὁλότησιν αὐτῶν, τὸ δὲ ἐν τοῖς γινομένοις καὶ ἀπογινομένοις πεπερασμένον ⟨καὶ⟩[40] τοῦτο ἢ κατὰ κύκλον, ὡς ἡ τοῦ ὅλου γενητοῦ περίοδος ἢ τοῦ ἡλίου εἰ τύχοι ἀπὸ τοῦ αὐτοῦ ἐπὶ τὸ αὐτὸ μία περιφορά, ἢ κατ' εὐθυπορίαν ὡς ἐπὶ τῶν ἀτόμων καὶ φθαρτῶν θεωρεῖται. οὕτω μὲν τὸν ῥέοντα χρόνον διεῖλε.

*****

Ταύτας τοίνυν τὰς ἀπορίας ὁ φιλόσοφος Δαμάσκιος λύειν ἐπιχειρεῖ τὸν ἐνεστῶτα χρόνον οὐ κατὰ τὸ ἀμερὲς νῦν λαμβάνειν ἀξιῶν· πέρας γὰρ χρόνου τὸ τοιοῦτο νῦν καὶ οὐ χρόνος. [...] [Fr. 8 = Simplicius, In Phys., 796.27–797.13 Diels] Θαυμάζω δὲ ἔγωγε, φησὶν οὕτως καὶ τοῖς ῥήμασι λέγων, πῶς τὸν μὲν Ζήνωνος ἐπιλύονται λόγον, ὡς οὐ κατά τι ἀδιαίρετον τῆς κινήσεως ἐπιτελουμένης, ἀλλὰ καθ' ὅλον βῆμα προκοπτούσης ἀθρούστερον, καὶ οὐκ ἀεὶ τὸ ἥμισυ πρὸ τοῦ ὅλου, ἀλλὰ ποτὲ καὶ ὅλον

---

[37] Cf. Plato, Timaeus, 28a 4–6: Πᾶν δὲ αὖ τὸ γιγνόμενον ὑπ' αἰτίου τινὸς ἐξ ἀνάγκης γίγνεσθαι· παντὶ γὰρ ἀδύνατον χωρὶς αἰτίου γένεσιν σχεῖν.
[38] Cf. Plato, Timaeus, 37d 5.
[39] scripsi : ἀεὶ σῳζόμενον codd.
[40] addidi.

the activity of the heaven is an inexhaustible circular motion [that becomes] again and again, so the time of the circular motion is the activity of the time that is there assembled into one. And how, someone may ask, does the time, which, as we say, is assembled into one, differ from eternity? Aristotle, for sure, would say that that "which contains each time that each time becomes" is eternity. And it is likely that Alexander [of Aphrodisias] probably follows Aristotle more in saying this. But one might retort to Alexander that it should be considered whether Aristotle would treat as identical the being and the everlastingness of the essence of the fifth body and [the being and the everlastingness] of the essence of the unmoved object of desire.[41] For if the latter is the cause and the former from the cause, as he himself agrees,[42] and if he demands that 'generation' be not predicated of corporeal sempiternity (for he says that this very name should de rejected), if, then, they differ, he would admit that the everlastingness is of two kinds, one being the cause, the other from the cause. But we [i.e. Platonists] who agree that whatever receives its existence from something else is generated and becoming[43] would reasonably not call this eternity, but time, positing this as the first image of eternity.[44]

[Fr. 7] One part [of the flowing time] is in the changing activities of the unchanging natures, whether psychic or corporeal, activities that preserve the everlastingness only in form. Another part [of the flowing time] is seen in the unendingly changing natures, whereby the everlastingness is formally preserved in their totalities. A third part [of the flowing time] is in the things that come to be and cease to come to be, and this [occurs] either in circle, like the revolution of the generated universe [i.e. the day and night] or, if you prefer, a single rotation of the sun from and to the same place, or else rectilinearly, as is seen in the individual perishable things. *That is the way in which he divided the flowing time.*

[II. Damascius' solution of Aristotle's aporiae]
The philosopher Damascius attempts to resolve these aporiae by claiming that the present time should not be understood in terms of the indivisible 'now'; for this kind of 'now' is not time but a limit of time [...]. [**Fr. 8**] I am astonished—*he says (and these are his very words)*—at how those who say that only the indivisible 'now' exists solve Zeno's argument by claiming that motion is not accomplished according to something indivisible, but rather progresses in a whole stride at once, and that it

---

41 That is, the unmoved mover of the heavens.
42 That is, Alexander, who would agree in that with Aristotle, *Metaphysics*, XII 7, 1072b 13–14: ἐκ τοιαύτης ἄρα ἀρχῆς ἤρτηται ὁ οὐρανός.
43 Cf. Plato, *Timaeus*, 28a 4–6.
44 Cf. Plato, *Timaeus*, 37d 5.

καὶ μέρος οἷον ὑπεραλλομένης, οὐ συνενόησαν δὲ οἱ τὸ ἀδιαίρετον μόνον νῦν εἶναι λέγοντες τὸ αὐτὸ καὶ ἐπὶ τοῦ χρόνου συμβαῖνον ἅτε συνόντος ἀεὶ τῇ κινήσει καὶ οἷον συμπαραθέοντος, ὥστε καὶ συμβηματίζοντος ὅλῳ πηδήματι συνεχεῖ καὶ οὐ κατὰ ⟨τὸ⟩ νῦν διεξιόντος ἐπ' ἄπειρον, καὶ ταῦτα κινήσεως μὲν οὔσης ἐναργοῦς ἐν τοῖς πράγμασι, τοῦ δ' Ἀριστοτέλους οὕτω δεικνύντος λαμπρῶς, ὅτι οὐδὲν ἐν τῷ νῦν κινεῖται οὐδὲ μεταβάλλεται, ἀλλ' ἐν τούτῳ μὲν κεκίνηται καὶ μεταβέβληται, μεταβάλλεται δὲ καὶ κινεῖται πάντως ἐν χρόνῳ. τὸ γοῦν ἅλμα τῆς κινήσεως μέρος ὂν κινήσεως τὸ ἐν τῷ κινεῖσθαι, οὐκ ἐν τῷ νῦν ἔσται κινούμενον, οὐδὲ ἐν μὴ ἐνεστῶτι χρόνῳ τό γε ἐνεστώς. ὥστε ἐν ᾧ κίνησις ἡ ἐνεστῶσα, χρόνος οὗτός ἐστιν ὁ ἐνεστὼς ἄπειρος ὢν τῇ διαιρέσει ἀπείρου οὔσης· ἑκάτερον γὰρ συνεχές. πᾶν δὲ συνεχὲς ἐπ' ἄπειρον διαιρετόν. *ταῦτα εἰπὼν καὶ τὴν Ἀριστοτέλους παρατίθεται ῥῆσιν,*[45] *ἐν ᾗ τὴν Ζήνωνος ἀπορίαν ἐπιλύεται ἔχουσαν οὕτως·* [fr. 9 = Simplicius, In Phys., 797.14–797.26 Diels] «Αἱ γὰρ αὐταὶ διαιρέσεις ἔσονται τοῦ χρόνου καὶ τοῦ μεγέθους καὶ εἰ ὁποτερονοῦν ἄπειρον, καὶ θάτερον, καὶ ὡς θάτερον, καὶ θάτερον, οἷον εἰ μὲν τοῖς ἐσχάτοις ἄπειρος ὁ χρόνος, καὶ τὸ μῆκος τοῖς ἐσχάτοις, εἰ δὲ τῇ διαιρέσει, τῇ διαιρέσει καὶ τὸ μῆκος, εἰ δὲ ἀμφοῖν ⟨ὁ χρόνος⟩, ἀμφοῖν καὶ τὸ μέγεθος. διόπερ καὶ ὁ Ζήνωνος λόγος ψεῦδος λαμβάνει τὸ μὴ ἐνδέχεσθαι τὰ ἄπειρα διελθεῖν ἢ ἅψασθαι τῶν ἀπείρων καθ' ἕκαστον ἐν πεπερασμένῳ χρόνῳ· διχῶς γὰρ λέγεται καὶ ὁ χρόνος καὶ τὸ μῆκος ἄπειρον καὶ ὅλως πᾶν τὸ συνεχές, ἤτοι κατὰ διαίρεσιν ἢ τοῖς ἐσχάτοις. τῶν μὲν οὖν κατὰ τὸ ποσὸν ἀπείρων οὐκ ἐνδέχεται ἅψασθαι ἐν πεπερασμένῳ χρόνῳ, τῶν δὲ κατὰ διαίρεσιν ἐνδέχεται. καὶ γὰρ αὐτὸς ὁ χρόνος οὕτως ἄπειρος. ὥστε ἐν τῷ ἀπείρῳ καὶ οὐκ ἐν τῷ πεπερασμένῳ συμβαίνει διιέναι τὸ ἄπειρον καὶ ἅπτεσθαι τῶν ἀπείρων τοῖς ἀπείροις, οὐ τοῖς πεπερασμένοις».

[Fr. 10 = Simplicius, In Phys., 797.35–798.9 Diels] *Ἀλλὰ τούτοις μᾶλλον προσεκτέον ὑπὸ τοῦ φιλοσόφου Δαμασκίου ῥηθεῖσιν καὶ ταῖς*[46] *αὐταῖς λέξεσι·* Τὸ δ' αὖ ἀεὶ μηδέποτε ὂν συνηγμένον εἰς ἕν, ἐν δὲ τῷ γίνεσθαι τὸ εἶναι ἔχον, τοῦτον εἶναι τὸν χρόνον ὡς ἡμέραν καὶ νύκτα καὶ μῆνα καὶ ἐνιαυτόν· οὐδὲν γὰρ τούτων ἀθρόον οὐδὲ [ὁ] ἀγών (καίτοι πάρεστιν ὁ ἀγών, ἀλλὰ κατὰ μέρος ἐπιτελούμενος) οὐδὲ ὄρχησις (καὶ αὐτὴ γὰρ κατὰ μέρος· ἀλλ' ὅμως ὀρχεῖσθαι λέγεταί τις ἐνεστῶσαν ὄρχησιν)·

---

45 Phys., VI 2, 233a 16–31.
46 scripsi : καὶ τοῖς ῥηθεῖσι codd.

does not always [cover] the half before the whole, but sometimes, as it were, leaps over whole and part, but did not realise the same thing happening in the case of time: for time always coexists with motion and, as it were, runs along with it, so that it strides along together with [motion] in a whole continuous jump and does not infinitely traverse a [series of] now[s]. And [they do not realise] this, while on the one hand motion is evident in things and on the other hand Aristotle has clearly shown that nothing moves or changes at the now but only has moved or has changed at it,[47] whereas, no doubt, things are changing and are moving in time. At any rate, the leap of motion, being a part of motion which occurs in the course of moving,[48] will not be moving at the now, nor will that which is present occur in time that is not present. So that in which the present motion occurs, this is the present time, and it is infinitely divisible, just as motion; for each is continuous. And everything continuous is infinitely divisible [i.e. in thought]. [**Fr. 9**] *Having said this Damascius also quotes the passage of Aristotle in which he solves Zeno's paradox, which runs as follows:* "For there will be the same divisions of time and magnitude. If either is infinite, so will the other be, and the one in the same way as the other; thus, if time is infinite in respect of its extremities, so is magnitude; if time is infinite in respect of divisibility, so is magnitude; if time is unlimited in both respects, so is magnitude. So Zeno's argument makes a false assumption that it is not possible for a thing to pass through or to come in contact with infinite things in a finite time. For magnitude and time and in general everything continuous is called infinite in two ways: in respect of divisibility or in respect of its extremities. So while it is not possible to come in contact with things quantitatively infinite in a finite time, it is possible in the case of things infinite in respect of divisibility; for in this way time itself is infinite. So it comes about that the infinite is traversed in an infinite and not a finite [time], and the contact with the infinite things is made by means [of parts of time] not finite but infinite".[49]

[**Fr. 10**] *But we should rather pay attention to these sayings of the philosopher Damascius in his own words:* Again, the everlasting, which is never gathered into one but has its being in becoming, this is time as day and night, as month, as year. For none of these comes all at once, neither a contest (although the contest is present, it is accomplished part by part) nor a dance (the dance too is accomplished part by part, but still a person is said to be dancing a present dance). In this way too, all time

---

47 Cf. Aristotle, *Phys.*, VI 6, 237a 14–15: ἐν δὲ τῷ νῦν οὐκ ἔστιν μεταβάλλειν, ἀνάγκη μεταβεβληκέναι καθ' ἕκαστον τῶν νῦν.
48 Thus, the leap of motion, which pertains to the being of motion and is measured, has to be distinguished from the (accomplished) motion, which is numbered.
49 *Phys.*, VI 2, 233a 16–31.

οὕτω δὴ καὶ τὸν σύμπαντα χρόνον ὑφεστάναι γινόμενον ἀλλ' οὐκ ὄντα (καὶ γὰρ τὰ κοινὰ τῶν εἰδῶν ἀίδια λέγειν ἡμᾶς ὡς ἀειγενῆ, καὶ ῥέοντα μὲν κατ' ἀριθμόν, ἑστῶτα δὲ τὰ αὐτὰ κατ' εἶδος) καὶ τὴν συνέχειαν κατὰ τοῦτο σῴζειν τριχῇ ταύτην διαιρουμένην ὡς πρὸς ἡμᾶς καὶ τὸν καθ' ἡμᾶς ἐνεστῶτα χρόνον. ἄλλοις γοῦν ἄλλος ὁ ἐνεστώς, ἐπεὶ καθ' ἑαυτόν γε ὁ χρόνος εἷς συνεχής, ἀδιαίρετος μὲν διαιρετὸς δὲ ἐπ' ἄπειρον οἷα συνεχής.

B Testimonia

[T. 1 = Simplicius, *In Phys.*, 778.20–29 Diels] [...] *εἰ ἔστι τις γένεσις καὶ κίνησις οὐκ ἐν τῷ γίνεσθαι τὸ εἶναι ἔχουσα οὐδὲ ἄλλο μετ' ἄλλο ἑαυτῆς μόριον, ἀλλ' ἅμα ὅλη ὑφεστῶσα (ὡς τὴν τῆς ψυχικῆς οὐσίας ἤ, εἰ μὴ ταύτης, τὴν γοῦν τοῦ οὐρανίου σώματος εἴποι τις ἂν γενητὴν μὲν εἶναι ὡς ἀπὸ μόνης αἰτίας ὑφεστῶσαν καὶ κινητὴν οὕτω κατὰ τὴν τῆς γενέσεως κίνησιν, καθ' ἣν τοῦ ὄντως ὄντος εἰς τὸ γινόμενον ἐξέστη καὶ ἀπὸ παραδείγματος εἰς εἰκόνα), εἴ τις οὖν τοιαύτην γένεσιν καὶ κίνησιν ὁρᾷ, ὡς ὁ ἐμὸς πολλάκις διετείνετο Δαμάσκιος, εἰκότως καὶ χρόνον ἅμα ὅλον ὁρᾶν φιλονεικεῖ μετρητικὸν τῆς τοιαύτης κινήσεως καὶ τοῦ εἶναι τοῦ ἅμα ὄντος.*

[T. 2 = Simplicius, *In Phys.*, 778.32–35 Diels] [...] *τὸ γινόμενον καὶ ἀπολλύμενον καὶ ἐπὶ τῶν ἀιδίων γενητῶν ἀμεταβλήτων δὲ κατ' οὐσίαν ἐξηγούμενος ὁ Δαμάσκιος μέσην ἔλεγε τοῦ ὄντος καὶ μὴ ὄντος τὴν τοιαύτην φύσιν, καὶ κατὰ μὲν τὴν εἰς τὸ ὂν ἀνάτασιν γινόμενον ἔλεγεν αὐτό, κατὰ δὲ τὴν εἰς τὸ μὴ ὂν ὑπόβασιν ἀπολλύμενον.*

[T. 3 = Simplicius, *In Phys.*, 787.29–788.5 Diels] *Ὁ δὲ Δαμάσκιος,*[50] *οἶμαι κἂν χθαμαλώτερον ἀλλ' οἰκειότερόν γε πρὸς τὴν Ἀρχύτου λέξιν,*[51] *ἀριθμὸν μέν τινος κινήσεως ἀκούει οὐ τῆς ὡς εἴδους καὶ ἀκινήτου, ἀλλὰ τῆς μεταβολικῆς, ὥστε οὐ τῆς ψυχικῆς μόνης, ἀλλὰ πάσης ὁμοίως μεταβολῆς, ἴσως δὲ καὶ ὅτι ἀτόμων ἀεὶ καὶ ἄτομος ἡ μεταβολή, διὰ τοῦτο 'τινός' (τὸ γὰρ καθόλου ἀμετάβλητον)· καθόλου δὲ διάστημα τῆς τοῦ παντὸς φύσεως, ὅτι οὐ μόνης κινήσεως ἀλλὰ καὶ ἠρεμίας, ὅπερ καὶ*

---

[50] Although I classify this passage as a testimony, I believe that it is a close paraphrase Damascius' text. As Simplicius adds no φησί, it seems that the οὖν at 788.6 introduces his own reflections on (pseudo)Archytas' text. Cf. also the expression καὶ ὅρα, which cannot but be by Simplicius himself. Moreover, the view that the time coordinate to generation is the *true* image of eternity (cf. Simplicius, *In Phys.*, 788.29–32: ἔοικεν οὖν καὶ Ἀρχύτας, ὥσπερ καὶ Ἀριστοτέλης, τὴν τῶν νῦν συνεχῆ καὶ ἀδιάκοπον ῥοὴν τίθεσθαι τὸν χρόνον καὶ τοῦτον μάλιστα παραδιδόναι τὸν τῇ γενέσει σύστοιχον καὶ κυρίως λεγόμενον χρόνον εἰκόνα ὄντως τοῦ αἰῶνος) cannot be shared by Damascius.
[51] Cf. Simplicius, *In Phys.*, 786.12–13: κινάσιος τι(νὸ)ς [scripsi cum Sonderegger : τις codd.] ἀριθμὸς ἢ καὶ καθόλου διάσταμα τᾶς τῶ παντὸς φύσιος.

exists in becoming but not in being (indeed, we call the common forms eternal, because they are always generated, they are flowing in number but, in form, they stand still and are the same) and preserves in this respect its continuity, which in respect to us and the time which is present for us is divided into three. Assuredly, the present time is different for different people, whereas in itself time is one and continuous,[52] indivisible but infinitely divisible [i.e. in thought] *qua* continuous.

B Testimonies

[T. 1] [...] *If there is some generation and motion which does not have its being in becoming nor one of its parts after the other, but exists simultaneously as a whole (as one might say that the generation of the psychic essence, or, if not this, then the generation of the celestial body was generated as existing from a single cause and is thus in motion in accordance with the motion of generation, in accordance with which it departed from true being into becoming and from being a paradigm into being an image), if then someone looks towards this sort of generation and motion, as my [master] Damascius often maintained, he has also a plausible claim to envisage also a time which is simultaneously a whole and measures that sort of motion and the being of what exists simultaneously.*

[T. 2] [...] *Damascius, explaining 'what comes to be and passes away' also with regard to the perpetual generated things, which are however unchanging in their being, said that* their nature is intermediate between being and not-being, *and that [in their case]* it comes to be qua raising towards being and passes away qua descending towards not-being.

[T. 3] *But Damascius—I think, if nearer the ground,*[53] *yet more suitably to the text of Archytas—interprets the* "number of a certain motion"[54] *as being* not of a motion as form and as unmoved, but of a changing motion; so that it is not of the psychic alone, but equally of all change; and very likely Archytas says 'a certain' because change always belongs to individuals and is individual (for the universal is unchangeable). [He says that] it is the universal extension of the nature of the universe because it measures not only motion but also rest, which Aristotle well

---

52 Cf. Alexander of Aphrodisias, *On Time*, 97.5 (Sharples 1982: 67).
53 This is said with regard to Iamblichus, whose 'more elevated' interpretation has been presented immediately before by Simplicius, *In Phys.*, 786.11–787.28.
54 Simplicius preserves Iamblichus' quotation of pseudo-Archytas' definition of time as "number of a certain motion or, else, universal interval of the nature of all" (*In Phys.*, 786.12–13).

Ἀριστοτέλης καλῶς νοήσας εἶπεν ὅτι «τοῦτό ἐστι» τῇ κινήσει «τὸ ἐν χρόνῳ εἶναι, τὸ μετρεῖσθαι αὐτῆς τὸ εἶναι· δῆλον ὅτι καὶ τοῖς ἄλλοις τοῦτό ἐστι τὸ ἐν χρόνῳ εἶναι τὸ μετρεῖσθαι αὐτῶν τὸ εἶναι ὑπὸ τοῦ χρόνου».[55] ὥστε καὶ τῆς ἠρεμίας ἡ τοῦ εἶναι διάστασις ὑπὸ τοῦ χρόνου μετρεῖται. ὥστε[56] καὶ εἰ τῆς κινήσεως ὁ χρόνος λέγεται, τῆς παρατάσεως λέγεται ταύτης τῆς τοῦ εἶναι τῆς ἐν γενέσει. καὶ ἔοικεν Ἀριστοτέλης τὸ διάστημα τῆς φύσεως εἰς τὴν παράτασιν τοῦ εἶναι τοῦ ἑκάστου μεταλαβεῖν.

[T. 4 = Simplicius, *In Phys.*, 791.32–33 Diels] *Ἐφιστάνει δὲ αὐτῷ* [sc. *τῷ Πλωτίνῳ*] *ὁ Δαμάσκιος ὡς ἀντὶ αἰῶνος τὸν αἰώνιον νοῦν παραδεδωκότι.*[57]

[T. 5 = Simplicius, *In Phys.*, 795.4–17 Diels] *Ἀλλὰ καὶ Πρόκλος ὁ ἐκ τῆς Λυκίας φιλόσοφος ὁ τῶν ἡμετέρων διδασκάλων καθηγεμὼν περὶ μὲν τοῦ χωριστοῦ χρόνου τὰ αὐτά πως τῷ Ἰαμβλίχῳ φιλοσοφεῖ καὶ οὐ μόνον νοῦν, ἀλλὰ καὶ θεὸν αὐτὸν ἀποδεικνύναι πειρᾶται, ὡς καὶ εἰς αὐτοψίαν ὑπὸ τῶν θεουργῶν κληθῆναι. τοῦτον δὲ τὰς μὲν εἴσω μενούσας ἐνεργείας ἀμεταβλήτους ἔχειν φησί, τὰς δὲ εἰς τὸ ἐκτὸς ἀποτεινομένας μεταβαλλομένας. περὶ μέντοι τοῦ μεθεκτοῦ καὶ ἀχωρίστου τῆς γενέσεως χρόνου τὰ αὐτὰ τῷ Ἀριστοτέλει διατάττεται νομίζων τὸν Ἀριστοτέλην κατὰ τὸ νῦν μόνον ὑφεστάναι λέγειν τὸν χρόνον. οἱ δὲ μετὰ Πρόκλον ἕως ἡμῶν σχεδόν τι πάντες οὐκ ἐν τούτῳ μόνον ἀλλὰ καὶ ἐν τοῖς ἄλλοις ἅπασι τῷ Πρόκλῳ κατηκολούθησαν. Ἀσκληπιόδοτον ἐξαιρῶ λόγου τὸν ἄριστον τῶν Πρόκλου μαθητῶν καὶ Δαμάσκιον τὸν ἡμέτερον· ὧν ὁ μὲν δι' ἄκραν εὐφυΐαν καινοτέροις ἔχαιρε δόγμασιν, ὁ δὲ Δαμάσκιος διὰ φιλοπονίαν καὶ τὴν πρὸς τὰ Ἰαμβλίχου συμπάθειαν πολλοῖς οὐκ ὤκνει τῶν Πρόκλου δογμάτων ἐφιστάνειν.*

[T. 6 = Simplicius, *In Phys.*, 800.19–21 Diels] *Ἀλλ' ὅτῳ ταῦτα πρὸς διάλυσιν μὴ ἀρκεῖ τῶν εἰρημένων, ἐντυγχανέτω τῷ τοῦ φιλοσόφου Δαμασκίου Περὶ χρόνου συγγράμματι.*

---

55 Aristotle, *Phys.*, IV 12, 221a 6–9.
56 scripsi : ὥσπερ codd.
57 Cf. Plotinus, *Enneads*, III 7, 3.

understood by saying that for motion *"this is what being in time means, that its being is measured; it is clear that this is to be in time for other things too, namely that their being is measured by time"*.[58] So in the case of rest, also, the extension of being is measured by time. So that, even if time is said to belong to motion, it is [actually] said to belong to the duration of being that occurs in generation.

[T. 4] *Damascius objects to Plotinus that he has delivered the eternal intelligence instead of the eternity.*

[T. 5] *But Proclus too, the philosopher from Lycia and professor of our own teachers, holds roughly the same philosophical view about the separate time as Iamblichus, and strives to demonstrate that it is not only intelligence but also a god, so that it has even been called on to appear by the theurgists. He says that this time has its internal activities unchangeable, whereas those directed externally are changing. However, with regard to the participated time that is inseparable from generation he maintains the same view as Aristotle, believing that Aristotle says that time subsists only in the now.*[59] *Proclus' successors right up to our time have followed him not only on this point but also in all other matters. I except Asclepiodotus, the best of Proclus' pupils, and our Damascius, of whom the former, because of his extreme cleverness, rejoiced in novel doctrines, while Damascius, through love of toil and his [intellectual] sympathy with Iamblichus, did not hesitate to reject many of Proclus' doctrines.*

[T. 6] *But let him who is not satisfied with the above as solutions of the aporiae read the treatise* On Time *by the philosopher Damascius.*

---

58 Aristotle, *Phys.*, IV 12, 221a 6–9.
59 That is, the present time (and not the indivisible now).

Bibliography

A Sources

Aristotle, *Categories* = L. Minio-Paluello (ed.), *Aristotelis Categoriae et liber De interpretatione*. Oxford: Clarendon Press, 1949.
Aristotle, *On the Heavens* = P. Moraux (ed.), *Aristote. Du ciel* [Collection des Universités de France], Paris: Les Belles Lettres, 1965.
Aristotle, *On the Progression of Animals* = A. Falcon/S. Stavrianeas/P. Golitsis (eds.), *Aristotle on How Animals Move. The* De incessu animalium*: Text, Translation, and Interpretative Essays*. Cambridge: Cambridge University Press, 2021.
Aristotle, *On the Soul* = W. D. Ross (ed.), *Aristotle. De anima*. Oxford: Clarendon Press, 1961.
Aristotle, *Metaphysics* = W. D. Ross (ed.), *Aristotle's Metaphysics*. Oxford: Clarendon Press, 1953.
Aristotle, *Physics* = W. D. Ross (ed.), *Aristotelis Physica*. Oxford: Clarendon Press, 1966.
Aristotle, *Politics* = W. D. Ross (ed.), *Aristotelis Politica*, Oxford: Clarendon Press, 1957.
Chaldean Oracles = É. Des Places (ed.), *Oracles chaldaïques* [Collection des Universités de France]. Paris: Les Belles Lettres, 1971.
Damascius, *On the Life of Isidore* = C. Zintzen (ed.), *Damascii vitae Isidori reliquiae*. Hildesheim: Olms, 1967.
Damascius, *The Philosophical History* = P. Athanassiadi (ed.), *Damascius: The Philosophical History. Text with Translations and Notes*. Athens: Apamea Cultural Association, 1999.
Damascius, *On the First Principles* = L. G. Westerink/J. Combès (eds.), *Damascius. Traité des Premiers Principes* [Collection des Universités de France], 3 vols. Paris: Les Belles Lettres, 1986–1991.
Damascius, *In Parm.* = L. G. Westerink/J. Combès (eds.), *Damascius. Commentaire du* Parménide *de Platon* [Collection des Universités de France], 4 vols. Paris: Les Belles Lettres, 1997–2003.
Hippolytus, *Refutation of All Heresies* = M. Marcovich, *Hippolytus. Refutatio omnium haeresium* [Patristische Texte und Studien 25]. Berlin: De Gruyter, 1986.
Michael Psellos, *General and concise exposition of the doctrines of the Chaldeans* = D. J. O' Meara (ed.), *Michaelis Pselli Philosophica minora* [Bibliotheca scriptorum Graecorum et Romanorum Teubneriana], vol. II: *Opuscula psychologica, theologica, daemonologica*. Leipzig: Teubner, 1989, opusculum 39 ('Ἔκθεσις κεφαλαιώδης καὶ σύντομος τῶν παρὰ Χαλδαίοις δογμάτων).
Philoponus, *In Meteora* = M. Hayduck (ed.), *Ioannis Philoponi in Aristotelis meteorologicorum librum primum commentarium* [Commentaria in Aristotelem Graeca, 14.1], Berlin: Georg Reimer, 1901.
Photius, *Bibliotheca* = R. Henry (ed.), *Photius. Bibliothèque* [Collection des Universités de France], 8 vols. Paris: Les Belles Lettres
Plato, *Parmenides* = J. Burnet (ed.), *Platonis opera*, vol. II. Oxford: Clarendon Press, 1900.
Plato, *Phaedrus* = J. Burnet (ed.), *Platonis opera*, vol. II. Oxford: Clarendon Press, 1900.
Plato, *Republic* = J. Burnet (ed.), *Platonis opera*, vol. IV. Oxford: Clarendon Press, 1900.
Plato, *Sophist* = J. Burnet (ed.), *Platonis opera*, vol. I. Oxford: Clarendon Press, 1900.
Plato, *Timaeus* = J. Burnet (ed.), *Platonis opera*, vol. IV. Oxford: Clarendon Press, 1900.
Plotinus, *Enneads* = P. Henry/H.-R. Schwyzer (eds.), *Plotini opera* [Museum Lessianum. Series philosophica 33–35], 3 vols. Leiden: Brill, 1951–1973.
Porphyry, *Launching Points towards the Intelligibles* = E. Lamberz (ed.), *Porphyrii Sententiae ad intelligibilia ducentes* [Bibliotheca scriptorum Graecorum et Romanorum Teubneriana]. Leipzig: Teubner, 1975.

Proclus, *In Remp(ublicam)* = W. Kroll (ed.), *Procli Diadochi in Platonis Rem publicam commentarii*, 2 vols. Leipzig: Teubner, 1899–1901.

Proclus, *In Timaeum* = E. Diehl (ed.), *Procli Diadochi in Platonis Timaeum commentaria* [Bibliotheca scriptorum Graecorum et Romanorum Teubneriana], 3 vols. Leipzig: Teubner, 1903–1906.

Proclus, *Théologie platonicienne* = H. D. Saffrey/L. G. Westerink (eds.), *Proclus. Théologie platonicienne* [Collection des Universités de France], 6 vols. Paris: Les Belles Lettres, 1968–1997.

Simplicius, *In Cat(egorias)* = K. Kalbfleisch (ed.), *Simplicii in Aristotelis Categorias commentarium* [Commentaria in Aristotelem Graeca, 8], Berlin: Georg Reimer, 1907.

Simplicius, *In Phys(ica)* = H. Diels (ed.), *Simplicii in Aristotelis physicorum libros quattuor priores commentaria* [Commentaria in Aristotelem Graeca, 9], Berlin: Georg Reimer, 1882.

B Translations

Aristotle, *Categories*, translated by E. M. Edghill, in: W. D. Ross, *The Works of Aristotle*. Oxford: Clarendon Press, 1928.

Aristotle, *On the Heavens*, translated by J. L. Stocks, in: W. D. Ross, *The Works of Aristotle*. Oxford: Clarendon Press, 1930.

Aristotle, *Physics*, translated by R. P. Hardie and R. K. Gaye, in: W. D. Ross, *The Works of Aristotle*. Oxford: Clarendon Press, 1930.

Hesiod, *Theogony*, translated by Hugh G. Evelyn-White. Cambridge, MA: Harvard University Press, 1914.

Plato, *Parmenides*, translated by B. Jowett, in: B. Jowett, *The Dialogues of Plato translated into English with Analyses and Introductions*. Oxford: Oxford University Press, 1892[3].

Plato, *Phaedrus*, translated by H. N. Fowler, in: *Plato in Twelve Volumes*, vol. 9. Cambridge, MA: Harvard University Press, 1925.

Plato, *Timaeus*, translated by W. R. M. Lamb, in: *Plato in Twelve Volumes*, vol. 9. Cambridge, MA: Harvard University Press, 1925.

Proclus, *Commentary on Plato's Timaeus*, vol. V, book IV: *Proclus on Time and the Stars*, edited and translated by D. Baltzly. Cambridge: Cambridge University Press, 2013.

Simplicius, *On Aristotle Categories 9–15* [Ancient Commentators on Aristotle], translated by R. Gaskin. London: Bloomsbury Academic, 2014.

Simplicius, *Corollaries on Place and Time* [Ancient Commentators on Aristotle], translated by J. O. Urmson, London: Duckworth, 1992.

C Secondary Literature

Ahbel-Rappe (2018) = S. Ahbel-Rappe, "Damascius the Platonic Successor: Socratic activity and philosophy", in: H. Tarrant / D. A. Layne / D. Baltzly / F. Renaud (eds.), *Brill's Companion to the Reception of Plato in Antiquity*. Leiden: Brill, 2018, 515–532.

Asmus (1911) = R. Asmus, *Das Leben des Philosophen Isidoros von Damaskios aus Damaskos*. Leipzig: Felix Meiner.

Bianconi/Ronconi (2020) = D. Bianconi/F. Ronconi (eds.), *La 'collection philosophique' face à l'histoire. Péripéties et tradition*. Spoleto: CISAM.

Craig (2000) = W. L. Craig, *The Tensed Theory of Time. A Critical Examination*. Dordrecht: Kluwer Academic Publishers.
Dalsgaard Larsen (1972) = B. Dalsgaard Larsen, *Jamblique de Chalcis, exégète et philosophe*. Aarhus: Universitetsforlaget I Aarchus.
Detel (2021) = W. Detel, *Subjektive und objektive Zeit. Aristoteles und die moderne Zeit-Theorie* [Chronoi, 2]. Berlin: de Gruyter.
Fonkič (1974) = B. L. Fonkič, "Zametki o Grečeskich Rukopisjach Sovetskich Chranilišč", *Vizantijskij Vremennik*, 36: 134–138.
Galperine (1980) = M.-C. Galperine, "Le temps intégral selon Damascius", *Les Études philosophiques*, 3: 325–341.
Glucker (1978) = J. Glucker, *Antiochus and the Late Academy* [Hypomnemata 56]. Göttingen: Vandenhoeck and Ruprecht.
Golitsis (2008) = P. Golitsis, *Les Commentaires de Simplicius et de Jean Philopon à la* Physique *d'Aristote. Tradition et innovation* [Commentaria in Aristotelem Graeca et Byzantina 3]. Berlin: de Gruyter, 2008.
Golitsis (2015) = P. Golitsis, "On Simplicius' life and works: a response to Hadot", *Aestimatio*, 12: 56–82.
Golitsis (2017a) = P. Golitsis, "Alexandre d'Aphrodise, Simplicius, et la cause efficiente de l'univers", in: A. Balansard / A. Jaulin (eds.), *Alexandre d'Aphrodise et la métaphysique aristotélicienne* [Aristote. Traductions et études]. Leuven: Peeters, 2017, p. 217–235.
Golitsis (2017b) = P. Golitsis, "La critique aristotélicienne des Idées en *Physique* II 2 et l'interprétation de Simplicius", *Revue des Sciences Philosophiques et Théologiques*, 101: 569–583.
Golitsis (2019) = P. Golitsis, "Simplicius, Syrianus and the harmony of ancient philosophers", in: B. Strobel (ed.), *Die Kunst der philosophischen Exegese bei den spätantiken Platon- und Aristoteles-Kommentatoren. Akten der Tagung der Karl und Gertrud Abel-Stiftung vom 4. bis 6. Oktober 2012 in Trier* [Philosophie der Antike 36]. Berlin: de Gruyter, 2019, p. 69–99.
Golitsis/Hoffmann (2014) = P. Golitsis/Ph. Hoffmann, "Simplicius et le 'lieu'. À propos d'une nouvelle édition du Corollarium de loco", *Revue des Études Grecques*, 127: 119–175.
Golitsis/Hoffmann (2023) = *Simplicius. Commentaire à la >Physique< d'Aristote. Digressions sur le lieu et sur le temps*. Édition critique, avec traduction et notes, par Pantelis Golitsis et Philippe Hoffmann [Commentaria in Aristotelem Graeca et Byzantina. Series Academica 9]. Berlin: de Gruyter, 2023.
Golitsis (forthcoming) = P. Golitsis, "Was ist die Form an sich (εἶδος καθ' αὑτό): Simplikios und die *Parmenides*-Exegese des Proklos und Damaskios".
Goulet-Cazé (1982) = M.-O. Goulet-Cazé, "Le programme d'enseignement dans les écoles néoplatoniciennes", in: L. Brisson *et alii* (eds.), *Porphyre. La vie de Plotin* [Histoire des doctrines de l'Antiquité Classique 16], t. I. Paris, 1982, p. 277–280.
Hadot (1992) = I. Hadot, "Aristote dans l'enseignement philosophique néoplatonicien. Les préfaces des Commentaires sur les *Catégories*", *Revue de théologie et de philosophie*, 124: 407–425.
Harlfinger (1987) = D. Harlfinger, "Einige Aspekte der handschriftlichen Überlieferung des Physikkommentars des Simplikios", in I. Hadot (ed.), *Simplicius. Sa vie, son oeuvre, sa survie*. Berlin: de Gruyter, p. 267–286.
Hoffmann (1980) = Ph. Hoffmann, "Jamblique exegete du pythagoricien Archytas", *Les Études philosophiques*, 3: 307–323.
Hoffmann (1983) = Ph. Hoffmann, "*Paratasis*. De la description aspectuelle des verbes grecs à une définition du temps dans le néoplatonisme tardif", *Revue des Études Grecques*, 96: 1–26.

Hoffmann (1994) = Ph. Hoffmann, "Damascius", in: R. Goulet (ed.), *Dictionnaire des philosophes antiques*, t. II. Paris: Éditions du Centre National de la Recherche Scientifique, p. 541–593.

Hoffmann/Golitsis (2016) = P. Hoffmann/P. Golitsis, "Simplicius' *Corollary on Place:* Method of Philosophising and Doctrines", in: R. Sorabji (ed.), *Aristotle Re-Interpreted. New Findings on Seven Hundred Years of the Ancient Commentators*. London: Bloomsbury Publishing, p. 531–540.

Karfík (2022) = F. Karfík, "L'être et le temps dans le *Parménide* et dans le *Timée* de Platon", *The International Journal of the Platonic Tradition*, 16: 134–151.

McTaggart (1908) = J. M. E. McTaggart, "The Unreality of Time", *Mind*, 17: 457–484.

McTaggart (1927) = J. M. E. McTaggart, *The Nature of Existence*, vol. II. Cambridge: Cambridge University Press.

Mesch (2003) = W. Mesch, *Die reflektierte Gegenwart. Eine Studie über Zeit und Ewigkeit bei Platon, Aristoteles, Plotin und Augustinus*. Frankfurt am Main: Vittorio Klostermann.

Owen (1966) = G. E. L. Owen, "Plato and Parmenides on the Timeless Present", *The Monist*, 50: 317–340.

Pellegrin (2000) = P. Pellegrin, *Aristotle. La Physique*. Paris: Flammarion.

Polansky/Cimakasky (2013) = R. Polansky/J. Cimakasky, "Counting the Hypotheses in Plato's *Parmenides*", *Apeiron*, 46: 229–243.

Roark (2011) = T. Roark, *Aristotle on Time. A Study of the Physics*. Cambridge: Cambridge University Press.

Sambursky (1968) = S. Sambursky, "The Concept of Time in Late Neoplatonism", *Proceedings of the Israel Academy of Sciences and Humanities*, 2: 153–167.

Seng (2016) = H. Seng, *Un livre sacré de l'Antiquité tardive: les Oracles Chaldaïques*. Turnhout: Brepols.

Sharples (1982) = R. W. Sharples, "Alexander of Aphodisias on Time", *Phronesis*, 27: 58–81.

Singer (2022) = P. N. Singer, *Time for the Ancients. Measurement, Theory, Experience* [Chronoi, 3]. Berlin: de Gruyter.

Siorvanes (1992) = Simplicius, *Corollaries on Place and Time* [Ancient Commentators on Aristotle], translated by J. O. Urmson, annotated by L. Siorvanes. London: Duckworth.

Sonderegger (1982) = E. Sonderegger, *Simplikios: Über Die Zeit. Ein Kommentar zum Corollarium de Tempore* [Hypomnemata 70]. Göttingen: Vandenhoeck & Ruprecht.

Sorabji (1983) = R. Sorabji, *Time, Creation and the Continuum*. London: Duckworth.

Spanu (2021) = N. Spanu, *Proclus and the Chaldean Oracles. A Study of Proclean Exegesis, with a Translation and Commentary of Proclus' Treatise on Chaldean Philosophy*. London: Routledge.

Stevens (2021) = A. Stevens, *Simplicius. Sur le temps. Commentaire sur la Physique d'Aristote, IV, 10–14 et Corollaire sur le temps*. Paris : J. Vrin.

Szlezák (1972) = T. A. Szlezák, *Pseudo-Archytas über die Kategorien*. Berlin: de Gruyter, 1972.

Trabattoni (1985) = F. Trabattoni, "Per una biografia di Damascio", *Rivista di storia della filosofia*, 40: 179–201.

Tresson-Metry (2012) = C. Tresson-Metry, *L'aporie ou l'expérience des limites de la pensée dans le Péri Archôn de Damaskios* [Philosophia antiqua 130]. Leiden: Brill, 2012.

Vargas (2021) = A. Vargas, *Time's Causal Power: Proclus and the Natural Theology of Time* [Philosophia antiqua 158]. Leiden: Brill.

Westerink (1959) = L. G. Westerink, *Damascius. Lectures on the Philebus wrongly attributed to Olympiodorus*. Amsterdam: North-Holland Publishing Co.

Westerink (1977) = L. G. Westerink, *The Greek commentaries on Plato's Phaedo*, vol. 2. Amsterdam: North-Holland Publishing Co.

Westerink/Combès (1997–2003) = L. G. Westerink/J. Combès (eds.), *Damascius. Commentaire du Parménide de Platon* [Collection des Universités de France], 4 vols. Paris: Les Belles Lettres, 1997–2003.
Westerink/Combès (1986–1991) = L. G. Westerink/J. Combès, *Damascius. Traité des Premiers Principes*. Collection des Universités de France. 3 Vols. Paris: Les Belles Lettres.
Zorzi (2019) = N. Zorzi, "Una Copista, Due Copisti, Nessuna Copista? Teodora Raulena e i Due Codici Attribuiti alla sua Mano", *Medioevo Greco*, 19: 259–282.

Index nominum

Antiqua

Achilles   59
Alexander of Aphrodisias   11, 47, 82, 101
Ammonius   4, 13, 15
Anaximander   1f.
(pseudo-)Archytas   2, 52, 71–75, 104f.
Aristotle   1–6, 12, 15–21, 23–25, 30, 32, 36f., 39–42, 48, 52–62, 65f., 70, 73, 75, 78, 82, 87, 91, 93, 95, 101

Calchas   88
Chosroes   11
Chrysippus   3, 40, 62, 73

Eudoxus   2

Hecate   6, 8
Hegias   12, 14
Hellanicus   1
Hercules   6
Hermeias   13
Hieronymus   1
Hippocrates   67

Iamblichus   2, 4, 16–19, 38, 51f., 63, 67f., 72–76, 86, 105
Isidore   12–15, 17

Marinus   12–15

Olympiodorus   12

Parmenides   14, 24, 61, 63, 69, 72, 85
Philoponus, John   15f.
Plato   2–6, 11–15, 17, 21–24, 27f., 47, 51f., 57f., 62f., 66, 68, 70f., 79, 80f., 84f.
Plotinus   12, 58, 85
Porphyry   3, 12, 15
Proclus   2f., 6, 8, 12–15, 17, 21f., 24, 27f., 31f., 35f., 47, 52, 73f., 86
Ptolemy   13

Simplicius   2, 5, 11–13, 15–17, 19f., 22–24, 26f., 28, 31f., 34, 44, 58, 63, 66f., 73, 91–93, 98, 104f.
Syrianus   12, 24

Zeno   14, 58f., 62, 70
Zenodotus   13–15
Zeus   88

Mediaevalia

Bessarion   12

George of Cyprus (Gregory II)   91

Ioannikios   91

Michael VIII Palaiologos   91

Photius   13f.
Psellos, Michael   12

Theodora Raoulaina Palaiologina   91

Moderna

Ahbel-Rappe, S.   13
Asmus, R.   15
Athanassiadi, P.   13–15, 17

Baltzly, D.   2, 8, 18, 22, 31, 47, 52, 73, 89
Bianconi, D.   12

Cimakasky, J.   24
Combès, J.   12, 15

Dalsgaard Larsen, B.   68
Detel, W.   6, 37
Diels, H.   23, 32, 92, 94, 96, 98, 100, 102, 104, 106

Edghill, E. M.   19
Evelyn-White, Hugh G.   88

Falcon, A.   43
Fonkič, B. L.   91
Fowler, H. N.   71

Galperine, M.-C.   60
Gaskin, R.   18, 67 f., 74
Glucker, J.   11
Golitsis, P.   5, 11, 15 f., 19, 69, 85, 91, 95
Goulet-Cazé, M.-O.   15

Hadot, I.   15
Hardie, R. P.   1, 6, 21, 38, 39–41, 53–55, 64
Harlfinger, D.   91
Hoffmann, Ph.   2, 5, 13, 16, 19, 45, 91

Jowett, B.   62 f., 72, 85

Karfík, F.   85

Lamb, W. R. M.   2 f., 21 f., 85 f.

Mesch, W.   85
McTaggart, J. M. E.   4, 45 f., 49, 54, 87 f.

Owen, G. E. L.   85

Polansky, R.   24
Pellegrin, P.   53

Roark, T.   37, 55
Ronconi, F.   12

Saffrey, H. D.   31
Sambursky, S.   4, 60
Seng, H.   8
Sharples, R. W.   47, 65, 105
Singer, P. N.   1, 67
Siorvanes, L.   24
Sonderegger, E.   104
Sorabji, R.   4, 60
Spanu, N.   8
Stevens, A.   37, 95, 99
Szlezák, T. A.   73

Trabattoni, F.   13
Tresson-Metry, C.   13

Urmson, J. O.   5, 83

Vargas, A.   2, 22

Westerink, L. G.   12, 15, 31

Zintzen, C.   14 f., 17
Zorzi, N.   91

Index locorum

Alexander Aphrodisiensis
De tempore (Sharples)
  94.35:   65, n. 58
  97.5:   105, n. 52

Anaximander (Diels-Kranz)
  12 A 11:   1, n. 1

Aristoteles
Categoriae
  6, 4b 20 – 25:   19, n. 39
  6, 4b 20 – 5a 37:   36, n. 50
Physica
  IV 10, 217b 33 – 34:   53, n. 7
  IV 10, 217b 33 – 218a 3:   54, n. 14; 87, n. 9; 94, n. 18
  IV 10, 218a 3 – 6:   53, n. 8
  IV 10, 218a 3 – 8:   48, n. 88
  IV 10, 218a 6 – 8:   53, n. 9
  IV 10, 218a 8 – 9:   53, n. 10
  IV 10, 218a 9 – 10:   53, n. 11; 65, n. 55
  IV 10, 218a 16 – 30:   54, n. 13
  IV 10, 218a 19 – 20:   60, n. 40
  IV 10, 218a 33-b 1:   2, n. 6
  IV 11, 218b 21:   55, n. 19
  IV 11, 218b 21 – 27:   6, n. 22
  IV 11, 218b 27 – 28:   55, n. 19
  IV 11, 219a 1:   55, n. 19
  IV 11, 219a 8 – 10:   92, n. 9; 94, n. 14
  IV 11, 219a 9 – 10:   93, n. 11
  IV 11, 219a 26 – 29:   64, n. 51
  IV 11, 219a 30 – 219b 2:   55, n. 18
  IV 11, 219a 32:   56, n. 20
  IV 11, 219b 1 – 2:   37, n. 54; 52, n. 3; 93, n. 11
  IV 11, 219b 10:   94, n. 15; 95, n. 25
  IV 11, 219b 10 – 15:   55, n. 17
  IV 11, 219b 31 – 33:   55, n. 15
  IV 11, 220a 10 – 11:   56, n. 22
  IV 12, 220a 27 – 32:   37, n. 52
  IV 12, 220b 14 – 16:   17, n. 32
  IV 12, 220b 15 – 19:   40, n. 68
  IV 12, 220b 23 – 24:   56, n. 24
  IV 12, 220b 32 – 221a 1:   24, n. 5; 37, n. 56
  IV 12, 220b 32 – 221a 9:   40, n. 67
  IV 12, 220b 33 – 221a 1:   59, n. 32
  IV 12, 221a 6 – 9:   76, n. 92; 106, n. 55; 107, n. 58
  IV 12, 221a 8:   38, n. 58
  IV 12, 221a 8 – 9:   92, n. 5; 93, n. 10
  IV 12, 221a 13:   39, n. 64
  IV 12, 221a 26 – 30:   39, n. 65; 94, n. 13; 95, n. 22
  IV 12, 221a 27:   83, n. 116; 94, n. 12; 96, n. 29; 97, n. 31
  IV 12, 221b 3 – 7:   40, n. 68; 83, n. 113; 94, n. 20; 95, n. 28
  IV 12, 221b 14 – 16:   41, n. 71
  IV 12, 221b 25 – 26:   24, n. 5; 37, n. 56
  IV 12, 221b 25 – 31:   40, n. 67
  IV 12, 222a 4 – 6:   83, n. 113; 94, n. 20; 95, n. 28
  IV 13, 222a 10 – 12:   56, n. 21
  IV 13, 222b 16 – 25:   1, n. 2
  IV 13, 222b 21:   32, n. 38
  IV 13, 222b 24 – 27:   41, n. 72
  IV 14, 223a 25 – 26:   3, n. 11
  IV 14, 223a 25 – 28:   57, n. 24
  IV 14, 223b 15 – 18:   40, n. 68
  IV 14, 223b 18 – 20:   3, n. 13; 21, n. 2
  VI 2, 232b 24 – 25:   38, n. 59; 92, n. 6
  VI 2, 233a 16 – 31:   102, n. 45; 103, n. 49
  VI 6, 237a 14 – 15:   59, n. 31; 103, n. 47
  VI 8, 239a 33 – 35:   64, n. 51
  VI 9, 239b 5 – 9:   70, n. 75
De Caelo
  I 1, 268a 6 – 7:   92, n. 6
  I 1, 268a 6 – 10:   66, n. 61
  I 9, 279a 25 – 27:   94, n. 16; 95, n. 26
De anima
  III 5, 430a 17 – 18:   25, n. 11
De incessu animalium
  2, 704b 19 – 22:   43, n. 74
Metaphysica
  XII 6, 1071b 19 – 22:   25, n. 11
  XII 7, 1072a 24 – 26:   25, n. 11
  XII 7, 1072b 7 – 8:   25, n. 11

XII 7, 1072b 13 – 14:   78, n. 97; 82, n. 109;
   101, n. 42
XII 7, 1072b 14 – 16:   25, n. 10
Politica
   VII 17, 1336b 40 – 1337a 1:   67, n. 64

Damascius
In Platonis Parmenidem
   I, 47.14 – 17:   25, n. 10
   I, 69.17 – 18:   25, n. 10
   III, 172.13 – 14:   48, n. 88
   III, 175.4 – 12:   80, n. 103
   III, 175.13 – 17:   76, n. 94
   III, 181.7 – 182.9:   8, n. 28
   III, 181.11 – 13:   8, n. 28
   III, 181.13 – 182.9:   76, n. 95
   III, 181.22 – 23:   30, n. 30
   III, 182.17 – 183.12:   61, n. 42
   III, 183.19 – 184.9:   71, n. 78
   III, 184.10 – 185.8:   64, n. 54
   III, 185.9 – 24:   48, n. 89
   III, 185.15 – 16:   80, n. 104; 86, n. 6
   III, 185.19 – 21:   70, n. 73
   III, 189.18 – 20:   33, n. 40
   III, 191.1 – 12:   65, n. 57
   III, 191.15 – 19:   72, n. 82
   III, 192.4 – 5:   58, n. 29
   III, 192.8 – 15:   68, n. 70
   III, 192.18 – 20:   59, n. 35
   IV, 53.10 – 14:   69, n. 71
   V, 122.8 – 123.8:   69, n. 72
Historia Philosophica (Athanassiadi)
   fr. 34 A: 17, n. 31
   fr. 34 D: 17, n. 31
   fr. 37 D: 14, n. 16
   fr. 38 A: 15, n. 23
   fr. 59 A: 14, n. 16
   fr. 145 A: 14, n. 17
   fr. 148 C: 15, n. 19
   fr. 150:   14, n. 17
   Test. III, 91 – 95:   13, n. 12
Vita Isidori (Zintzen)
   fr. 33:   17, n. 31
   fr. 85, lin. 5 – 10:   14, n. 16
   fr. 77:   17, n. 31
   fr. 131 – 133:   14, n. 16
   fr. 226:   15, n. 19

De primis principiis
   III, 160.17 – 161.8:   1, n. 1

Hesiodus
Theogonia
   lin. 36 – 38:   88, n. 10

Hippolytus
Refutatio omnium haeresium
   I, 6.1 – 8:   1, n. 1

Homerus
Iliad
   A, lin. 69 – 70:   88, n. 10

Ioannes Philoponus
In Aristotelis Meteora
   44.21 – 36:   16, n. 27
   97.20 – 21:   16, n. 27
   116.36 – 117.39:   16, n. 27

Oracula Chaldaica
   fr. 54:   77, n. 95
   fr. 57:   8, n. 27
   fr. 199:   89, n. 11

Parmenides (Diels-Kranz)
   28 B 8, lin. 5 – 6:   85, n. 1
   28 B 8, lin. 26 – 30:   85, n. 2

Photius
Bibliotheca
   cod. 181, 127a 10 – 14:   13, n. 12
   cod. 181, 126b 40 – 127a 10:   13, n. 15
   cod. 181, 242:   15, n. 19· 17, n. 31

Plato
Sophista
   244d 14:   28, n. 21
   245b 7 – 8:   24, n. 8
Respublica
   VII, 529d 2 – 3:   22, n. 2
   VIII, 546a 3:   22, n. 2
   VIII, 546b 3 – 4:   21, n. 2
Timaeus
   27d 5 – 28a 4:   26, n. 12
   27d 6:   79, n. 100

28a 4–6:   11, n. 4; 82, n. 110; 100, n. 37; 101, n. 43
31b 1:   8, n. 28
36e 4–5:   47, n. 85
37c 6-d 7:   21, n. 1
37c 6–38a 8:   57, n. 27
37d 3:   30, n. 32
37d 5:   11, n. 3; 82, n. 111; 100, n. 38; 101, n. 44
37d 6:   35, n. 46
37e 4–5:   7, n. 24
37e 5–38a 2:   6, n. 23
38a 1–8:   85, n. 3
38a 7–8:   17, n. 33; 87, n. 8
38b 6:   2, n. 7
38b 6–7:   22, n. 3
38c 1–2:   30, n. 32
38c 1–3:   86, n. 5
38c 3:   47, n. 85
38c 3–4:   77, n. 95
38c 4–6:   21, n. 2
38c 6:   3, n. 9
39b 4–7:   2, n. 4
39c 1–2:   2, n. 8
39c 3-d 2:   3, n. 10
39d 2–7:   21, n. 2
40b 8-c 2:   76, n. 94

Parmenides
127b 6:   14, n. 17
137c 4:   61, n. 43
137c 4–5:   24, n. 7
137c 4–142a 8:   24, n. 7
141d 6-e 6:   85, n. 3
142b 1–155e 4:   24, n. 8
142b 3:   61, n. 43
142b 5:   61, n. 43
142b 5-c 7:   24, n. 8
142c 7-d 9:   35, n. 47
142d 1:   28, n. 21
142d 1–2:   24, n. 8
142e 11–12:   24, n. 7
149d 8–151b 7:   61, n. 41
151b 7-e 2:   61, n. 41
151e 2–155e 3:   61, n. 41
152a 4–5:   61, n. 44
152b 2-d 4:   62, n. 46
152b 3:   66, n. 62

152b 3–4:   52, n. 4; 64, n. 52
152b 5-c 6:   60, n. 39
152b 6-c 1:   65, n. 56
152c 3–5:   64, n. 53
152d 4–8:   72, n. 80
152d 8-e 10:   63, n. 50
152e 1–2:   48, n. 87

Phaedrus
247d 1-e 2:   71, n. 77

Plotinus
Enneades
III 7, 3:   106, n. 57
III 7, 8.53–56:   58, n. 30
V 1, 1.3–7:   26, n. 14

Porphyrius
Sententiae ad intelligibilia ducentes
§44, lin. 45–46:   3, n. 12

Proclus
In Platonis Rempublicam
II, 12.8–11:   21, n. 2
In Platonis Timaeum
III, 9.15–18:   51, n. 2
III, 17.22–30:   31, n. 35
III, 19.14–28:   22, n. 2
III, 19.28–32:   2, n. 4
III, 20.22–30:   17, n. 35
III, 20.25–21.5:   89, n. 12
III, 21.5–6:   3, n. 12
III, 27.13–15:   22, n. 3
III, 27.32–28.6:   52, n. 2
III, 32.25–27:   73, n. 85
III, 34.8–10:   22, n. 3
III, 40.8–13:   47, n. 85
III, 40.21–24:   89, n. 12
III, 42.16–43.24:   7, n. 25
III, 50.28–51.1:   47, n. 85
Theologia Platonica
III 1, 5.16–6.1:   28, n. 20
III 7, 29.22–25:   28, n. 19
III 8, 31.2–3:   24, n. 8
III 8, 32.8–13:   27, n. 18
III 8, 33.4–7:   35, n. 45
III 9, 36.22–23:   27, n. 18
III 12, 45.13–15:   28, n. 23

III 12, 46.5–10:   29, n. 28
III 12, 46.9–10:   29, n. 26
III 14, 50.24–25:   27, n. 18
III 14, 51.18–19:   28, n. 25
III 14, 51.27–52.6:   29, n. 27
III 14, 52.7–11:   27, n. 18; 28, n. 24
III 15, 53.22–54.9:   29, n. 27
III 16, 54.22–55.6:   30, n. 32
III 16, 55.11–14:   35, n. 45
III 16, 56.6–7:   30, n. 29
III 17, 58.6–9:   30, n. 31
III 20, 72.17–18:   35, n. 45
III 20, 72.19:   28, n. 22
III 21, 77.19–22:   28, n. 26
III 26, 89.4–11:   29, n. 28
III 27, 94.21–24:   35, n. 48

Psellus, Michael
Philosophica minora
II 39, 146.9–12:   8, n. 27

Stoicurum Veterum Fragmenta (von Arnim)
II, 165:   63, n. 48
II, 509, 3–4:   72, n. 81
II, 509 (p. 164.15–17):   3, n. 14
II, 509 (p. 164.17–18):   40, n. 67
II, 510:   62, n. 47

Simplicius
In Aristotelis Categorias
130.14–19:   19, n. 40
352.2–6:   74, n. 87
353.16–19:   74, n. 89
354.24–27:   67, n. 66
354.26–27:   67, n. 67
355.4–14:   67, n. 68
361.15–20:   18, n. 37
In Aristotelis Physicam
624.18–20:   5, n. 18
624.38:   13, n. 11
625.1:   12, n. 5
625.1–3:   5, n. 18
625.4–27:   33, n. 41
625.9–11:   41, n. 70
625.26–27:   92, n. 8
625.28:   32, n. 37
626.4–17:   43, n. 75

627.16–628.2:   44, n. 76
632.33–633.6:   22, n. 4
638.29–34:   23, n. 4
640.29–30:   24, n. 6
644.25–26:   17, n. 30
644.26–34:   66, n. 59
644.35–645.4:   66, n. 61
700.19–21:   2, n. 5
773.19–774.24:   26, n. 16
773.29–31:   34, n. 43
773.33:   24, n. 9
773.34–774.5:   57, n. 28
774.19–20:   32, n. 39
774.28–35:   34, n. 42
774.30–31:   16, n. 29
774.35–775.21:   38, n. 63; 92
775.9–10:   76, n. 93
775.12–16:   51, n. 2
775.17–19:   43, n. 73
775.22–23:   24, n. 6
775.23–24:   92, n. 7
775.24–26:   89, n. 13; 92
775.31–34:   20, n. 41; 51, n. 1
776.2–33:   94
776.20–24:   83, n. 114
777.7–10:   22, n. 4
777.12:   70, n. 72
778.20–29:   104
778.32–35:   104
779.14–32:   84, n. 117; 96
779.26:   79, n. 99
780.1–12:   78, n. 96· 98
780.5:   5, n. 19
780.12–19:   78, n. 98; 100
780.20:   98, n. 33
780.20–781.1:   81, n. 107
780.20–781.13:   98
780.33–781.1:   87, n. 7
781.1–13:   82, n. 112
781.11–13:   11, n. 2; 77, n. 95; 81, n. 105
782.27–28:   66, n. 63
784.18–22:   18, n. 36
785.2–3:   74, n. 86
785.15–16:   73, n. 83
785.16–17:   52, n. 6
786.11–13:   52, n. 5; 73, n. 84
786.11–787.28:   105, n. 53

786.12–13: 104, n. 51; 105, n. 54
786.13–22: 73, n. 86
786.22–29: 74, n. 87
786.30–33: 52, n. 2
787.10–17: 75, n. 90
787.17–21: 38, n. 60; 75, n. 91
787.29–788.4: 75, n. 92
787.29–788.5: 104
788.6: 104, n. 50
788.29–32: 104, n. 50
791.32–33: 106
794.18–20: 17, n. 34
795.4–17: 106
795.15–17: 17, n. 31
796.32–797.13: 59, n. 33
796.27–797.13: 100
797.14–797.26: 102
797.35–798.9: 102
798.4–9: 47, n. 85
798.8: 56, n. 23
798.18: 79, n. 102
800.19–21: 106
800.20–21: 17, n. 30

Suidae Lexicon
III 324, 16: 15, n. 23

www.ingramcontent.com/pod-product-compliance
Lightning Source LLC
Chambersburg PA
CBHW070317240426
43661CB00057B/2671